The Role of Mexico's *Plural* in Latin American Literary and Political Culture

From Tlatelolco to the "Philanthropic Ogre"

John King

First published in 2007 by
PALGRAVE MACMILLAN™
175 Fifth Avenue, New York, N.Y. 10010 and
Houndmills, Basingstoke, Hampshire, England RG21 6XS
Companies and representatives throughout the world.

PALGRAVE MACMILLAN is the global academic imprint of the Palgrave Macmillan division of St. Martin's Press, LLC and of Palgrave Macmillan Ltd. Macmillan® is a registered trademark in the United States, United Kingdom and other countries. Palgrave is a registered trademark in the European Union and other countries.

ISBN-13: 978–1–4039–8078–6
ISBN-10: 1–4039–8078–0

Library of Congress Cataloging-in-Publication Data

King, John, 1950–
    The role of Mexico's *Plural* in Latin American literary and political
culture : from Tlatelolco to the "philanthropic ogre" / by John King.
        p. cm.—(Studies of the Americas series)
    Includes bibliographical references and index.
    ISBN 1–4039–8078–0
        1. Mexican literature—20th century—History and criticism. 2. Spanish American literature—20th century—History and criticism. 3. Paz, Octavio, 1914–1998—Political and social views. 4. Mexico—Civilization—Periodicals. 5. Plural (Mexico City, Mexico) I. Title.

PQ7153.K56 2007
860.9'97209034—dc22   2007013294

A catalogue record for this book is available from the British Library.

Design by Newgen Imaging Systems (P) Ltd., Chennai, India.

First edition: December 2007

10   9   8   7   6   5   4   3   2   1

Printed in the United States of America.

For Dimitra

Contents

Acknowledgments

Research trips to Mexico and the United States were funded by the British Academy, the AHRC, the University of Warwick, and the Fundación Octavio Paz. A research leave grant from the AHRC enabled me to complete the writing of the book.

Many people in Mexico discussed this project with me, in particular Aurelio Asiáin, Carmen Boullosa, José de la Colina, Adolfo Castañon, Enrique Krauze, Carlos Monsiváis, Elena Poniatowska, Alejandro Rossi, Guillermo Sheridan, Danubio Torres Fierro, Gabriel Zaid. Alberto Ruy Sánchez, and Margarita de Orellana were a consistent source of good company and good ideas. Margo Glantz offered friendship and hospitality on numerous occasions. Octavio Paz and Marie-José Paz made me welcome, as I explain in the introduction. Thanks to Gabriel Pérez Barreiro and Sumiko Sakai for the color illustration of one of Kazuya Sakai's finest paintings. James Dunkerley offered encouragement and good advice, as always. Efraín Kristal and Gerald Martin worked very hard to give earlier versions of the manuscript more coherence: I have benefited in many ways from their friendship. Finally, the greatest thanks to Dimitra, for everything.

Introduction

The original project of Plural was (and still is) to edit a Latin American journal in Mexico, that would be open to the world.
—Octavio Paz to Tomás Segovia, 27 January 1972.

In its issue of July 1999, the cultural journal *Letras Libres*—which had begun publication following the death of Octavio Paz in 1998 and the subsequent closing down of Paz's magazine *Vuelta*—sought to claim its place within Mexican cultural traditions and institutions. It printed an "árbol hemerográfico" ("A family tree of little magazines"), with a growth span of almost one hundred years. At its base stood the cultural group known as the Ateneo de la Juventud and the literary magazine, *Contemporáneos* that appeared in Mexico between 1928 and 1931. Just above the base of *Contemporáneos,* we find *Barandal* (1931–1932) and *Taller* (1938–1941), magazines that Paz himself was involved with in his youth and in his early years as a poet. Toward the top of the trunk are *Plural* (1971–1976), *Vuelta* (1976–1998), and *Letras Libres* (1998–), the two magazines that Paz personally edited in the final three decades of his life, and this new journal that, following his death, openly declared its adherence to his legacy. In this particular mapping of the field of twentieth century Mexican cultural history, Paz—in his work as a poet and critic but also, crucially, in his role as an editor of journals—is seen as central. Indeed the critic Guillermo Sheridan has argued that Paz's work as an editor and promoter of literary journals should be considered almost on a par with his life as a poet.[1] The present book seeks to analyze the first of these central journals, *Plural*, edited by Paz between October 1971 and July 1976, and published as part of the *Excélsior* newspaper group, then directed by Julio Scherer.

In his introduction to this "árbol hemerográfico," Christopher Domínguez Michael asks other critics to draw up their own genealogies, "planting and tending to other trees."[2] I had been working on a similar enterprise some twenty years earlier, preparing a book on the Argentine cultural journal *Sur* (1931–1970), which I also argued was at the heart of the "family tree" of Argentine cultural and literary journals. I said in my introduction to that book that I follow the cue of the critic Raymond Williams who has argued that "the critic of a literary magazine or a cultural group must establish two factors: the internal organization of a particular group and its proposed and actual relations to other groups in the same area of enquiry and to the wider society."[3] My own reading of twentieth-century Argentine cultural history had therefore been through the prism of a cultural journal and it was this particular reading that I wished to apply to Mexican culture in the seventies.

I was well aware of the existence of *Plural* when I was working on *Sur* for my doctoral thesis in Oxford. The Taylor Institution library had a subscription to the magazine, thanks to the interest of the then Fellow in Latin American literature, David Gallagher, who, I would later discover in the *Plural* archive, was someone that Paz wanted as a literary correspondent for the magazine in the United Kingdom. I would read *Plural* both for general interest in the mid-seventies, as a neophyte in the emerging interest in the field of Latin American literature in Britain, and as a guide to my own research on Argentina. I benefited greatly from the series of interviews published by the Uruguayan critic Danubio Torres Fierro with the main writers in *Sur*—Victoria and Silvina Ocampo, José Bianco, Adolfo Bioy Casares, Alberto Girri—writers who were rarely interviewed at that time, unlike the "boom" novelists of the sixties. I knew of the close bond of friendship between Paz and José Bianco, the managing editor of *Sur*, and the important contributions that Paz made in *Sur*, in particular his denunciation of the concentration camps in the USSR in 1951, based on the work of David Rousset. It seemed to me that *Plural* was the natural successor to *Sur*, which had ceased regular publication in 1970, although I always found *Plural* more engaging than the overtly more serious *Sur*, especially the "Letras, letrillas, letrones" section at the end of the magazine, which commented on cultural and political life in a humorous and often sardonic way.

I also found *Plural* a very useful source of information on Latin American art as I worked, simultaneously, on a book on the Di Tella Arts Center in Buenos Aires, the center of "swinging Buenos Aires" in the 1960s.[4] I found that the managing editor of *Plural*, Kazuya Sakai, had exhibited in the Di Tella Institute in the early sixties before moving to Mexico, and that Octavio Paz, from his post as Ambassador in India, had found the time to write to some young conceptual artists in the Di Tella about a media happening that they were staging in Buenos Aires.[5] In the pages of *Plural* there was also a regular "artistic supplement," with color illustrations introducing the work of contemporary Mexican and Latin American artists to its readers. There was thus a very clear affinity between the Argentine cultural institutions that I was working on and Octavio Paz's magazine.

As I struggled to finish my Argentine projects, I met Alejandro Rossi, the Mexican philosopher and essayist, in Oxford in 1983. I discovered that he was one of the regular columnists in *Plural* and later in its successor *Vuelta*, and he shared with me his own insights into Argentine culture and into overt and more arcane links between cultural groups in Argentina and Mexico. When, with the books on *Sur* and the Di Tella finally written, I received a letter from Alberto Ruy Sánchez—who I had met a few years earlier at a conference on film in Manchester—telling me that he was now working in the offices of *Vuelta*, it seemed to me somehow inevitable that I would write on Octavio Paz and cultural magazines in Mexico.

My first introduction to Mexican culture came in July–September 1985. I thought I should try to do some detailed work on *Plural* before approaching Paz and Alberto Ruy Sánchez managed to borrow for me Paz's copies of *Plural*. I was surprised, flicking through the pages, at the number of annotations there were in the margins and the text, in Paz's hand, correcting every typographical error with exclamations of impatience, on occasion commenting on the texts themselves. Here, evidently, was an editor passionately involved with a journal at every point of production. When later I plucked up the courage to ring Paz, I was further surprised when he picked up the phone himself: I had been expecting a secretary, a maid, someone who would be an initial buffer. I was still more surprised when, after stammering out my introduction, he invited me to meet him the next day. It quickly became clear as I settled into my first coffee, in his airy glass-fronted, plant fringed, study, that Paz himself read the history of Mexican literature through an analysis of literary groups, literary generations, and little magazines. As he mapped for me the antecedents of *Plural*, in a way not dissimilar to *Letras Libres*'s later "árbol genealógico," he seemed to have almost total recall of events that had taken place some fifty years earlier, in the 1930s: the different fractions and *cénacles* of intellectuals and poets, the continuities and breaks with the past. He had always been, from his earliest times as a writer, a person strongly identified with literary magazines, and he was very willing to cooperate with my research, through conversation and later by making available to me his own collection of letters on

Plural and also the *Plural* archive. In a memorable first trip to Mexico, I met many of the protagonists of the *Plural* years. I remember in particular an interview with the legendarily elusive Gabriel Zaid, who told me that he could give me forty-five minutes and that we would meet at a Sanborns restaurant at a specific time. I had been told by several people to be punctual, and indeed Zaid arrived at the precise minute of the agreed interview time. He then proceeded to eat and give me a most insightful and engaging overview of the magazine's place in Mexican letters. When he finished his last mouthful and left, I knew, without looking at my watch, that exactly forty-five minutes had elapsed: a memorable example of erudition and time management that I would struggle ever to approximate.

What struck me forcibly as a major difference with my work on *Sur* was that in Mexico there was no equivalent of the rich cultural Maecenas in Mexico, like the writer Victoria Ocampo, who funded the magazine, and the publishing house *Sur*, for more than forty years out of her own private fortune. I would sometimes ask Victoria Ocampo whether her magazine made any money, but she always refused to answer this question, implying that it was too uncouth. Of course, she must have lost money with every issue, but this did not deter her. In contrast, the main cultural Maecenas in Mexico is the state—that state which Paz would later come to call "the philanthropic ogre"—and, to a lesser extent, certain powerful newspapers, which themselves were in close relationships with the government and the ruling party of Mexico's then one-party state. Octavio Paz himself was alluding to this when he mentioned the case of the short-lived Mexican little magazine *Taller*: "Why did *Taller* cease publication? In the first place through lack of resources: in Mexico there was no way of keeping going an independent publication such as ours and there was not a single talented administrator amongst us. Literary magazines, until the appearance of *Vuelta*, had been supported or published by a public institution or by a newspaper conglomerate. The only exception was *Letras de México*, edited by Octavio G. Barreda."[6]

Thus, any work on *Plural* and its antecedents would, of necessity have as a necessary focus the relationships between writers, cultural institutions, and the state in twentieth-century Mexico.[7] It was interesting to discover, for example, that Mexico's great man of letters, Alfonso Reyes wrote to Victoria Ocampo asking her if he could work in her publishing house during a lull in his different state-sponsored activities. In a letter to Ocampo dated 15 August 1938, and sent from Rio de Janeiro, he confesses: "I need a salary to live. I have had offers from some Yankee universities. But to accept them would be to bury myself for life in an environment that I am not suited to and which would not sit well with my European and French view of life...I would like to think of another possibility: the development of your publishing house."[8] That proposed Ocampo-Reyes collaboration could have been a most interesting development in Latin American letters, but it proved to be a fleeting idea, as President Cárdenas brought Reyes back to help set up the Casa de España, later to become the Colegio de México.

It was also clear to me on my first visit to Mexico, and became even clearer in subsequent trips, that while the Mexican cultural and political scene was at one level very stable—there were defined parameters that people worked within—there was still a great deal of movement within and among cultural groups, with shifting alliances. If I was looking to define a moment of *Plural* in the early to mid-seventies, then, I would need to be careful to separate those years from the more overtly polemical years of the eighties and nineties when I was conducting my research, by which time ideological differences that had previously been latent were much more openly—and irremediably—apparent. It seemed disconcerting, for example, to be working on a literary figure, Octavio Paz, who could receive a Nobel Prize for Literature in 1990 and also be burned in effigy in Mexico City in anti-US demonstrations, accused of being the friend of Ronald Reagan for his criticism of the Nicaraguan revolution. In this shifting field, certain writers involved in the *Plural* project would later find themselves outside the Paz orbit. In issue 82 of the magazine *Vuelta*, October 1983, Paz wrote an article on Tina Modotti entitled "Tina Stalinísima" that was interpreted as a direct attack on Elena Poniatowska, who was then researching a novel on Modotti, and who had been close to Paz from the fifties. Some years later the friendship between Paz and Carlos Fuentes that reached back to 1950 was seen publicly to come to an end as the deputy director of *Vuelta*, Enrique Krauze, launched a frontal assault on Fuentes in the magazine in June 1988.[9] Some of these rifts were temporary, others were not.

From the mid-eighties, I began to find that the study of literary magazines in Latin America was no longer such a solitary task as it had been when I began my work in this field in the mid-seventies. An invitation by Claude Fell to the Sorbonne in 1987 found me in the midst of a group of international scholars all working on magazines throughout the region. Two writers in particular from Mexico, Carlos Monsiváis and Guillermo Sheridan, would become especially significant to my work. Monsiváis, as I had already discovered, occupied a central position in Mexican intellectual life, different to that of Octavio Paz, articulating a world of Mexican culture in which the comic Cantinflas should be given as much attention as a poets or novelists. Sheridan offered a more specifically "literary" lesson in how to write the cultural history of Mexico, especially through the perspective of little magazines.[10] Thanks to the initiative of Claude Fell, the Sorbonne would host several international conferences on the study of magazines mapping a period from post-World War I to the late twentieth century.[11] From the late eighties, monographs, PhD theses—especially in the United States—and articles would begin to appear with a certain regularity on the topic of little magazines in Latin America.[12]

I returned to Mexico in the late eighties but by then my own research had taken a different turn: perhaps spurred on by reading Monsiváis on such screen idols as Dolores del Río and Tin Tan, I had been commissioned to write a general history of cinema in Latin America, a project that I thought would be a temporary diversion from my pursuit of little magazines, but that occupied most of my attention for the next decade or more. I spent most of my time in the screening rooms at IMCINE, the Mexican Film Institute, with occasional forays into different literary archives in Mexico.

Fortunately however, as I struggled to keep up my research on *Plural*, I was aided by the fact that the state publishing house, Fondo de Cultura Económica, under literary critic José Luis Martínez, had, from the late seventies, begun a policy of republishing literary magazines from the twenties and thirties in Mexico in facsimile editions Thanks to the generosity of Adolfo Castañon, the then managing editor of Fondo, I found myself boarding a British Airways flight back to London staggering under the weight of two huge boxes of literary journals that evaded excess baggage duty due to the cooperation (and cultural enthusiasm) of ground staff in Mexico City. While that ambitious publishing scheme would eventually run out of funds, my work was further facilitated by the later independent publication of facsimile editions of the journals *S.Nob* and *Libre*. There have been other attempts in Latin American countries to make available the cultural heritage of little magazines through facsimile editions and more recently through digitization, though no other country as yet can match Mexico's commitment to this area. The publication of these facsimile editions had the added bonus, for a researcher, of their publication being commented on, mainly in the pages of *Vuelta*, by Paz himself and by critics such as Castañon and Sheridan. There was thus a lively debate about the continuities and breaks with the past, with

Paz in particular revisiting some of the defining moments of his early years through his memory of such journals as *Taller*.

The greatest source of primary material was the correspondence of Octavio Paz himself, relating to *Plural,* which he had photocopied for me from his own archive in his study. All the letters I have from him have a neat JK at the top of every page. Getting to the letters was a long and fascinating process because he read extracts of every one of them to me, punctuating his reading with comments like, "Look how angry I got with x.," "Look at how we exposed the Soviet Union here," "Look at this letter to Pepe (Bianco)." He was reliving those times through reading out his letters, very focused, very enthusiastic. I wondered why there were so many letters written from abroad about the magazine until he explained the chronology of his frequent, and often protracted visits to the United States as a visiting professor in Harvard and later in the University of California. For example, he left for the States a few days after the publication of the first issue of *Plural* and spent the next six months in Harvard sending regular letters, combining exhortation, satisfaction, and discontent at the developing project of the magazine. And these are rarely short letters: they are often several pages of tightly packed, single spaced typescript, revealing a total attention to every aspect of the magazine, from the infuriating typos that crept into the text to comments about literature and politics, to the tensions between literary groups. Thus what is usually the secret life of a magazine—the strategies, agreements and differing interpretations that are usually discussed on the phone or in offices or private houses—is here shown in sharp relief. And, as mentioned above, Paz also gave me access to the *Plural* archive that was made available in a series of boxes and files brought to the *Vuelta* offices, where I was made welcome by Enrique Krauze and Aurelio Asiáin and benefited from the skills of Javier Aranda, who was classifying the archive. These files read as a Who's Who of international culture in the early seventies, from Butor to Lévi-Strauss, from Susan Sontag and John Cage to Julio Cortázar and Mario Vargas Llosa. There were also a number of letters, especially from the managing editors Tomás Segovia and Kazuya Sakai mapping out the every day myriad and complex issues involved in keeping this magazine in regular publication.

In hindsight I should have spent more time listening to Paz reading from his letters in the early to mid-nineties and less time looking at masked wrestler films and into María Félix's eyes, but there was always the sense with Paz that somehow his energy and passion would make him immune to the wearing of time, and that I could take the study at my own, rather crabbed, pace. Certainly whenever he spoke to me, he was always affable and never showed what must have been an irritation that all this was taking rather too long. When last I spoke to him in Mexico City in April 1995, I told him that the Argentine filmmaker María Luisa Bemberg—who had adapted his biography of Sor Juana Inés de la Cruz for the screen, in the film *I the Worst of All* (1990)—was dying of cancer and he vowed to send her a note immediately. I had no idea that the same fate awaited him not many months later. Indeed when he came to Oxford University in June 1996 to give a talk on his recent book on art and eroticism, *La llama doble* (*The Double Flame*), he looked and sounded in good form.

After his death, his widow Marie-José Paz and the board of the Fundación Octavio Paz gave me a last push toward focusing on and completing the project by giving me a grant that I used to do concentrated archival work at the University of Texas in Austin in 2001 and 2002. Here in the extraordinary Nettie Lee Benson library was the most complete collection of Mexican literature, criticism, and little magazines, all on open access, and staffed by both subject experts in the field and helpful students anxious to guide one through the spaces of the library, with corridors running for hundreds of yards, where the uninitiated might fall victim to the characters in Borges's "Library of Babel," lost forever in the space between S for Segovia and Z for Zaid. Here I realized what other foreign scholars of Mexican culture had probably known all along: that going to Mexico City is about meeting the protagonists of the work, having access to their thoughts and personal archives, while the painstaking archival work can as easily be done in one of the splendid research libraries in the United States, instead of battling with hangovers, smog, and Mexico City traffic to reach a research archive in that city.

But of course the most abiding memories are those gleaned from Mexico City. The mornings I spent in the house of Carlos Monsiváis reading through his bound collection of *La Cultura en México* taught me more about the status of intellectuals in Mexico than the many interesting books and articles on the topic. The mornings would start well enough. Sharing Monsiváis's views that cats know a thing or two, I would take down volumes and open them up in different places: then, in a feline *coup de dés*, depending on how many of his dozen cats came to sit on my lap or on the bound copies of the magazine, I would concentrate on certain issues. Then the phone started ringing, insistently, every few minutes. Most often, it was answered by someone in the house, and the range of requests was legion, from invitations to international symposia to very local requests to support a young poet, or attend a specific political rally. Radio interviews were in the main conducted over the telephone, while camera crews, mainly from television news channels, would wander in and out, their arc lights illuminating different parts of the house showing to good effect Monsiváis's collection of political cartoons. And somehow, in the gaps, Monsiváis was writing regular columns and books, with a sardonic humor that he had made his own. Once again, as I had done with Paz, I wondered at the energy and the range of topics that Monsiváis and others would be forced to cover on a daily basis. Every major (or indeed minor) political and cultural event would need to be passed through the filter of their opinion and they seemed not to resent this, but rather to see it as their civic and intellectual duty. Other writers, most notably Carlos Fuentes and Elena Poniatowska, are subject to similar media interest and it is not surprising that Fuentes has lived for a number of months a year abroad, most recently in London, where the anonymity of the city is conducive, at least, to writing and reflection.

Somewhere, in this tangled skein of personal and political stories lies the moment of *Plural* between 1971 and 1976, and the object of my study. Readers will have noticed that in the book title, I offer a slightly longer time frame taking the area of study as a ten-year period, from the student massacre at Tlatelolco in 1968—arguably one of the most important moment in Mexican history since the beginning of the revolution itself in 1910—to the tenth anniversary of that massacre, and the publication of perhaps the most quoted essay that Paz ever wrote, "The Philanthropic Ogre" in 1978. This framework allows me to explore the reaction of Paz to the events at Tlatelolco, and their aftermath, that leads directly to his setting up *Plural* some three years later. Ending the research in 1978 also enables me to study not just the closure of the magazine in July 1976, due to government pressure, but also to chart the early development of the magazine *Vuelta* that Paz founded as an independent venture some months later.

This book is organized into six chapters. The first chapter explains the centrality of Octavio Paz to the history of twentieth-century Mexican letters and gives a brief overview of Paz's political and aesthetic development from his years as a student in Mexico City in the early thirties. The chapter is divided into three parts. The first section traces Paz's career up to the early fifties, examining his work through the prism of the little magazines to which he contributed enthusiastically from 1931. It covers in particular the formative moments of Paz's political development: the Spanish Civil War and his break with Soviet-led politics and culture in the thirties and forties. The second section offers a panorama of Mexican culture in the fifties and sixties, mapping the different cultural institutions that formed the relationship between Mexican writers and the state. This section also surveys a range of cultural protagonists and the growth of different cultural manifestations: a pro-Cuban intelligentsia after 1959, the internationalization of Latin American literature through the novel in the 1960s known as "the boom," and the growth of a specifically Mexican countercultural movement known as the "onda" or new wave. The third section focuses more specifically on the boom and Paz's early plans to form a Latin American magazine that would reflect or filter these different interests.

Chapter two takes up the story in 1968 and explores Paz's reaction to the massacre of Tlatelolco and his resignation from the diplomatic service, a move that would require him to rethink his life as a man of letters without any institutional affiliations, a radical departure for a writer and critic whose life and career had been defined by the realities and institutions of postrevolutionary Mexico. The chapter also concentrates on political developments in Mexico and in Latin America widely. In Mexico, following the brutality of the Díaz Ordaz regime, a new president, Luis Echeverría, would look to mend fences with the intellectual community by offering blandishments and state support for the universities and for cultural programs. Another assault on student demonstrators in the early months of the regime, however, would put a question mark over the reformist intentions of the government. In the broader cultural field, the "Padilla affair" in Cuba was to open up many complex questions about the nature of politics and commitment and would shatter for many the somewhat utopian idea of Cuba as a place of progressive reforms in the social and cultural spheres. Cuba—the first revolution of continental importance after Mexico's own historic process—would cast a long shadow over all debates about culture in Mexico, debates that Paz's new magazine, *Plural,* would seek to explore. Paz was offered the directorship of *Plural* by the editor of the liberal newspaper *Excélsior,* Julio Scherer: it was to be an independent journal, housed in and financed by *Excélsior.*

The following three chapters explore the content and orientation of the magazine over the five years of its publication. Chapters three and four analyze political and cultural criticism in the journal. Chapter three explores, in the main, three illustrative moments: the debate concerning the writer and the state sparked by the Echeverría government; the military coup in Chile on 11 September 1973, which brought to an end the Chilean road to socialism and underlined, for some, the validity of Cuba's more ruthless form of revolution; and Paz's sustained attack on the policies of the Soviet Union—to which Cuba was by then economically and perhaps politically mortgaged—as centered around debates about the Gulag and the writings of Solzenitsyn, amongst others. Chapter four analyzes what the magazine saw as the key areas of literary and cultural criticism. It isolates which writers became regular critics within the magazine and explores their different interests ranging from Paz's reading of Fourier to Mario Vargas's Llosa's reappraisal of Flaubert and Camus. Particular attention is given to the magazine's analysis of modern art in Latin America. Chapter five explores which works of poetry and fiction were published in the magazine and assesses how broad a spectrum the magazine could offer of contemporary international Mexican and Latin American literature.

The concluding chapter discusses the circumstances surrounding the closure of the magazine and charts the development of a new cultural journal, *Vuelta*. It explores the ways in which *Vuelta* can be seen in terms of both a continuity and a break with *Plural*: sketching out a moment in which the image of "plurality" no longer had the same optimistic credence of the early seventies, ushering in a more polemical time. The titles of the two magazines are thus very significant and we will explore in the main the claims to "plurality" suggested in the one title, and also the challenging title of *Vuelta* that implied both a swift return to independent publishing after overt government censorship and also a more personalist (and less pluralist) title: "We/I are/am back." An analysis of the role of Paz and his magazines, therefore, can hopefully offer an illuminating focus on the complexities of culture and politics at a watershed moment in Mexican history.

Chapter 1

Mapping the Field: Paz, Politics, and Little Magazines, 1931–1968

In September 1974, Octavio Paz published in issue 38 of *Plural* an autobiographical poem, "Nocturno de San Ildefonso" ("Nocturne of San Ildefonso"), in which a mature poet—Paz was sixty at the time of writing—looks back, through a memory tunnel, to Mexico City, circa 1932 and discovers his seventeen-year-old self walking from the Zócalo in central Mexico City to the Preparatory School in San Ildefonso. Paz adds a footnote to the title and explains that, "In 1932, The National Preparatory School was housed in San Ildefonso, a building that that formerly been a Jesuit school."[1] We will see later in this book that in 1974 Paz was immersed in a very intense reappraisal of the impact of revolutionary thought in Mexico and in the wider world, in particular pointing out the harmful effects of Soviet communism which, he felt, still beguiled the young. This poem therefore, is an attempt to explore—on a sleepless night, as his wife lies sleeping by his side—his own personal political (and poetic) journey that had begun some forty years earlier.

In the poem, ideas are seen to be "burning"; "adolescent conversation" also burns. The young students are caught up in the fervor of exploring new ideas, seeking "good," looking to set the world to rights. Enrique Krauze puts it well: "The generation of young men born during the Mexican Revolution did not only dream about repeating the destiny of their fathers and grandfathers but about going beyond it to mark their struggle on the road to the true and final revolution: the Bolshevik revolution."[2] Paz's students were "inventing fates," facing "the century and its cliques." These admirable proposals, however, were to be crushed by developments in history, as the poem later argues. Innocence itself is seen as the greatest guilt, and every year the piles of bones mounted up and people are forced into "conversions," "retractions," "excommunications," "apostasies," "bewitchments," "deviations." This, the poet argues, is *his* history. After this anguished confession, the poet eventually achieves sleep trusting in the life-affirming presence of his wife.

Without reprising the entire intellectual history of the thirties we should begin by looking at several key moments in Paz's intellectual development which marked his later work so profoundly.

The Early Decades

The armed phase of the Mexican Revolution was little more than a decade in the past when Paz joined the Preparatoria in 1930. During the Revolution, Paz was brought up in his grandfather's house in Mixcoac, while his father, a lawyer, followed the fortunes of Emiliano Zapata. His grandfather, a key figure in the formative period in his early years, had been at different times in his long life (he died in 1924, aged eighty-nine) a soldier, an intellectual with contacts to President Porfirio Díaz, the editor of the newspaper, *La Patria*, a writer, and a well known liberal figure. In his extensive library Paz would start his own journey through Mexican history and world literature. In the political discussions and conflicts that doubtless occupied his father and grandfather in the early 1920s, Paz would have been immersed in the history of those recent times, which profoundly marked him. Indeed Enrique Krauze argues that his later *El laberinto de la soledad* (*The Labyrinth of Solitude*, 1950) is an attempt at dialogue with his own frequently absent, solitary father, and that his father's revolutionary affiliation would mark his own definition of the Revolution: "Deep inside, His Revolution is the Mexican, the egalitarian, the utopian, the communitarian, the true, the Zapatista, Revolution. Paz would always be, in the literal sense of the word, a son of the Mexican Revolution."[3] In his later life, Paz would return insistently to definitions of the term "revolution" in the political and artistic fields. These family conversations would also give Paz some inkling of the reconstruction of the Revolution under the presidency of General Obregón (1920–1924), and in particular the work of his indefatigable Education Minister, José Vasconcelos. They would doubtless have talked about the cultural nationalist ambitions of Vasconcelos, his support for state education, book publication and libraries, his utopian dream that Mexico and indeed the whole of South America could see the development of a "cosmic race" that would meld all different ethnic groups. A Department of Fine Arts would look to foster new work in painting and music, and commissions were given to artists to act as mural painters, to cover acres of walls with monumental and didactic art. Paz would doubtless have seen the beginnings of these mural projects in family visits to the center and he would, years later, constantly engage with the issue of visual arts and revolution, praising the muralists for their technical abilities, but increasingly rejecting their ideological blinkeredness.[4] Paz was doubtless precocious enough to have read the 1923 Manifesto of the Union of Workers, Technicians, Painters and Sculptors, signed by the "big three" of Siqueiros, Rivera, and Orozco, and others, which declared a faith in the popular arts of Mexico.[5]

Vasconcelos left office in 1924, to be replaced by the more explicitly ideological nationalism of President Calles. Paz was fourteen, and already buying magazines, when a group of writers—Jorge Cuesta, Salvador Novo, Carlos Pellicer, José Gorostiza, Xavier Villaurrutia, Jaime Torres Bodet, and others—began a magazine in 1928 that they entitled *Contemporáneos*. Lorenzo Mayer takes up the story: "All, to greater or lesser degree, bore the mark of Vasconcelos and all were savagely attacked as 'intellectuals of bad faith,' 'traitors to the country,' *descastados* (untouchables); they were, in fact, fighting the cultural nationalism of Calles, a caricature of that of Vasconcelos, demanding absolute freedom of expression and declaring that Mexico must open its doors to all cultures, particularly from Europe. They devoted a large part of their time to translating, with considerable expertise, the most important writers of the twentieth century."[6]

In the effervescent years of the Preparatoria, the way that Paz and his friends found to nurture and then express their ideas was through the medium of literary magazines. The first literary journal that Paz cofounded was *Barandal* ("Balcony") in August 1931. Guillermo Sheridan, who has written the most complete and incisive account of Paz's literary and political activities in the 1930s and 1940s, makes the important point that even though this was a moment of intense political radicalism at the Preparatoria—Paz participated in its debates as a member of the student movement, the UEPOC (The Pro-Worker and Peasant Student Union)—when he came to start a literary journal, he thought in terms of the model of the *Contemporáneos* group of writers: "When everything would have pointed to them thinking of a political journal or at least a journal full of politicized literature, they opted from the outset to keep literature outside the realms of dispute."[7] This enterprise also caught the imagination of the older generation, Salvador Novo, Carlos Pellicer, José Gorostiza, and, in particular Xavier

Villaurrutia. The magazine was therefore conceived not just in the spirit of *Contemporáneos* but also as a dialogue with that group. The magazine published seven issues between August 1931 and March 1932. Paz would also participate in another short-lived magazine *Cuadernos del Valle de México* (two issues, September 1933 and January 1934) when he had joined the university proper as a reluctant student of law. Through little magazines his fame as a poet began to grow, whilst he was still immersed in the large ideological debates of the time: the growth of fascism, the Spanish republic, the Spanish Civil War. Indeed, Paz was later to remark that, "my generation was the first, in Mexico, to live the history of the world as its own history, especially the international communist movement. Another distinctive note of our generation: the influence of modern Spanish literature."[8] Two significant moments mark his career: an involvement with the agrarian reforms of President Cárdenas, which took him to Mérida in the Yucatán for six months in 1937 as a rural schoolteacher—he abandoned his Law degree and the family home when his father died in 1936—and, more significantly, his invitation to attend the Second International Writers' Congress for the Defence of Culture in Valencia in 1937, which was to meld both his enthusiasm for the antifascist movement and also consolidate his links with modern Spanish poetry.

The Spanish Civil War would have a marked effect on Paz's life and poetry. Perhaps the most quoted of all his poems, "Piedra de sol" ("Sunstone," 1957), for example, has at its center a concrete date, "Madrid 1937" and posits a utopian moment when the entwining of two lovers' bodies can transcend the horrors of the war. He did indeed travel with his first wife Elena Garro to the war, with an invitation received directly from Spain, from Rafael Alberti and Pablo Neruda, not through the official pro-Soviet, Marxist organization of the LEAR (Liga de Escritores y Artistas Revolucionarios; League of Revolutionary Writers and Artists), founded in Mexico in 1933 as a popular front movement, akin to those in Europe. At the Congress, the twenty-three-year old Paz was surrounded by some of the most respected literary figures of the age. Most of the debates, however, were exhortatory and were conducted along simple, Manichaen lines on the assumption that the threat of Hitler and Franco was so great that any criticism of the left would be seen as playing into the hands of fascism. Thus Gide was condemned for his rather timid criticisms of the Soviet Union in his book *Retour de l'URSS,* in particular by the Spanish writer José Bergamín, without anyone standing up in his defense.[9] Paz also made close friends with the writers grouped around the Spanish magazine *Hora de España*, and the debates in the international forum, in the midst of the savagery and heroism of war, would bring him face to face with the complex question of "commitment" and its relationship to poetry.

On his return to Mexico from Spain, he would continue to support the antifascist movement and would do everything he could to incorporate Spanish writers into Mexican cultural initiatives. He was almost immediately involved in starting up a new poetry magazine, *Taller* (1938–1941) that would later include the Spanish exiles of the *Hora de España* group when large-scale Spanish exile migration to Mexico followed the fall of the Republic in March 1939. This Spanish exile community would help to transform Mexican culture in the following years, as recent studies have shown.[10] Paz saw *Taller* as a "confluence," bringing together different generations of writers from Mexico and Spain, and putting them alongside the significant names of international modernism. As he himself would later recall: "In *Taller* we published the *Contemporáneos* writers, who, with the exception of Novo, were pleased to work with us. We published the first collection of poems of T.S.Eliot in the Spanish language, with an introduction by Bernardo Ortiz de Montellano and translations by Rodolfo Usigli, Juan Ramón Jiménez, Angel Flores, León Felipe, Octavio G. Barreda, and Ortiz de Montellano."[11] Not everyone found this "confluence" of writers to be sufficiently "committed" to the dominant orthodoxies of the day and Paz would become embroiled, from his earliest years, in debates about the social responsibility of literature and of the writer. He made his own position clear when he wrote in *Taller*, as early as May 1939, that the writer had an obligation to remain true to himself, over and above the demands of the times.

Indeed certain key events in national and international affairs were to further shake his already uneasy modus vivendi with the pro-Soviet left. On 23 August 1939 Hitler and Stalin signed a nonaggression pact and on 1 September Germany invaded Poland. Paz comments: "I felt that not only had they clipped our wings but also our tongues: what could we say? A few months earlier I had been asked to denounce Trotsky as a friend of Hitler and now Hitler was the ally of the Soviet Union."[12] Less than a year later, in May 1940, the artist Siqueiros—who had become a friend of Paz in Spain—led an unsuccessful armed attack on Trotsky's house in Mexico City. A few months later, on 20 August 1940, an assassin Mornard completed the work. This led to Paz's further isolation from the militant cultural field.

A significant parting of the ways was to occur shortly after with Pablo Neruda, who, as Guillermo Sheridan reminds us, arrived in

Mexico City as consul for Chile on the same day that Trotsky was murdered. Rumors that Neruda was in some way implicated in the assassination circulated for many years, but no convincing evidence was ever found. For some months Neruda and Paz maintained their Spanish Civil War "truce," though it was clear that their ideological positions were moving far apart. The simmering differences became explicit over a publishing venture, *Laurel,* that looked to bring together a compendium of Spanish American and Spanish writers. A dispute about who should be included led to a famous confrontation, when Neruda apparently came up to Paz, fingered a white shirt he was wearing and added that the shirt was cleaner than Paz's conscience. A scuffle ensued. Over the next months the disagreements between the two reached the little magazines and extended into a feud that was to last for the next thirty years. Paz would always assert that Neruda declared war on him from that moment, expelling him from the *cénacle* of revolutionary poets. This tension with Neruda, which was at once very personal but also referred to a much wider problem about poetry and "commitment," will recur throughout this book. It cannot of course be separated from the implicit rivalry between the two men as *poets* and it must be said that, first, Paz rarely wins in critical polls as to which was the greater poet and second, that Neruda is always seen as the quintessential *Latin American* poet. On the other hand Paz's pre-eminence as an essayist—indeed as an essayist of Latin America and the world—is fully comparable with Neruda's poetic prestige. If it is considered that Paz is also an undeniably great poet by any international measurement it is easy to see why the rivalry was both intense and complex and, indeed, why both men were eventually worthy winners of the Nobel Prize for Literature.

While being an indefatigable founder of and contributor to little magazines in Mexico, Paz was also attracting the attention of major Spanish language journals in Latin America. Indeed, he would declare that his "coming of age" in the world of international letters was when José Bianco, the managing editor of the Argentine cultural journal *Sur,* then the most significant journal in Latin America, asked him to contribute a review of a book by Villaurrutia. Paz saw his rite of passage in chivalric terms: "For my part, I feel that literature is like an order of chivalry. To be a writer, you have to go through certain trials, which end in recognition; both of these aspects, the trials and the recognition, bring to mind the ceremonies that were organized for knights. More fortunate than Don Quixote, one day in 1938, I was dubbed a writer, not by a roguish innkeeper, but by José Bianco, who invited me to write for *Sur.* My ordeal was to write my first article for that magazine."[13] Paz contributed several other notes on contemporary Mexican letters to *Sur* in the early forties—on José Revueltas, Leopoldo Zea, and Xavier Villaurrutia—as well as publishing two major poems that he would later include in revised form in *Libertad bajo palabra*, "Mediodía" and "La caída," as his literary friendship with Bianco developed. In the ideological turmoil of Mexican letters, the world of *Sur* must have been seen by Paz as a literary haven.

Paz's last major project of the early forties as an editor, before he left Mexico in 1943, was to participate in the formation of the journal *El Hijo Pródigo* that first appeared in April 1943. First appearing at the height of the Second World War, the journal eschewed the historical, sociological and "Latin Americanist" focus of the recently formed *Cuadernos Americanos*, founded by Jesús Silva Herzog, and published, in the main, original works of poetry, essays on poetic theory, and criticism of poetry. This was not seen by the contributors as turning away from the issues of the moment, but rather they asserted that literature, in particular poetry, was a privileged vehicle for expressing, in the magazine's terms, "imagination and reality."

Sheridan has argued that one can read the parable of the "prodigal son" as a commentary on Paz's own aggressive-defensive attitude toward literature and the nation and toward little magazines themselves. It is very likely, although the piece is unsigned, that Paz wrote the first editorial printed in *El Hijo Pródigo* in April 1943. In it we find the following commentary:

> Sooner or later, every son of God is a prodigal son (We are all prodigal sons, according to Donne). But if we preserve our imagination, our natural return would not be a return as such. And whoever might want to make us return, and might succeed in doing so for a moment, could never really make us return in the true sense of the word. We would return, but we would not return. And this paradox must be our secret, our inalienable right that can never be taken from us: to return without returning; reality and imagination. An intense life in the world of the imagination and an eye and an ear finely tuned to the reality of everyday life. This combination, we feel, is the only thing that can free us and provide us with an integrated and human literature.[14]

In Sheridan's persuasive interpretation, each literary magazine would be, for Paz, a prodigal son: it must share in the curiosity of exploring outside the confines of the home and then bring these new experiences back in a return that could never be a simple return since the experiences of the journey have worked their transformations on individuals and on institutions.[15]

Paz is central to this first issue of the magazine: apart from almost certainly writing the editorial, he publishes two poems (pp.18–20), and his recent work is reviewed on pages 44–48, a collection entitled *A la orilla del mundo* ("On the Banks of the World"), which picks up the earlier metaphor of the prodigal son: the unsanctioned journey and the homecoming. Here the poet is a pilgrim or a wanderer who suddenly finds himself back unexpectedly at a home port, and has to distil the experiences of the journey. A few issues later Paz would make explicit his poetics in an essay entitled "Poetry of Solitude and Poetry of Communion": "But poetry continues to be a force that is capable of revealing to man his dreams and of inviting him to live them in the daylight...Poetry, by expressing these dreams, invites us to rebellion, to live our dreams while awake. It points us to a future golden age and calls us to freedom."[16] Paz would not contribute greatly to the magazine after the first half a dozen issues. He was looking to travel, to follow the lead of the prodigal son, and to extend his horizons beyond Mexico.

When Paz departed Mexico in November 1943, with a Guggenheim grant for study at Berkeley, and later joined the Mexican diplomatic service in the United States, José Bianco asked him to interview the poet Robert Frost in Vermont. This interview was published in *Sur* in November 1945. Although many years later, in particular from the late sixties, the intellectual life of east coast America would become a major focus for Paz, at the end of the Second World War, there was only one place that he wished to live: Paris. He arrived there in November 1945 and stayed for six years occupying different positions in the diplomatic service.

Much criticism of Paz has focused on his encounters in Paris with the surrealists. And of course, Paz would make constant reference to surrealism throughout his work. One analysis that he would always look to ridicule was the widely held view that somehow surrealism had run out of steam by 1940. To the contrary, Paz would always argue that surrealist works would be published or painted to the mid-sixties at least, and that during his time in Paris, it was perhaps the most important creative impulse. In one of his most satirical and impassioned pieces published in *Plural* in 1973, Paz would ridicule the exhibition catalogue printed for the MOMA touring exhibition of the "Art of Surrealism," displayed in the Instituto de Bellas Artes in Mexico. As a corrective to the truisms and inaccuracies of the catalogue, Paz would provide his own "Chronology of Surrealism," showing the continued importance of the movement, and inscribing key Latin American painters and poets—including himself—into this chronology. In this version his own, *¿Aguila o sol?* (*Eagle or Sun?*) of 1951 is one of the landmark texts.[17] A number of essays and literary supplements published in *Plural* in the seventies can be seen as a corrective to what Paz perceived as the widespread ignorance of the origins and influence of surrealism.

In his own key poems and essays in this period—including *El laberinto de la soledad* (1950) and *¿Aguila o sol?* (1951)—he is looking to explore the "dialectic of solitude," the need to break with one world and the search to create another world through solidarity and eroticism. He is doing this in a dense weave of writings that includes the exploration of pre-Columbian and modern myths, the rereading of Mexican painting through the work of Tamayo, and the exploration of the function of poetry as communion and embrace. In *¿Aguila o sol?* he argues that, "the poem prepares a loving order. I foresee a man-sun and a woman-moon, the one free from his power, the other free from her slavery, and implacable loves lighting up the black space."[18] Here, as Efraín Kristal has argued, "myth and poetry open the doors to a *return,* a return to the world of men and women through communion."[19]

Another important dimension to his time in Paris was his meeting with writers from all over Latin America. Paris in the aftermath of the war was once again a magnet for writers and artists: it became the meeting place for those whose previous point of contact had most likely been the pages of little magazines. The Peruvian painter Fernando de Szyszlo and his wife, the poet Blanca Varela, for example, began a lifelong friendship with Paz at the end of the forties in Paris.[20] Paz took them along to see Breton, for by then, according to Szyszlo, "Octavio was one of the leading figures of cultural life in Paris. Once a week we met in the Café Flore to plan a magazine with Octavio and Cortázar."[21] Even in his early thirties, Paz could be seen by Szyszlo as both an influential writer and intellectual and also as a bridge between Mexican, Latin American, North American, and European writers and artists. These friendships and connections would remain strong and would reappear some twenty-five years later in *Plural.* These would include other expatriates living in Paris including Emile Cioran and the Greek philosopher and political scientist Kostas Papaioannou. Paz would credit Papaioannou for clarifying for him certain "mysterious" areas of Marxism as philosophy and in practice, as Paz grappled to understand the nature of the Soviet Union in the postwar period.[22]

It was the Argentines connected to the *revista Sur* who were making the most concerted transatlantic crossings after the war. Paz comments on this cultural "invasion": "Many years ago, at the beginnings of the Peronist regime, I coincided with José Bianco, a dear friend and a notable writer, in Paris. Thanks to him I got to know Adolfo Bioy Casares and Silvina Ocampo. Shortly afterward, Victoria Ocampo arrived. We used to call her 'Queen Victoria.' "[23] One can see from this remark the regard in which Paz always held the somewhat self-effacing Bianco, who had come to Paris to reestablish contacts and to prepare, along with Victoria Ocampo, the founder and main editor of *Sur*—a special bumper edition of *Sur* on French literature: *Sur* 147–149, published in January–March 1947. Victoria Ocampo's style, by contrast, he found to be somewhat peremptory and regal, while the seductive Bioy Casares would add a further major complication to his already problematic marriage with Elena Garro.[24] Paz has always acknowledged his interest in the writers of the *Sur* group and recognized the importance of the magazine: "For me *Sur* was what the *Nouvelle Revue Française* was for European readers: literature conceived as a world of its own: not apart from, or taking precedence over, other worlds, but also never subservient to these worlds."[25] He would always claim, however, that his "own" journals would be more dynamic and less sedate than *Sur*.[26]

Paz considered his most important contribution to *Sur* to be the publication, in issue 197, March 1951, of a dossier drawn from the work of David Rousset on concentration camps in the USSR that he had written in October 1950. Paz's growing disillusionment with policies in the USSR from the late thirties and throughout the forties was informed by such independent revolutionary thinkers as Victor Serge, whom Paz had met in Mexico City on a number of occasions in the early forties, when Serge was living a somewhat precarious, highly fortified exile from 1940 until his death in 1947. Guillermo Sheridan, observes that while Serge was already denouncing Russian concentration camps, alongside the Nazi camps, in the early forties, "It would take Paz a further six years to acknowledge that there were concentration camps in Siberia, when, in Paris, in 1949, he read *L'Univers concentrationnaire* by David Rousset. That might seem late, but it was in fact much earlier than many others and premature if we think in terms of the slowness of the Latin American intelligentsia."[27] Rousset's publication and analysis of Soviet documents relating to concentration camps caused a furor in Paris, where he was attacked by the procommunist weekly journal *Lettres Françaises* as being anti-imperialist and also of falsifying the documents.

When Paz came to include his essay in his *Obras Completas* in the mid-nineties, he wrote a revealing footnote commenting on the subsequent legal battle between Rousset and *Lettres Françaises* that vindicated Rousset's analysis: "The courts found against the Communist weekly and fined two of its editors on the grounds of public defamation. Some years later, one of these editors, Pierre Daix, recognized his mistake and has written brave and lucid studies on the Soviet totalitarian regime. Daix's example has not been followed much in Mexico or in other Latin American countries."[28] He is clearly commenting on his own relationship with the "old left" in Mexico and Latin America, and on what he saw as the left's inability to revise their own entrenched positions. He often said that he published his dossier in *Sur* because no publication in Mexico would touch it, and he dates his fracture with the pro-Soviet left to this publication, referring in particular to Pablo Neruda and Neruda's Mexican friends as his main critics. It would always be his argument, however, that the left abandoned him rather than him abandoning the left, and certainly his afterword to the *Sur* dossier of the early fifties makes a clear plea in favor of a more democratic socialism: "It is not correct to say that the Soviet experience condemns socialism...The crimes of the bureaucratic regime belong to that regime and not to socialism."[29] When Paz came to edit the cultural journal *Plural* in the 1970s, as we shall see, he brought out a special issue on the concentration camps, issue 30, March 1974, in which he revised his views on the camps, seeing them not as exploitative economic units but rather as institutions of terror.

Soon after publishing this dossier, Paz's secondment in Paris came to an end and he was moved to India and Japan, before returning to Mexico in the final weeks of 1953, an absence of almost ten years. He would remain in Mexico for five years, until 1959, working as the director general of International Organisations. Although this would prove to be a most productive period in his creative life—he published two books of essays and four volumes of poetry as well as contributing regularly to newspapers and magazines—he would not start up another journal of his own at this time. The reasons for this seem clear. He had a full-time job in the diplomatic service that left him some time for his own work, but little else. He had also been out of the country for many years and did not feel any particular affinity to a group or aesthetic project in the country. Indeed, he felt somewhat beleaguered, under attack from those who did not share his views on the Soviet Union and were also wary of his increasingly influential views on aesthetics and politics. How can we describe this cultural field in Mexico in the mid-fifties through the sixties, a field that Octavio Paz was destined to dominate in the decades to come?

Mexican Literary Culture at Mid-Century

Elena Poniatowska would remember the impact that Paz had on younger writers on his return to Mexico: "You saw that Mexico had changed a great deal and you remarked on this with ever increasing surprise. I looked on you with devotion. The impact you had on us, on Carlos Fuentes, Marco Antonio Montes de Oca, Tomás Segovia, Gabriel Zaid, Juan García Ponce, Salvador Elizondo, José Emilio Pacheco, Homero Aridjis, was very considerable."[30] In an interview with Poniatowska conducted within a few weeks of his return, Paz complained of the poverty of literary criticism in Mexico and declared what would almost be an early manifesto for *Plural*: "By sincerely drawing attention to important works, critics should create a small circle of readers that can grow and form a true reading public. It is a pity that in Mexico there are no good journals capable of analyzing our literary production with dignity, rigor and generosity."[31] At this time, rather than organizing a magazine himself, as he would might well have done a decade earlier, he now threw down the gauntlet to younger writers and critics. He would support different magazines and enterprises that were beginning to emerge at this time.

For example, the first issue of the *Revista Mexicana de Literatura*, September–October 1955, edited by Emmanuel Carballo and Carlos Fuentes, has at its lead presentation one of Paz's finest poems, "El cántaro roto" ("The Broken Jar," pp.1–5). In the same way that little magazines in the thirties and forties would often contain an essay by Alfonso Reyes as a mark of respect and affiliation, as would be the case of the *Revista* in its second issue (November–December 1955), so too a younger generation of writers showed their respect for Paz's work and also for his policy of openness toward the world of universal letters. It is interesting that later in the same issue, in a roundup of literature throughout the world entitled "Talón de Aquiles" ("The Achilles Heel"), the magazine quotes approvingly the famous essay by Borges on the Argentine writer and tradition, in which he argues that no camels appear in the quintessential "Arab" text, the Koran. For Borges, Argentines should seek to emulate Muhammed's example, and offer an Argentine literature without local color ("Nacionalismo camellero," p. 90). Borges and Paz: here were two precursors for a new generation. Issue 8 of the *Revista* would also include two long reviews of Paz's *El arco y la lira* (*The Bow and the Lyre*) by Tomás

Segovia and Manuel Durán, examples of a balanced criticism that Paz had argued was so sadly lacking in Mexico.

In the same issue of the journal, José Luis Martínez offered a "map of contemporary Mexican culture." In it he points to the importance of cultural magazines: "The extraordinary proliferation of cultural journals in Mexico is conditioned by the traditional poverty—in terms of resources, readers and a 'market'—that our culture has always experienced, and by the need that writers feel to make public their recent work, to learn about the production and opinions of their contemporaries and to register events that are important to the life of the spirit." He counts sixty-four *revistas* in publication, but notes that most of them are precarious financially and—in agreement with Paz—of very varied quality with only flashes of intelligence and "authentic intellectual passion." He talks of the emergence of weekend cultural supplements in certain newspapers existing alongside cultural magazines brought out by young writers.[32] This is a world in the mid-fifties where, according to Daniel Cosío Villegas quoted in a footnote by Martínez, less than ten thousand people regularly read and bought books.

When Martínez refers to cultural supplements, he is thinking in particular of *México en la Cultura*, a weekly supplement to the newspaper *Novedades*, founded and edited by Fernando Benítez, that was issued between 1949 and 1961. When the conservative newspaper *Novedades* objected to the prorevolutionary stance taken by Benítez and his staff after 1959, Benítez resigned and took his group of writers across to the weekly journal *Siempre!* directed by José Pagés Llergo. A new supplement, *La Cultura en México*, would appear in that magazine throughout the sixties and seventies and would become an important focus for writers and critics. These two successive supplements were for many, in the words of the poet and essayist José Emilio Pacheco, "our open university, our invitation to read, to write and to think." Pacheco offers a snapshot of *México en la Cultura* in 1956, when he was seventeen years old. "Every Saturday I waited for the supplement to arrive and I read it word for word, including the advertisements. That year they referred to the old Colonia Juárez as the 'zona rosa' (the pink district) or the 'district of art and good taste.' "[33] Pacheco would later become the managing editor of the newly formed *La Cultura en México* in the sixties, until December 1971, "when Benítez made me director and I, like the Duke of Windsor, immediately abdicated the throne in favor of Carlos Monsiváis. My resignation seemed to me a good move since it allowed the supplement to be renewed with the arrival of a new generation."[34] Cultural supplements, in newspapers and magazines, offered employment for writers, a much wider audience for their essays, poems, or short stories than in little magazines—an audience of tens of thousands rather than, at best, a thousand or so—and the possibility of promoting their books to this wider audience. Even though the odd voice was raised in objection—the poet Tomás Segovia warned against the influence of journalist-writers[35]—few writers would turn their back on contributing to an enterprise that was to showcase established Mexican writers and artists and the activities of Mexican publishing houses, in particular Fondo de Cultura Económica under the directorship of the Argentine Arnaldo Orfila. The supplements would also help foster a "new journalist" style, with the interviews and chronicles of Elena Poniatowska, the mordant explorations of high and popular culture by Carlos Monsiváis, and the witty, irreverent essays of the poet Gabriel Zaid.

Indeed, when Fernando Benítez wrote the introductory statement in the first issue of *La Cultura en México* in 1961, he posited a community of supportive readers that stretched from students to magazine editors and to President López Mateos himself: "Men of science, artists, writers, liberals, students in the provinces, everyone who understood the significance of our modest but lively attempt to showcase the essential values of Mexico were with us when we faced this difficult moment. We should say that the first person to come to our aid, in a disinterested fashion, purely because he wanted our cultural work to continue uninterrupted, was the President of the Republic." On the following page, a series of greetings from writers and intellectuals in Europe and the Americas—C. Wright Mills, Alejo Carpentier, Juan Goytisolo, Pablo Neruda, Augusto Roa Bastos, Arnaldo Orfila Reynal—joined with Mexicans such as Paz, Yáñez, Tamayo, Siqueiros, and Alfonso Caso to celebrate the new publication and to support Benítez's enterprise.[36] An early admirer, who was to withdraw his support when *La Cultura* published an account of the murder by the military of the agrarian organizer Rubén Jaramillo along with his family in 1962, was the president, López Mateos. Indeed, according to Gabriel Zaid in an essay first published in *Plural* in April 1975, the president tried, unsuccessfully to shut the supplement down altogether, but Pagés Llergo resisted such open intervention.[37]

Studies by the critics Kristine Vanden Berghe and Deborah Cohn have analyzed the writers contributing to these two magazines and their links with the wider intellectual field that was dominated by a range of state-funded cultural institutions. They both make the convincing case that, in Cohn's words, "Mexican literature and cultural activity were the supplements' staples: weekly columns...were devoted to reviewing what *Mexican* authors were doing, how *Mexican* books were being received, both home and abroad, what and whom *Mexican* journals and publishers were publishing and how the *Mexican* publishing industry was flourishing, both nationally and internationally."[38] Certain names recur in these pages, as Vanden Berghe has charted: the film critic Emilio García Riera, the critic Emmanuel Carballo, the writers Juan Vicente Melo, Carlos Monsiváis, Juan García Ponce, Carlos Fuentes, Jose Emilio Pacheco, Elena Poniatowska and Julieta Campos, the poets Ali Chamucero, José Emilio Pacheco, and Gabriel Zaid. These names would recur in different cultural institutions throughout Mexico City.

The relationship between cultural institutions and the state remained close throughout the history of twentieth-century Mexico. The French critic Annick Lempérière has given a coherent overview of the different, interlocking spheres of interest.[39] In the fifties, the cultural enterprises of the state national university, UNAM were significant. The poet and essayist Jaime García Terrés headed the Dirección de Difusión Cultural (Cultural Outreach) at UNAM, and he was also responsible for editing the university journal, the *Revista de La Universidad de México* between September 1953 and August 1965. In 1964, García Terrés published with the UNAM university press, an anthology of the *Revista* entitled, significantly, *Nuestra Década (La cultura contemporánea a través de mil textos)* ("Our Decade: Contemporary Culture Through a Thousand Texts"). The *our* in the title reflects not just his editorship within the overall history of the university magazine, but also his optimism in the achievements of the cultural field, in Mexico and in the wider world (especially in the years following the Cuban revolution), from 1953 to 1963. In this volume, selected by García Terrés as his most significant achievements as an editor, we find that Paz was a regular contributor, publishing six poems and an essay, "Saludo a Sri Radhakrishna" in 1954, his first year back in Mexico, and a significant essay on surrealism two years later, as well as a number of essays that would later comprise his book *Corriente alterna* (*Alternating Current*), published in 1967.

In a conversation with Alvaro Matute, recorded in 1983, García Terrés talks of his agreeable surprise at revisiting the early issues of the *Revista* after an absence of thirty years:

> I was surprised at the things that appeared at that moment on a regular basis: "look, Cernuda has given us a poem to publish, Dámaso Alonso sent us a poem, Octavio Paz also sent in something. Look out for this young writer who is going to publish something important." Of course

that young writer was Gabriel García Márquez and it was Tito Monterroso who brought me one of his stories. These were the times when Rulfo began publishing. In one of the first issues we carried a chapter of a novel that was called, or was about to be called "Los murmullos." It later became *Pedro Páramo* although that novel was published without the chapter that I have just mentioned.[40]

The links between the *Revista* and *México en la Cultura* were close. García Terrés worked in both publications and the collaborators were often the same people, although a *suplemento* was a more immediate and a *revista* a more considered form of publication. He was, however, happy to point out that the "discoveries" of the period (Carlos Fuentes and Jorge Ibargüengoitia) were published first in the *Revista de la Universidad*, and that all the writers who were to, "construct the new Mexican literature (Fuentes, Ibargüengoitia, Arreola, Juan García Ponce, José Emilio Pacheco) all published early work in the *Revista*."[41]

The indefatigable García Terrés initially employed Carlos Fuentes at a pittance to help him run UNAM's Difusión Cultural, which soon began to organize film screenings (chiming with the growth of the cine club movement throughout the world), theater events, literary readings and lectures and seminars on culture. The focal point of this activity became the Casa del Lago, an arts center founded in 1959. In his conversation with Jaime García Terrés, Alvaro Matute spoke of the advantages of being a UNAM student in the early sixties: "In the Casa del Lago you could listen to lectures by Carlos Fuentes, Ramón Xirau, Juan García Ponce, Salvador Elizondo and many others...You also got to hear about the great names of twentieth-century culture, Einstein, Freud, Stravinsky, Picasso. In short, the university cultural outreach department was going through one of its best periods, in modest locations like the Casa del Lago itself, the Caballito Theater, The Auditorium of the Faculty of Medicine—where the Sunday concerts were held—and the university cine club in Justo Sierra."[42] In the same way, new publishing houses were set up to complement work of the expansive Fondo de Cultura Económica: Era (1960), Joaquín Mortiz (1962), and Siglo XXI (1965). All these initiatives showed the marked influence of Spanish exile writers and intellectuals.[43]

Perhaps the most lyrical, nostalgic, evocation of the moment of the late fifties and sixties can be found in Juan García Ponce's *roman-à-clef*, *Pasado Presente* ("Past Present").[44] In it there is mention of some of the defining moments of the period and an evocation of different cultural spaces. We find an active Jaime Pérez Torres (García

Terrés), who is "very intelligent" and "full of brilliant ideas" organizing poetry readings with his friend César Salazar (Paz), a handsome famous writer recently returned from Europe (p.129). It was César who would come up with the idea of producing poetic theater, *Espacio poético* (the movement *Poesía en voz alta)*, to which he contributed translations of French avant garde poetry and a short theatrical piece of his own, based on a Hawthorne novel. This theatrical piece is introduced by a young writer Adalberto Arroyo (Carlos Fuentes), who works with Salazar in the Foreign Office. After the show, the novelist's main protagonist Lorenzo (García Ponce) is invited to a party back at the home of Adalberto's parents, who are absent on diplomatic business, which turns into a rather wild event with the painter Julián Solana (Juan Soriano) smashing up a dining table, with broken glasses and cigarette burns on the carpets and drunken revelers strewn throughout the house (pp.133–134). As the character Lorenzo gradually gains in literary (and sexual) experience, we find him moving through the different cultural institutions in Mexico from the mid-fifties to the mid-sixties. He begins as a playwright, but then becomes more attracted by fiction. He publishes a short story in the university *Revista* and collects a copy of the magazine from the new department of Difusión Cultural in the Torre de Rectoría at the university (p.253). He receives a grant from the Centro Mexicano de Escritores (an organization sponsored by the Rockefeller Foundation to encourage young writers), and he is also given a job in Difusión Cultural.[45] He takes up the coeditorship of the *Revista del Valle de México* (in "reality" the *Revista Mexicana de Literatura)*. At the same time another narrator, with a life remarkably similar to that of Salvador Elizondo, becomes involved in the *Nuevo Cine* movement, edits a magazine called *Spleen (S.Nob)* and wins the Villaurrutia prize for a novel in 1965 (with César Salazar on the jury). All the young writers and artists appear in this novel, that describes a close-knit intellectual field, with writers publishing in supplements and little magazines, attending cine clubs and gallery vernissages giving and attending lectures at the Casa del Lago, competing for the attention of intellectual mentors such as Salazar (Octavio Paz), and being encouraged by such figures as Jaime Pérez Torres (Jaime García Terrés).

Garcia Terrés did find jobs for a number of aspirant writers. Emmanuel Carballo ran the department of literature in Difusión Cultural, while Juan García Ponce and José Emilio Pacheco worked as managing editors at the *Revista de la Universidad*. Huberto Batis worked in the Imprenta Universitaria, while Juan Vicente Melo ran the Casa del Lago. In the area of political culture, Carlos Fuentes and a group including Jaime García Terrés, Victor Flores Olea and Luis Villoro founded the journals *El Espectador* (1959) and *Política* (1960–1964). What the state helped to provide, in terms of a blossoming of cultural activities, the state also could look to take away. Huberto Batis, the editor of the journal *Cuadernos del Viento* in the early sixties, talked of the pressure that editors and publishers could come under. Speaking of the publisher Manuel Marcué, he remarks: "difficult time would come for Manuel when *Política* began to upset the government; the electricity was cut off...and the presses were ruined by thugs breaking in and throwing talcum powder on the machines so that all the grease congealed and blocked up the works."[46]

Política's espousal of the Cuban revolution, in particular in the arena of international affairs, but more particularly its flirtation with the Movimiento de Liberación Nacional under the revived political leadership of Cárdenas would be the main reason behind these attempts at sabotage. A more overt case of state intervention came in 1965, when the Argentine intellectual, Arnaldo Orfila, the director of the government-owned publishing house, Fondo de Cultura Económica, was sacked by the recently elected president, Gustavo Díaz Ordaz, for publishing Oscar Lewis' anthropological account of life in a Mexican neighborhood tenement, *The Children of Sánchez,* because the president considered that the book painted Mexico in too negative a light. In this case, the intellectual groups supporting the enlightened editorial policies of Orfila protested against his dismissal. Elena Poniatowska offered Orfila space in her house to launch a new venture[47] and there was a public campaign to sell shares in a publishing project, directed by Orfila, that was to become the most important publishers in Latin America for nonfiction works in the next decade: Siglo XXI. One of the first books published by Siglo XXI was an anthology of contemporary Mexican poetry, *Poesía en movimiento, 1915–1966,* edited by Octavio Paz, Ali Chumacero, José Emilio Pacheco, and Homero Aridjis.

These writers and artists became known as a "mafia." In 1967, the Argentine writer, Luis Guillermo Piazza enshrined the term by writing a scarcely disguised *roman-à-clef* about the writers who contributed in the main to *La Cultura en México,* entitled *La mafia.* It is a title that stuck, and it contained certain elements of truth, as we have seen. Of course, some of the main protagonists laugh away the claim. Carlos Monsiváis wrote in 1965: "It was reading *México en la Cultura,* in the great period when it was edited by Fernando Benítez, Gastón García Cantú and Vicente Rojo, that I discovered the existence of a 'mafia' which, as a star struck adolescent, I assumed had to be completely inaccessible, surrounded by moats and drawbridges and adorned by the figure of a princess, Elenita Poniatowska, of course. Later on I realized that the mafia was just the name that people who were failures or who were still trying to make it gave to those who were working and were successful."[48] Pace Monsiváis, the same names do recur, in the *suplementos,* the little magazines, and the different cultural enterprises of UNAM. But it was a group that renewed itself, adding members all the time. Let us return to the case of the *Revista Mexicana de Literatura.* It first appeared, as we have already noted, under the editorship of Carlos Fuentes and Emmanuel Carballo, with an advisory committee that included Ali Chamucero, Antonio Alatorre, Archibaldo Burns, José Luis Martínez, Marco Antonio Montes de Oca, and Ramón Xirau. This lasted from 1955–1957. Between 1958 and 1960, Alatorre, a university lecturer and the Spanish poet Tomás Segovia would direct the journal, while from 1960 until its demise in 1965, Juan García Ponce took over as editor. Each "phase" offers a somewhat different nuance to the *revista*'s overall direction: it was a Mexican journal of literature, not an exclusive journal of Mexican literature. The opening issues, benefiting from Fuentes's effortless cosmopolitanism and his range of international contacts and readings, showed that the "nopal curtain" had been well and truly lifted. The first issue, for example, features Paz, the anti-Peronist short story by Borges and Bioy Casares, "El hijo de su amigo," an essay by Malraux, an essay on Rulfo, and contributions by García Ascot and Xirau. The section "Talón de Aquiles" offers widespread commentaries on literary events throughout the world. This first issue could also announce that in its subsequent issues, there would be contributions from different generations of Mexican writers, Alfonso Reyes, Daniel Cosío Villegas, Juan Rulfo, and Ali Chamucero, and from different writers in Latin America—the Argentines Julio Cortázar, José Bianco, Silvina Ocampo, and Enrique Molina, the Peruvian poet, Emilio Westphalen, the Nicaraguan Ernesto Cardenal, the Cubans José Lezama Lima and Cinto Vitier—as well as North Americans and European writers from Cummings and Muriel Rukeyser to André Breton, Simone Weil, and Kostas Papaioannou. The magazine made a point of offering special sections, such as on contemporary North American poetry (issue 5, May–June, 1956) and on new Mexican writers. At the end of its first year, in issue 6 (July–August 1956), the magazine listed all its contributors with a bibliographical note and declared: "The number and proportion of the authors published (73 in total: 33 Mexicans, 18 writers from Spain and Latin America, 22 foreign writers) makes us think that the two aims of the magazine—to have our writers known abroad and to publish foreign writers in Mexico—are being met. We would like to acknowledge the support we have received in different publications: *Mito* in Bogotá, *Orígenes* in Havana, *Papel Literario* in Caracas, *The Times Literary Supplement* in London and the French journals *L'Esprit des Lettres* y *Les Lettres Nouvelles*."[49] This sense of cultural bridge building across a network of international writers and publications would be continued under Juan García Ponce through special editions (on eroticism, North American writers and Borges, to give a few examples), and through Mexican writers such as Jorge Ibargüengoitia, José de la Colina, and Carlos Monsiváis, along with new residents in Mexico like Gabriel García Márquez, being put alongside contemporary writers and essayists, from Yevtushenko to the critical theorists of mass communications, Adorno and Marcuse. The *Revista* remained a decorous literary journal throughout.

The same was true of the journal *Diálogos,* edited by Ramón Xirau. In the first issue of the magazine (November–December 1964), Xirau would write:

> *Diálogos* believes in the need to open doors to writers of all nationalities; it believes that this need is, in our times, an obligation. It believes that, alongside the natural collaboration of Mexican authors—dialogue begins at home—that it is absolutely necessary to have the constant collaboration—in every issue—of writers from Spanish America. This is the time for us to get to know each other; it is the time to do away with false distances and false geographical barriers. We hope that writers from Mexico, Spanish America, Europe, The United States and the new nations of the world see *Diálogos* at least as a room within a shared house.[50]

For a time, especially in its early years, the magazine did fulfill many of its declared intentions.

It was in little magazines such as the short-lived *S.Nob,* edited by the novelist Salvador Elizondo, along with the film critic Emilio García Riera and Juan García Ponce, that the more caustic and experimental aspects of early sixties culture could be found. Elizondo would remark in an interview: "We wanted to publish a literary magazine, but one that was not exclusively literary, because our generation liked having fun…We wanted to be snob anarchists. We wanted to talk about everything, about Pound, sex and drugs…"[51] The film producer Gustavo Alatriste would bankroll the endeavor for a short time—leaving García Márquez to edit his profitable women's magazines—allowing a group of writers, film directors, artists, and critics, that included the Colombian Alvaro Mutis and the Chilean writer, and later filmmaker, Alejandro Jodorovsky, to offer a caustic, irreverent view of modern culture. In fact it is difficult to think of any magazine published anywhere in the world at this time as prepared as *S.Nob* to take things to the edge. They mixed *maudit* writers such as Genet, Arrabal, and Sade, with humorous essays and stories exploring such diverse issues as lycanthropy and incest. Notes on modern film, theater, and music appeared alongside poems and line drawings by Leonora Carrington, and freewheeling cartoons appeared on every page. It was all effortlessly hip, up to date and scabrous. It was also a financial drain and Alatriste withdrew funding after seven issues. Echoes of this magazine—in particular the analysis of *maudit* writers and eroticism, and some of the humor—would later resound in *Plural*, as we shall see.

Another slightly younger, equally irreverent generation was also beginning to emerge that would later become known as *la onda*, a term that initially referred to the influence and appropriation of rock music.[52] The novel that has been seen to start a countercultural *literary* movement was Gustavo Sainz's *Gazapo* (1965). Both he and José Agustín, another quintessential *onda* writer, were two of six writers featured in the "New Twentieth Century Mexican Writers Introduced by Themselves" series, a group of short autobiographical texts. Another writer in that series, Carlos Monsiváis, was emerging as the main new journalist of the sixties, a flâneur and cartographer of Mexico City, equally at home in high culture and in counterculture. He edited another volume of Mexican poetry, *Antología de la poesía mexicana del siglo XX* in the same year as the volume that Paz coedited with Siglo XXI, including 45 poets born between 1862 (F. González de León) and 1940 (Homero Aridjis). This deliberate melding of high culture and popular culture, of asserting the place of the popular in "serious" literature would become an increasingly important factor in the developing field.

This was the literary climate, between 1953 and the mid-sixties, in which Paz would play such an influential part in shaping, from inside Mexico in the mid-fifties, and later from India, where he occupied the post of ambassador. At the time the most energetic and influential figure of the sixties, in Mexico and in the wider world of Latin American literature, appeared to be Carlos Fuentes. He wrote a series of influential novels and was an indefatigable literary critic and political commentator, a movie scriptwriter and film critic, an eloquent, polyglot, speaker, and a person of great personal charisma. It is through Fuentes that this overview of the Mexican cultural field must broaden out to consider wider trends in Latin America in the sixties: the literary movement that has been given the name of "the boom."

The Boom and its Magazines

In 1983, the *New York Times* published a watercolor by the Mexican painter and cartoonist, Abel Quezada entitled "The Boom," which depicts seven writers sitting in a café. The main focus of Quezada's sketch is a large table, around which are grouped six Latin American writers. Even in New York, by the time of Quezada's painting in the early eighties, their features are immediately recognizable, for the image and personal circumstances of the writers had been marketed as vigorously as their works. To the front and slightly to the side of the main group sits the Argentine Jorge Luis Borges, in a characteristic pose, leaning on his walking stick and seemingly glancing with wide myopic eyes, outside the frame. Behind him is the rather intense figure of the Mexican Carlos Fuentes, next to the tall, boyish-looking, rather impassive Argentine, Julio Cortázar, who has his arm around—in the center of the picture—a smiling, colorfully dressed, Gabriel García Márquez. Alongside García Márquez, facing out of frame, is the only poet in the group, the Mexican Octavio Paz. Next to and just in front of Paz is the very dapper figure of the Peruvian Mario Vargas Llosa, wearing slightly rakish two-tone shoes. Behind Vargas Llosa, sitting on his own at a smaller, more remote table, is the somewhat morose figure of the Mexican Juan Rulfo. In a few brush strokes, Quezada offers a plausible and persuasive depiction of the dynamics of the boom. There is an eccentric precursor in Borges, four major, central novelists supported by a poet who was also an essayist and a strong promoter of the modern in many influential articles, and a figure like Rulfo who, despite his talents, never wanted to sit in the limelight of the central table. The picture is also significant in what it does not depict: there is no writer from Brazil and quite clearly there are no women. There is also no reference to Pablo Neruda.

The café is a male space set somewhere in an imagined Latin America. On the wall behind the writers is a poster of a shadowy military man in dark glasses who has something to do with a presidential campaign, and two further pictures of a football team and of scantily dressed dancing ladies. There has always been a close identification between literary groups and cafés in the capital cities of Latin America. Many of the vanguard movements of the 1920s, for example, were identified with certain little magazines and with particular bars or cafés. Borges talked often of sitting up through the night in bars in Buenos Aires listening to the bewitching conversation of Macedonio Fernández, or meeting the boisterous *Martín Fierro avant garde* group of writers and painters at dinners or lunches. Although women writers were often part of these groups, they were often delegated to the role of child or muse as was the case of Norah Lange with the *Ultraistas* and *Martin Fierristas* in Buenos Aires. Mexican writers from the sixties, as we have seen, would favor certain cafés in the *zona rosa* of Mexico City.

Quezada's imagined café is somewhat anachronistic for several reasons. Whilst certain city spaces, and cafés in particular, would continue to be associated with modern cultural movements in the sixties and beyond, the boom cut across these national literary topographies. It would be very unlikely to find these writers in the same café in the sixties, unless it was in Paris, or Barcelona or, in some cases, Havana. Indeed Gerald Martin has pointed out that the first time all the boom writers (not including Paz) met under the same roof was in the country house of Julio Cortázar in 1970 in Saignon, when they all assembled from different parts to attend the premiere of Fuentes' play *The One Eyed Man is King* at the Avignon Festival.[53] The intimacy of the national and the local that café culture might imply gives way in the sixties to something that is more fluid and restless, the space of an airport lounge, for example (although this reality is ironic because at least three of the writers, Fuentes, Vargas Llosa, and García Márquez had a deep fear of flying). Indeed Mario Vargas Llosa recalls that his first meeting with García Márquez in 1967 was when their planes touched down almost simultaneously in Caracas airport.[54] Whilst few of the writers would have agreed wholeheartedly with the *boutade* of Jacques Vaché to André Breton quoted at the beginning of Cortázar's novel *Rayuela* (*Hopscotch*, 1963)—"rien ne vous tue un homme comme d'être obligé de represénter un pays"—the national would certainly become a more porous and malleable term. The painting is, however, correct in suggesting a shared intimacy, at least for a few years, perhaps a decade. Leaving aside the two "precursor" figures of Borges and Rulfo, the central protagonists of Quezada's illustration were certainly friends throughout the sixties and were each other's most supportive critics. It was Carlos Fuentes who would be the natural leader of this group. Pressures of politics, stardom, and conflicting egos would take their toll on these friendships in later years, but in the period of the boom, there was a sense of a shared project. The boom was mainly associated with the novel, so it was a movement that Paz was somewhat peripheral to, although the visibility of his own poetry and criticism increased enormously in the sixties, especially in the United States and throughout Latin America as part of the wider movements described below. In the world of the boom *novelists*, Fuentes was the natural leader.

Beginnings are notoriously difficult to define: what we have in literature are continuities and breaks with the past. Did the boom begin when Jorge Luis Borges was awarded, along with Samuel Beckett, the Formentor Prize of 1961 that guaranteed his translation into different European languages? Or when the youthful Mario Vargas Llosa won in 1962 the Biblioteca Breve prize offered by the Spanish publishers Seix Barral for his manuscript *Los impostores* that would later be retitled *La ciudad y los perros* (*Time of the Hero*)? When Carlos Fuentes published *La muerte de Artemio Cruz* (*The Death of Artemio Cruz)* in 1962? When Julio Cortázar brought out *Rayuela* (*Hopscotch*), his extraordinary Baedeker of the new, in 1963, or when the Mexico-based Gabriel García Márquez first published *Cien años de soledad* (*One Hundred Years of Solitude*) in Argentina in 1967? Whatever inaugural date different critics might put, this chapter deals with developments from the late fifties to the late sixties.

Cultural historian Marshall Berman gives an evocative reading of sixties culture: "All the modernisms and anti modernisms of the 1960s, then, were seriously flawed. But their sheer plenitude, along with their intensity and liveliness of expression generated a common language, a vibrant ambience, a shared horizon of experience and desire...The initiatives...sprang from a largeness of spirit and imagination and from an ardent desire to seize the day."[55] While it is obviously dangerous to generalize across continents and across cultures, we can argue that Latin America shares to some degree this optimism that Berman associated with the sixties. Indeed we have already marked out a particularly vibrant Mexican cultural field. Two different political projects helped to modernize and radicalize the political and cultural climate: the Cuban Revolution and the rhetoric and realities of what economists at the time called "developmentalism."

We should not, with over forty years of hindsight and in a very different political climate, underestimate the achievements and also the hope offered by the Cuban Revolution. It was held by most at the time in Latin America to be an exemplary nationalist and anti-imperialist movement that seemed to demand an intellectual and practical commitment and offered the utopian promise of uniting the artistic and political vanguards. In the early years at least, Cuba invited young writers, awarded literary prizes, published new work in their journal *Casa de las Américas*, and organized symposia and round table discussions. There is no doubt that writers such as Carlos Fuentes and Mario Vargas Llosa sympathized with this early promise of social and cultural change. Carlos Fuentes wrote part of *La muerte de Artemio Cruz,* his quintessential boom novel, while in residence in Havana, while Vargas Llosa would persuasively argue in his acceptance speech at being awarded the Rómulo Gallegos prize in 1967—evocatively and significantly entitled "Literature is Fire," a statement that could almost be read as a manifesto of a group—that the underdevelopment of Latin America could only be solved through radical means.[56] He was wrong, of course, in his analysis, but the passion and commitment of the argument illustrates that specific time.

Fear of another Cuba would, of course, dominate U.S. foreign policy in the 1960s in Latin America, and would lead to policies that form part of any overall definition of the boom. These policies ranged from support for modernizing, nonrevolutionary regimes such as those of Frondizi in Argentina, Frei in Chile, or Kubitschek in Brazil, to the development of support of certain forms of modern art by cultural foundations such as Ford and Rockefeller, to the establishment of centers of study on Latin America in the United States and in Europe—that were fundamental in generating critical works on the boom and on many other aspects of politics and culture—to the support of translations of Latin American fiction. British critic Jean Franco's most recent book—and Franco, it must be acknowledged, was an important disseminator of knowledge about Latin American literature from the sixties, along with higher profile academics of the time like Emir Rodríguez Monegal who actively disseminated the works of the boom in his magazine *Mundo Nuevo* and in subsequent publications—gives a reading of Spanish American literary texts in the context of the Cold War.[57] This context is clearly important to our overall understanding of the internationalization of the boom writers, but it would be wrong to label their work as "export-led" or their importance as merely a U.S. marketing strategy. Before the novelists had a visibility in world markets, they had found their own Latin American audience.

The sixties, sandwiched in Latin America between populist regimes of the forties and fifties and a wave of military dictatorships in the early to mid-seventies, showed many signs of cultural innovation and modernization (to use another term of the time). Some snapshots of the period must suffice as illustrations. The most impressive, perhaps overblown symbol of the new was the building of the city of Brasília. In a project led by the enthusiastic and charismatic president of Brazil, Juscelino Kubitschek—who promised his country "fifty years of progress in five"—and designed by the architects Oscar Niemeyer and Lúcio Costa, Brasília took shape from the late 1950s and through the 1960s. The ambition and beauty of the project caused Kubitschek to herald it in 1960 as an extraordinary *Brazilian* achievement: "We imported neither architects nor town planning experts to design Brasília. We planned and built it with our own native talents—Niemeyer and Costa—and the laborers who erected it, from the contractor down to the 'candango'…were all our own people. That is why Brasília depicts, more eloquently than words can convey, our level of civilization and our enterprising spirit."[58] Here is an early expression of the optimism of the time, which could be summed up in Octavio Paz's famous phrase that Latin Americans were now contemporaries of all mankind sharing the banquet of civilization on equal terms. The boom, in the same way as Kubitschek described Brasília, would be both formally innovative and "rooted" in a Latin American experience.

Moving to another city—the city of Victoria Ocampo's *Sur*—the late fifties and early sixties in Buenos Aires were marked by innovations in many fields, from the selling of washing machines and washing powders, to new wave cinema, to the introduction of television and mass media advertising, to the growth of psychotherapy and analysis. In literature, a change was taking place in readership, a change noted by the writer and cultural Maecenas Victoria Ocampo. Ocampo had edited the influential literary magazine *Sur* from the early 1930s and *Sur* had been a showcase for the best of Argentine and international literature through the magazine and associated publishing house. For Ocampo, the domain of literature and culture was that of a civilizing minority, an embattled and beleaguered minority, a family affair. Ocampo was still resisting the fact that through the 1960s many more people had access to what had previously been conceived as high-brow culture. Critic Angel Rama—himself a very vocal part of critical debates in the sixties and early seventies—has provided revealing figures of sales of Cortázar novels in the 1960s. If an expected print run was one or two thousand copies for a novel published in 1960, by the end of the decade, sales for each novel would be in the tens of thousands or, in the case of García Márquez's runaway success, *Cien años de soledad*, in hundreds of thousands.[59] The boom helps to cause but also benefits greatly from this growth in middle-class readership in Latin America. One cannot just talk of a qualitative difference in the work of the novelists who published in the 1960s with respect to their predecessors, for it is in this decade, also, when Borges—who would often joke that he sold thirty-seven copies of *Historia universal de la infamia* (*Universal History of Infamy,*

1935) in the 1930s, which was about the number of people that he could personally thank—began to sell in large numbers, in Buenos Aires and throughout Latin America.

A number of factors contribute to this increase apart from obvious demographic changes and growth in urbanization. The story of the boom is linked to the open and aggressive policies of certain publishing houses, in Spain and throughout Latin America. In Barcelona, Carlos Barral set up the Biblioteca Breve prize, which guaranteed widespread distribution for the winner's novel. Within Latin America, some of the larger houses, especially in Argentina and in Mexico—Losada, Sudamericana, Espasa Calpe, Siglo XXI, Joaquín Mortiz, Era—increased their representation and distribution of Spanish American texts and smaller publishing houses grew up and supported contemporary authors. In Barcelona the literary agent Carmen Balcells also began to represent these young, successful writers, adding another marketing dimension—as well as support and shrewd literary guidance—to her literary charges. In an autobiography, as full of fable as of fact, García Márquez spoke of the traveling salesmen who would arrive in Baranquilla in the late forties with books from Argentine publishers such as Losada and Sur: "Thanks to them we were early admirers of Jorge Luis Borges, Julio Cortázar, Felisberto Hernández and the English and American novelists, well translated by Victoria Ocampo's group."[60] But such distribution was infrequent and print runs were small.

The Chilean writer José Donoso would write his own "personal history" of the boom in 1972.[61] In it he repeatedly emphasizes the centrality of this vibrant city, Buenos Aires, in his literary formation, as he escaped from what he experienced as the claustrophobia of cultural life in Chile. Though the driving force behind his own success was in great part his friendship with Carlos Fuentes, who encouraged him and put him in touch with the literary world with great generosity, Donoso also argued that the literary journal *Mundo Nuevo*, established in Paris in 1966 by the Uruguayan critic Emir Rodríguez Monegal, was a key factor in promoting the boom. Unlike the Cuban journal *Casa*, *Mundo Nuevo* avoided discussion of concrete political commitment, and treated contemporary novelists as part of a cultural renaissance free from ideological disputes. It favorably reviewed the latest texts, conducted interviews with authors—the first issue in July 1966 had a long interview with Carlos Fuentes—and printed short extracts of new work. The "inaugural" interview with Fuentes is interesting because it also looks to establish the writer (and perhaps also the interviewer) as an international, cosmopolitan "star."

Rodríguez Monegal prefaces the interview with a laudatory pen portrait. After describing Fuentes's expressive features—building up the star persona—he remarks: "The personality of Carlos Fuentes is almost as incandescent as his novels...He is a natural communicator in several languages. He is one of the most lively and polemical figures in contemporary Latin American letters."[62]

Mundo Nuevo chimed with the U.S. Cold War support of literary modernism and it perhaps came as no surprise when the body supporting the magazine, the Congress for Cultural Freedom, was found to receive its funds from the CIA. As we have argued above, this is a further example of the boom attracting, for the space of a decade, the support of both politically engaged and culturally modernizing groups. The honeymoon, in particular with Cuba, would end quite abruptly for some, in the early seventies, as we shall see in chapter two. In the early issues, however, some writers seemed unaware of the ideological storm clouds building up around the magazine and García Márquez would be happy to receive advance publicity for *Cien años* in the magazine, even though he would later argue that Monegal had misled him (had "cuckolded" him) about the funding of the enterprise. Fuentes was sent the first seventy pages of *Cien años* and he declared in a letter to García Márquez, the day after his interview with Rodríguez Monegal for *Mundo Nuevo*, that the work was a masterpiece (Fuentes to García Márquez, Paris 15 April 1966). A year later, having read the entire novel, he would write enthusiastically to García Márquez (and to Cortázar within this letter), reaffirming this view and also his belief in a community of supportive writers in Latin America: "And what a sense of relief, Julio: don't you think that every successful Latin American novel liberates you a bit, allows you, amidst the enthusiasm, to map out your own territory, to deepen your own vision, with the fraternal knowledge that others are fashioning their own vision, in a sort of dialogue with you?" (Fuentes to García Márquez, 22 July 1967).[63] It was this community that *Mundo Nuevo* sought to foster, address, and promote, but it could not contain the inevitable ideological schisms.

In the months before the publication of *Mundo Nuevo*, the editor of *Casa de las Américas*, Roberto Fernández Retamar launched a very public attack on the magazine, which was syndicated throughout Latin America in different supplements and little magazines including *México en la Cultura* and *Marcha* in Uruguay. After Rodríguez Monegal had written to him on 1 November 1965 announcing a "literary magazine in Paris for Latin America" and saying that the journal was "linked to the Congress for the Freedom of Culture, but not dependent on it," Retamar replied that the Congress was financed by the United States and that its only "mission was not the 'freedom of culture' but the defense of US imperialist interests.'" The debate covered five letters ending in a dialogue of the deaf, with Rodríguez Monegal refusing to be branded as anti-Cuban and offering *Mundo Nuevo* to the best Cuban writers, and Retamar reaffirming his belief that Monegal was at best just naïve.[64] The Cubans in *Casa*, of course, would have been rubbing their hands when they could read in the *New York Times* in April 1966 of the links between the CIA and the Congress for Cultural Freedom. While the journal was influential for a period—and marked a beleaguered space of cultural modernization—it was surrounded by increasing debate and Rodríguez Monegal would soon resign.

An event that received coverage in the first issues of *Mundo Nuevo* was the 1966 P.E.N Club Congress held in June in New York. It was attended by a number of Latin American writers and Rodríguez Monegal was involved in chairing certain sessions. Once again the Cubans rounded on the event castigating writers for attending an event in the "belly of the monster" of U.S. imperialism. They singled out for particular opprobrium the Chilean poet Pablo Neruda, arguably the most important social poet in Latin America and a distinguished member of the Communist Party, along with Carlos Fuentes.[65] If the broadside against *Mundo Nuevo* seemed to many to be justified, the attack on Neruda was widely regarded as gratuitous and insulting, a clear demonstration of a narrowing of outlook, after the heady days of the honeymoon period with Cuba in the early sixties. Certainly Neruda would never forgive the slight. Fuentes put it well in a letter to Neruda. After expressing his disbelief at the accusation of the Cubans, he remarks that: "NOBODY can question the extent of your commitment. We thought that the paranoid spirit of Zhdanov was a thing of the past. I don't think this comes from people like Alejo (Carpentier), who are above such things, but rather from individuals like Retamar and Desnoes whose revolutionary consciousness is more recent and more naïve, but not as solid as their desire to climb the bureaucratic ladder. I find it intolerable that they dare give you of all people lessons about revolution. But what is worse is that in their desire for bureaucratic promotion, they look to belittle, or are incapable of understanding... the victory that your trip to the United States represents. For isn't it a victory that you read the poems that we heard in the very heart of the empire? Isn't it a victory for everyone that left wing North American writers managed to get the bureaucrats to let you into the country…Isn't it a victory that these honest men, friends of Latin America, feel that they are not alone, that they can count on our support? Isolating people, undermining them, abandoning them, that's the game that Yankee imperialism plays."[66]

The attacks on Fuentes over the P.E.N conference would certainly help to cool his enthusiasm for the Cuban regime. Fuentes must have felt somewhat beleaguered at that moment since he often found it difficult to obtain a visa to enter the United States because of the clauses of the McWarran Act that excluded "Communist" sympathizers. At the same time, however, he was being pilloried by the Cubans for being a lackey of U.S. imperialism. He was beginning to find the rather simple solutions offered by the Cubans as inappropriate, as he remarked in the same letter to Pablo Neruda. He ridicules the statement by Retamar and colleagues in their open letter to Neruda that any socialist revolution has to pass through a phase of guerrilla struggle. "For me, in my country, the fight against imperialism means to fight for internal transformations, based on Mexican reality. And I'm not thinking of sacrificing this strategy on the altar of the paranoid deliria of two or three freshly minted revolutionary Cubans: I do more for the revolution in Mexico, speaking from New York, attacking the mask of 'revolutionary prestige' that the right wing government in Mexico shelters behind, than struggling up the Sierra Maestra to eat a pepper omelet. Enough. You know all this better than I do."[67] This from a writer full of enthusiasm for the revolution in the late fifties and early sixties, who would support the cultural center at Casa de las Américas and the journal of the same name as it attracted writers from all over Latin America and would help to define the debates concerning culture and the imaginative proximity of revolution that had so engaged the younger Octavio Paz in the thirties. Yet here, by 1966, was a clear example of a hardening of opinions.

In any event, Paz had always treated the Cuban revolution with a certain caution. Some three decades following his political engagement in the mid-thirties and beyond, Paz was much more skeptical about the nature and definitions of "revolution" in general and about the vanguard claims of Cuba in particular. If we consider the enormous output of his poetry and essays in the sixties—the nonpoetic work alone ran to eight full-length books, from *Cuadrivio* in 1965 to *Conjunciones y disyunciones* (*Conjunctions and Disjunctions*) in 1969, including major analyses of the work of Claude Lévi-Strauss and Marcel Duchamp[68]—then the lack of support for Paz in the pages of *Casa* is quite striking.

Paz Quest for a Personal Vehicle

From his post as Ambassador in India, with visits back to Mexico and Europe for different cultural events, Paz was supportive of the different cultural outlets and enterprises in Mexico, while being up to date with journals such as *Mundo Nuevo* and the newsweekly journal *Primera Plana* in Argentina, which, in the style of *Time* or *Newsweek,* offered a new style of political and cultural commentary in the 1960s in Argentina: other magazines would subsequently copy its format all over the continent. From its first issue in 1962 that carried on its front cover an image of J.F. Kennedy, the magazine would exude sophistication and modernity and was up to date with all the latest fashions. In the section on books, the world of authors and books became news, beyond the domain of small literary groups or *cénacles.* And what could be more fashionable than this seemingly new writing coming from all over Latin America, or the success of home-grown talents. In *Primera Plana,* as in *Mundo Nuevo,* primacy was given to the interview, to highlighting the writer as star. A striking example of this new journalism can be found in issue 234 of the magazine (20–26 June 1967), which displays Gabriel García Márquez on the front cover, followed by an interview with García Márquez and a review by Tomás Eloy Martínez of the recently published *Cien años de soledad. Primera Plana* was a model to be emulated in the sixties and early seventies: it helped, along with the *suplementos* in Mexico, as we have seen, to break the mold of cultural criticism as the bastions of a small civilized minority, publishing in little magazines for a few.

What has clearly emerged in the publication of the correspondence between Octavio Paz and the publisher Arnaldo Orfila was that Paz was seriously exploring the possibility of launching his own literary magazine in Mexico, along with Carlos Fuentes and Tomás Segovia. There is a letter dated 16 November 1967 from Paz in New Delhi to Orfila talking about recent conversations in Mexico. Paz was on an autumn visit to Mexico in 1967, between August and October. The letter picks up on this conversation, by talking about a need to raise money in Paris for the magazine. We know from other articles by Paz and from interviews, that Paz had had a conversation with Malraux, De Gaulle's minister of culture about the need to launch an ambitious magazine, in Spanish, on Latin American culture and politics, and that Malraux had advised him that the French government might be prepared to offer some financial assistance. The Paz-Orfila letters reveal how detailed these plans were and how much Paz was looking to return to a world of magazine editing. We have seen that there was clearly space for a journal of this sort. The little magazines in Mexico had limitations in terms of readership and resources. The "internationalist" journal *Mundo Nuevo* had foundered. The Cuban *Casa* was becoming increasingly inflexible and dogmatic. In terms of personnel, Segovia had great experience of magazine editorship; Fuentes had a range of international contacts and was becoming disenchanted with both *Mundo Nuevo* and *Casa*; while Paz was clearly imagining a life outside the diplomatic service. There was a strong bond between Fuentes and Paz: it seemed a very practical and viable arrangement. Paz had clearly asked Orfila, in Siglo XXI, to publish and distribute the magazine for him—Orfila had already published *Poesía en movimiento* and *Corriente alterna* and was publishing Fuentes's *Zona sagrada* (*Holy Place*), dedicated to Octavio and Marie-José Paz—and to work out some precise costing that Paz could take to the French. The practical and experienced Orfila was enthusiastic about the project, but said that it could only work if Paz was back living full time in Mexico: he probably remembered the difficulties that had emerged in trying to get the four editors of *Poesía en movimiento* to agree to a final selection of poets, with Paz, an engaged and critical commentator, based in India. With Paz potentially in another continent, and the other editor, Carlos Fuentes, known to be an inveterate globetrotter, the principle of a settled editorship was obviously important to Orfila. Paz wrote to Orfila on 12 December 1967, from New Delhi: "Once we have resolved the fundamental problem: to assure the funding for the magazine for at least two years, we will deal with the other problem that bothers you (and me as well): my return to Mexico. On this matter I can only say that my decision will rest on two things: the first, the magazine; the second, my being able to obtain in the University or in some other place a decent amount that will allow me to get by decorously and have some time for my own work."[69] In a later letter dated 19 February 1968, he wrote that, "Gastón García Cantú has made certain proposals to me that I am minded to accept once the issue of the magazine becomes clear."[70]

In the event, the money from France came with too many strings attached—the magazine was seen as an extension of French cultural propaganda funded by the Ministry of Foreign Affairs—but Paz was still anxious to explore the possibility of funding within Mexico. In a letter of 5 April 1968, he gives Orfila an outline of the proposed magazine to take to the editorial board of Siglo XXI. He remarks that he and Fuentes,

> ...think that our magazine must be, above all else, a magazine of criticism. This word is applicable to the sphere of thought and to the spheres of art, literature, politics and society. A critical revision of the ideas that surround us; a rigorous examination—and I don't mean petty, quite the reverse—of literature and art in Latin America and the world; a criticism of social and political structures; a criticism of the reality of our continent. Even creative literature, as I conceive it, is criticism...We want to edit a literary magazine, a magazine of new, Spanish American literature. We want to engage with what is new in other languages and our pages will be open to like-minded writers from Europe and the United States. It will be a Spanish American and a Latin American magazine: the new writers from Brazil will have the preferential coverage they deserve...We will not fall into the trap of nationalism. We are cosmopolitan by fate, by birth: we are of this time.[71]

In this correspondence there is no detailed analysis of what the content of this journal might be and how the different interests of Paz and Fuentes might be fused. Paz's work in the sixties had taken him from an exploration of Mexican myths, to an appreciation of the cultures of the East. In Eastern cultures, and in the ethnographic work of Claude Lévi-Straus, he had found strong bases for a critique of the idea of progress in modern culture. Lévi-Strauss offers a model, but does not give enough attention, for Paz, to the erotic. In Paz's own analysis modern societies degrade sexuality and he associates the deterioration of the erotic principle in the West with its celebration of technology and progress. He is thus drawn to artists such as Duchamp who look to criticize this aspect of modern culture through his focus on the machine as the critical symbol of modernity.[72] How these concerns, and Paz's dominant interests in modern poetry, would have dovetailed with Fuentes's energetic promotion of the modern novel, his work on Faulkner, and his support for the internationalization of the boom, and what space they both might have found for the blend of popular and high culture represented by Carlos Monsiváis, are questions that, in the end, are never answered. But they would recur again when Paz was given the opportunity to shape his own journal some years later. As we have seen in this chapter, Paz, Fuentes and Monsiváis represent three different ways of seeing Mexican and international culture, and each had his own strong ideas that would not readily blend or coexist with those of the other two.

Right up to letters dated the end of August 1968, the subject of a new *revista* remains central to this correspondence, as Paz and Orfila try to come up with funding alternatives. Orfila is talking to people within different Mexican Ministries, as well as suggesting that certain public sector companies, or semi-official organizations such as banks and utility companies might be persuaded to invest, although he points out the perennial problem of "independence" within a state system. He remarks in a letter dated 10 May 1968 that government officials have told him that "these public service institutions would be very cautious when it came to agreeing to help a magazine that might be critical of certain aspects of the nation."[73] Paz wonders whether it might be possible to assimilate already existing magazines like *Diálogos*—which, according to Orfila had a print run of 1,000 copies—or *Cuadernos Americanos,* but Orfila argued that it would be best to start afresh rather than seeking to take over and revive an existing publication. The matter was still unresolved when, on 21 September, Paz wrote in a postscript that he had just heard that the army had occupied UNAM. He remarks that, "I continue to think that we have entered the final phase of the crisis: there will either be reforms (more substantial than those sought by the students) or the state of unrest will spread to other groups and classes with unpredictable consequences."[74] Mexico was about to change in a most dramatic way and Octavio Paz was to become a central—if not the central—interpreter of these changes for Mexican readers.

Chapter 2

The Genesis and Birth of *Plural*

Octavio Paz Post-1968

A crucial watershed in contemporary Mexican history and, by extension, in the diplomatic career of Octavio Paz, came with the massacre in Tlatelolco on 2 October 1968. We are not looking here to reprise the vast literature existing on the student movement of 1968 and its tragic outcome, or even the reaction of intellectuals to the events of 1968.[1] The thread guiding us through this period will be the actions and selected writings of Octavio Paz, because the events of 1968, and more widely the question of politics and democracy in Mexico, would from this time become a constant preoccupation in his work.

A year earlier, in an interview conducted with Elena Poniatowska on a brief visit to Mexico in October 1967, the ambassador in India was talking enthusiastically about the expansiveness of sixties culture. He had just returned from poetry festivals in London and Spoletto. In Poniatowska's words, "Ever since Octavio Paz has been back in Mexico, he has been talking a great deal about poetry festivals, in Spoletto and London, about the community of poets and about how now, more than ever before, poets from different language backgrounds have got to know each other and understand each other. 'In London the other night, we read our poetry in front of ten thousand people,' says Octavio enthusiastically, 'It was extraordinary.'"[2] International poetry, sixties rock, Lévi-Strauss and French structuralism, the lessons of India, a theoretical discussion of the different terms, *revolution, revolt* and *rebellion* taken from his new work *Corriente alterna*, all pointed in this interview to a mood of optimism. Paz was still recognized as arguably the most important cultural figure in Mexico, a critical conscience, a prophet and a guide, although we have seen that his place was disputed by different tendencies: the pro-Cuban left; the boom novelists and the countercultural *onda* writers and critics. Carlos Monsiváis, in one of his many articles on the experiences of 1968[3]—he was one of the founder members of the AIAE, the Assembly of Intellectuals, Artists and Writers affiliated to the student movement—chose to include interest in the work of Paz and other writers as a mark of the "modernity" of the student movement: "A significant minority enjoyed reading novels and poems as prophecies. We can call science students modern if, in their leisure time, they immerse themselves in Cortázar's *Rayuela* or Paz's *La estación violenta*."[4]

Since Paz was in India in 1968, he was not following or experiencing the student movement on a daily basis. In any event, his post as a diplomat would have circumscribed what he could have said. But it is clear that he paid close attention to the 1968 movements in Paris and the United States and that he saw them as in some ways similar to the aspirations and the protests of the surrealists in the 1930s. What better call to a long-standing surrealist than slogans such as, "Dessous les pavés c'est la plage." It was this enthusiasm for the new energies that had made him start discussing ideas for a literary magazine with André Malraux, Carlos Fuentes and Tomás Segovia. As the student movement gained in popularity and clashed with government forces throughout the summer—as is outlined most vividly in issue 340 of *La Cultura en México,* entitled "México 68. ¿Represión o democracia?"—the Mexican Foreign Ministry asked Paz to send them his assessment of how India had dealt with similar situations to those occurring in Mexico. Paz replied on 6 September that the situation in Mexico was distinct: "It is not a social revolution, even if a number of the leaders are radical revolutionaries. It is a question of reforming our political system. If we do not start now, the next decade will be violent."[5] When, one month later, Díaz Ordaz did not heed his warning, Paz looked to resign immediately after the massacre. The somewhat labyrinthine processes of the Mexican diplomatic corps meant that Paz had to declare himself *en disponibilidad,* the only form of "resignation" open to him. The official Mexican press would later try to slur Paz with the term *en disponibilidad,* suggesting that he was more interested in pension rights than in principles. Paz also cancelled a lecture series at the Colegio Nacional scheduled for 15 October. His most resounding form of protest was a short poem, dated 3 October, which he sent to the Cultural Programme of the XIX Olympics (having previously refused to participate in the poetry reading organized as part of the Olympic Games celebrations). His poem, "México: Olimpiada de 1968" ("Mexico: 1968 Olympics"), and letter to the committee was published in the 30 October edition of *La Cultura en México*, after the imposed *tregua olímpica* (Olympic truce), when the government looked to shut out all bad news during the time of the games. The poem also appeared in the Argentine magazine *Sur* (issue 314, September–October 1968). The central part of the poem, in italics, summed up what many thought but few expressed: that if the shame felt by every individual Mexican over the massacre could become a collective force, then it would have great power, and become a "crouching lion."

In a government bureaucratic system of some three million employees, Paz's resignation was an isolated event. Other writer-state officials in prominent positions—Agustín Yañez, the Secretary of Public Education and Martín Luis Guzmán, who held a state job in the cultural field and was also the director of the journal *El Tiempo*—continued in place. Guzmán, indeed, was one of the most vigorous opponents of the student movement and would put his pen and the resources of his magazine to the defense of the actions of Díaz Ordaz. Closer to Paz, both his former wife Elena Garro and his daughter Helena Paz made declarations in the conservative newspaper *El Universal* attacking him and implicating intellectuals as the true authors of the 2 October killings, by inciting students to rebel.[6] At the same time, government sources circulated a version that Paz had been misled by false versions of the massacre circulated by the foreign press.

By contrast, the editorial team of *La Cultura en México*—Fernando Benítez, José Emilio Pacheco, Carlos Monsiváis, and Vicente Rojo—wrote a statement, in defense of Paz published in early November. After ridiculing the idea that Paz had fallen victim to misinformation from the outside, they stated:

> Furthermore, Octavio Paz has always represented our country in the best possible way. After resigning not just from a brilliant career and an Ambassadorial post, but also from a secure future—which was no mean thing—he assumed his age-old responsibility as a poet and as a Mexican, which implies a total commitment. On the one hand we have the bureaucratic language of people who never resign from anything, putting an end to an honorable twenty five year career and, on the other hand, a brief poem expressing anger and disgust with blinding clarity. The tremendous weight of this poem has tipped the balance in favor of justice and truth, in an unequivocal fashion, which is the

privilege of a great poet. *La Cultura en México,* which has been fortunate to count Octavio Paz among its most distinguished contributors, would like to openly express to him our support, our appreciation and our fraternal affection.[7]

On 30 October, José Emilio Pacheco would also publish in *La Cultura* a poem entitled "Lectura de los 'Cantares Mexicanos'," which can be read as a direct commentary on the events of 2 October, albeit framed as a rewriting of ancient Nahuatl texts. *La Cultura en México,* and the magazine *Siempre!* maintained its integrity before and after 2 October, as did the newspaper *Excélsior* under its new editor Julio Scherer, who was appointed in September 1968. Scherer, of course, would later become central to the next stage of Paz's career.

Paz gave interviews to the *Le Monde* correspondent in India that appeared in mid-November.[8] In it Paz, now free from diplomatic ties, could declare that the PRI had ritually sacrificed its students in an act of pure state terrorism, and that the way forward for Mexico was a curb on the personal power of each president and the disintegration of the single party system. He had particularly harsh words for writers who remained as state lackeys: Martín Luis Guzmán, the former great writer and comrade of Pancho Villa, was now publishing "monstrous" statements about what had happened on 2 October. Later in the year, he would leave India for Paris and not return to Mexico until after the presidential term of Díaz Ordaz. As he left New Delhi, he wrote to Orfila on 23 October that he would like to write an account of press coverage of recent events, in partnership with Fuentes, a sort of "black book" of Mexican journalism.[9] In a later letter, dated Nice 12 December 1968, he expressed an interest in developing the idea of a collaborative book on the events in Mexico that would include a chronicle of the times, and a mixture of documents and theoretical texts. In a letter to Orfila dated 23 January, he outlined a very detailed plan for the book. In his reply, Orfila expressed his caution that perhaps it would be too early, in the current climate, to publish such a book in Mexico. In the event it would be Elena Poniatowska who would carry through a similar project, *La noche de Tlatelolco* (*Massacre in Mexico*), published in the next presidential term in 1971. In the letter of 12 December, Paz spoke of being met at the quayside in Barcelona by Fuentes, García Márquez, Carlos Barral, and others. Fuentes still wanted to continue with the magazine, but by now Paz was finding his ideas rather ambitious and impractical.[10]

For the next two and a half years, Paz would spend time at the family home of his wife in Nice and then move to Paris before taking up a post as a visiting professor at the university of Pittsburgh. The university circuit in the United States—which had greatly expanded in the area of Latin American studies through the 1960s—flooded Paz with offers. He remarked in the letter dated 12 December to Orfila that he had received more than fifteen proposals from different universities. From Pittsburgh he moved to the University of Texas in Austin. It was in Austin on 30 October 1969 that he gave the Hackett Memorial Lecture dedicated to an analysis of contemporary Mexico as a "postscript" to the publication of *El laberinto de la soledad* in 1950. He would later revise and extend this paper into a short book, *Posdata,* written in Austin (the date and place of the prologue is Austin, 14 December 1969), and published in Mexico in 1970. In the calendar year of 1970, Paz was the Simón Bolivar Visiting Professor at the University of Cambridge, England, where he would write to his publisher Orfila about the reception of *Posdata.* It was Orfila's wife who had come up with the title *Posdata:* Paz had initially favored the much more directly political title, *Olympics and Tlatelolco,* which later became one of the subheadings of the book. Orfila is at pains to point out to Paz that discretion is advisable, that even at the end of November 1969, "although there might be more openness in certain respects, the issue about which the authorities are hyper sensitive is precisely the words 'Tlatelolco-2 October.'"[11]

With a prologue and three sections—"The Olympics and Tlatelolco," "Developmentalism and other Mirages," and the "Critique of the Pyramid,"—Paz moves from a consideration of the student movement and the recent massacre in Mexico, to an overview of Mexican politics since the Revolution, to a speculation about the continuities between the Aztec past and the current regimes, in term of a unconscious savage, subterranean "intra" history that recurs throughout the centuries, demanding blood sacrifices. Most criticism has concentrated on the poetic/metaphoric third section, giving little attention to the earlier part of the analysis, where Paz is very clear in his criticism of the brutality of the current regime and the undemocratic nature of the political system.[12] Indeed, the essay opens with a clear sense of outrage at backwardness and underdevelopment in Latin America, that Latin Americans are the uninvited dinner guests who have come in through the back door of the West, intruders reaching modernity when the lights were about to go out, always late. And yet, despite this, the poets and writers of the subcontinent were on a par with any writers the world over.[13] Paz states that his analysis might be both a postscript to *Labyrinth* and an introduction to a future book on the nature and development of Latin America. Of course, this was a book that he would never write, yet it was an idea that would reverberate in the cultural journals that he would later edit. The key word in this introduction to *Posdata* is "relationship": "We are nothing except a relationship: something that cannot be defined unless it is part of history. The question what is Mexico is inseparable to the question about the future of Latin America which, in turn, is part of the wider question of the relations between Latin America and the United States" (p.271). We should remember that this is a lecture given initially in the United States at a moment when Paz would become a very regular visiting professor.

Posdata also contains a strong critique of the PRI. It is a party that has had no ideas and no program in forty years of existence (p.283). It has no internal democracy and is dominated by hierarchical groups that pay blind obedience to the president of the day. The PRI has never acted as a critical voice with regard to the power of the president: "In Mexico there is a horror that it would not be excessive to call sacred of anything that could be seen as criticism and intellectual dissidence; a difference of opinion becomes instantly and imperceptibly turned into a personal dispute. This is particularly true of the president: any criticism of his policies is sacrilege" (p.285). In the third section, Paz develops his theory of two Mexicos, one developed, the other underdeveloped and he equates this "other Mexico" as David Brading has usefully observed, as a continuation of Sarmiento's civilization and barbarism debate, with the other Mexico as a form of primitive barbarism, only too quick to pick up the obsidian knife and plunge it into its sacrificial victims.[14] If some critics found the metaphors used in this third section somewhat fanciful, there could be no denying the vigorous criticism of the earlier sections and the desire for engagement with political and historical processes. Paz was particularly irritated that Gastón García Cantú, in a "serious and honest" review had accused him of offering a mythical interpretation of Mexican history. Quite the reverse: "for me the 'critique of the pyramid' is a critique of myth and its *unconscious* foundations. My critique of the pyramid is not anti-Marxist. Far from it: it is part of that criticism of ideology that Marx considered was fundamental to all criticism."[15]

With almost twenty-five years of hindsight (and of increasing criticism), on his eightieth birthday Paz talked to Julio Scherer of the impact of *Posdata*. He saw it as the moment when the Mexican left declared his "civil death": "My ideas were severely criticized by both government spokesmen and by left wing intellectuals. The former were looking to preserve the status quo, while the latter were looking to set up a socialist regime through revolutionary means. The reaction of this first group is natural; the reaction of the intellectuals of the parties of the student movement less so. None of them seemed to be aware of the contradiction between their revolutionary passion, the cult of Che Guevara or any other left wing icon, like Mao, and the real meaning of the process they were involved in: the democratic process."[16] We will explore in later chapters whether this "civil death" did occur quite so quickly, if at all. A writer that Paz would later identify as one of his detractors, Carlos Monsiváis, offers a less conflictive retrospective assessment of this work. In an article written soon after Paz's death, Monsiváis argued that, "The social and cultural left admire Paz. Whether or not they accept his views in *Posdata*, his analysis of '68, they study them very seriously . . . They are devoted to his poetry and even if they are often irritated by some of his attitudes, they have great respect for his lyrical power, the excellence of his prose and his gift for images."[17] Obviously Monsiváis writes this article in the late nineties, not in the heat of the journal wars of the early seventies, where a measured assessment such as this proved more difficult to formulate. But it is certainly the case that, for a number of different reasons, Paz found it wise not to return to Mexico until after the end of the Díaz Ordaz regime.

His choice of teaching in the States and taking up a short-term professorship in Cambridge meant that he was not following the Paris/Barcelona axis of the boom writers and the marked conviviality in the late sixties. The year 1968, for example, found Fuentes, Cortázar, and García Márquez heading for Prague together to see the results of the stifling of the "Prague spring." By 1970, Vargas Llosa had left London for Barcelona ending up a few doors away from García Márquez. Paz thus felt somewhat marginalized when that group began to discuss forming a literary magazine to replace the fading *Mundo Nuevo*, meeting, as we have seen, in a party at the country home of Cortázar in 1970.

Libre and the Padilla Affair

According to Paz's account, the project for a journal had been taken over by Fuentes's enthusiasm:

> Rather hurriedly Fuentes had spoken about our plan to a number of South American and Spanish writers who lived in that city or passed through there [Paris]: Juan Goytisolo, Cortázar, Vargas Llosa, García Márquez and I don't know who else. When I got to Paris at the end of

1968, I found that the idea of a magazine had become too widespread and had lost its original purpose. The group was very heterogeneous and disparate. Goytisolo found a backer who was prepared to pay for the first few issues. But I decided not to get involved. I told Goytisolo that I felt (and still feel) that there is an affinity between our outlooks. The same was true of Vargas Llosa and Sarduy. But I could not (and cannot) feel the same about some of the people invited by Fuentes. Those invited decided to meet in Cortázar's house in the country to develop the project. Even though the woman who was subsidizing the magazine asked me to come to that meeting—and Goytisolo and Sarduy also insisted that I should be there—I chose not to participate. I mistrusted some of the last minute invitees, like García Márquez, who were too linked to Havana. I felt, also, that my proposal had been distorted. During the meeting García Márquez proposed that a friend of his should be the managing editor. Perhaps he did not know that from the outset it had been agreed that Tomás Segovia would be the managing editor. Goytisolo came up with a good title: *Libre*. That was the best bit of the magazine."[18]

In a letter to Orfila dated 20 October 1970, written in Cambridge, Paz sounded the death knell to an enterprise that had occupied their correspondence for some three years: "In one of your letters, you speak of the Magazine. It isn't what I wanted and I am sad that this project that was initially mine has little by little become something else. I do not want to be part of the committee for this publication and I will tell the organizers so when they are in touch with me."[19]

It is significant that by this time, thanks to Fuentes's promotion of him as one of the Latin American boom writers,[20] the Spaniard Juan Goytisolo had become a central spokesperson for the group. Goytisolo gives a somewhat different account to that of Paz: that he was approached to edit a political cultural journal aimed at a Spanish-speaking readership by Albina de Boisrouvray, "who was then a very young, exceedingly beautiful woman, with a passion for literature and cinema, whose origins—her maternal grandfather, Patiño had been the famous Bolivian 'king of tin'—explained her familiarity with the real problems in the world."[21] Goytisolo saw this as an opportunity to work for what he called the "demilitarization of culture," to thaw the "cold war atmosphere in the field of Hispanic letters," and to support the Havana regime from the outside that would help avoid the cultural isolation of the regime and support the position of those inside who were fighting for "freedom of expression and real democracy."[22] That was the message that he gave to the writers assembled at Cortázar's house in Provence, who found it, according to Goytisolo, both interesting and opportune. But it was already clear from Cortázar's vigorous opposition to the inclusion of Cabrera Infante in the magazine that Cuba would be the main stress point of the enterprise and that Goytisolo's plans to build bridges between Cuba and the non-Communist left in Europe and Latin America would become increasingly utopian.

Paz's comments also show the cracks that were already beginning to appear in the seeming camaraderie of the boom: tensions over Cuba and conflicting personalities are uppermost in Paz's defense of his initial project. In a facsimile edition of the magazine published in 1990 the managing editor referred to by Paz, Plinio Apuleyo Mendoza, looked back on the brief span of the magazine. In keeping with a now much more polemical climate in 1990, he brushes aside Paz's claim to authority: "The earliest idea of the magazine came from Octavio Paz, who wanted to call it *Blanco*. But the real force behind it was Juan Goytisolo."[23] The tensions in the planning stage, in 1969 and 1970, however, became a major fissure by the time the first issue of *Libre* was published. The first issue (September–November 1971), one might say, contained the seeds of its own destruction, for it included a dossier on what became known as the "Padilla Affair" at the heart of its text. It was "Padilla," for Goytisolo that would cause the divisions: "A black cat had inopportunely passed through the magazine's home: the famous Padilla affair. The consequence of this shattered our original attempts at dialogue and discussion. Hatred, aggression and attacks would henceforth transform the Spanish cultural community into a world of goodies and baddies worthy of a Wild West film."[24] It was an ironic, though no doubt inevitable outcome, not least because he suggests that the original concept—with Paz but without García Márquez and associates—was the more promising way forward. In the event the magazine alienated both left and right: the center could not hold.

What are these events in Cuba that would cause a rather public ideological parting of the ways? In the early seventies, a siege economy, the failure of the much vaunted ten million ton sugar harvest, counterrevolutionary violence, and political isolation helped to form an embattled mentality on the island. In these circumstances a poet, Heberto Padilla, was imprisoned and later subjected to a rather shameful show trial, in early 1971, in which he made an abject personal recantation of his antirevolutionary writing. This infuriated a number of intellectuals, from Latin America, North America, and Europe, who wrote two open letters to the Cuban regime complaining about Padilla's shoddy treatment.[25] Fidel Castro replied in a furious manner, castigating bourgeois intellectuals who were the lackeys of imperialism and agents of the CIA, while the literary critic and poet Roberto Fernández Retamar wrote an aggressively polemical essay, *Calibán*, which contrasted willfully nationalist Calibans standing up to Prospero's colonial rule with Ariel-ist intellectual writers like Carlos Fuentes or critics like Emir Rodríguez Monegal whose critical brilliance masked a servility to their imperial masters.[26]

Interestingly, the Cubans did not attack Paz: this was a clear sign that they felt they had already lost Paz to the cause many years earlier. It was Fuentes and Vargas Llosa who provoked the greatest anger from the Cubans. Of the core boom group, the gratuitous attack on Fuentes would further distance him from the cultural policies of the island, if not from revolutionary politics in general. Vargas Llosa was also savaged by the regime and this probably helped to accelerate his reconsideration of revolutionary socialism as a panacea and the revolutionary function of literature. Cortázar and García Márquez, by contrast, defended the Cuban regime, and Cortázar's work took on a more overtly political tone. *La Cultura en México* brought out an edition dedicated to the Padilla case (issue 484, 19 May 1971), where a number of Mexican intellectuals expressed their disquiet. Paz, with a reference to the horrific show trials in Russia in the thirties, saw the Padilla affair, by contrast, as "history as literary gossip." He did see, however, two points of contact between the two show trials: "this obsession with seeing a foreign hand in the slightest manifestation of criticism . . . the other the disturbing and disconcerting religious tone of the confessions." For Paz, all this was yet another indication that, "in Cuba the fatal process that turns the revolutionary party into a bureaucratic caste and the leader into a Caesar is already in motion."[27] In a mordant, sarcastic essay, Carlos Fuentes remarked that Cuban socialism could not make such grubby errors, since it had a responsibility to be exemplary: "We cannot overlook a shoddy mistake which undermines our ability to defend Cuba; we cannot overlook it because of the future that we desire for socialism in Mexico. We speak from Mexico, where one of our best writers, José Revueltas, remains unjustly imprisoned and where hundreds of free, thoughtful, promising young people were assassinated in Tlatelolco by the repressive forces of President Díaz Ordaz. We cannot trivialize these prisons, these deaths, with a Stalinist caricature of socialism."[28]

This did not mean, of course, that longstanding literary friendships would deteriorate immediately, or even slowly, over Cuba, but it did point to a hardening of attitudes and positions that the easy internationalism of the sixties was coming to an end. Goytisolo put it more trenchantly. He spoke of his increasing "moral distancing from *Libre* whose hesitating direction and defensive attitudes were less and less in keeping with the original ambition behind the idea. The four issues that came out—coordinated after mine by Semprún, Petkoff and Adriano González León, and, finally, Vargas Llosa—undoubtedly contain worthwhile creations and essays, exemplary interviews and surveys, but, at the same time, texts and articles that were obviously the fruit of compromise and which I am ashamed to read today."[29] Here Goytisolo is saying quite openly that he is ashamed at not confronting the issue of Cuba more openly, for having been something of a "fellow traveler" in the sixties and in not having condemned the Cuban regime more forcibly, in the pages of *Libre* and elsewhere. Plinio Apuleyo Mendoza has pointed out that the limits of the word "freedom" for the editorial board of *Libre* came with a contested figure such as the Cuban Guillermo Cabrera Infante, one of the most widely read and experimental writers of the sixties, with his novel *Tres tristes tigres* (*Three Trapped Tigers*), but also a vociferous opponent of the Castro regime, from his exile in London: "The precarious unity around the project was close to breaking point: writers sympathetic with the Cuban regime threatened to withdraw if Cabrera Infante were published in *Libre*."[30]

Another issue raised by the journal *Libre* was the always problematic question of how to finance an expensive enterprise like a literary magazine. We have seen that Paz's initial idea for a journal had first faltered when De Gaulle, at the recommendation of Malraux, had agreed to fund the magazine, but only if it appeared as part of the Ministry of Foreign Affairs budget, that is, as part of the French government's *mission civilisatrice*. Paz had declined. We have seen how *Mundo Nuevo*'s finances had been seen to have a dubious provenance, while *Casa de la Américas*, funded by the state, became increasingly a mouthpiece for Cuba's internal and international policies. *Libre*'s start-up funds came from Albina Boisrouvray, a French radical filmmaker who, paradoxically, was also the granddaughter of the ruthless Bolivian tin magnate, Simón Patiño. However much *Libre* might argue that Boisrouvray had nothing to do with the family concerns and was a devout supporter of radical causes in Latin America, the Cubans and other radical groups throughout Latin America would argue that the magazine was tarnished by the abuses suffered by Bolivian miners. The opportunity for Paz to edit a journal would come from Julio Scherer, the new, liberal editor of the longstanding daily newspaper, *Excélsior*. It is here that our analysis should return to developments in Mexico.

Mexico, a Change of President

The new president of Mexico elected in 1970 was Luis Echeverría. In an engaging book analyzing how Mexican presidents chose their successors, Jorge Castañeda discusses how Diaz Ordaz came to decide on Echeverría, his Minister of the Interior. Castañeda has rehearsed all the conspiracy theories over this succession, how Echeverría outmaneuvered his rivals for the presidency, and how the need to deal with the aftermath of the student massacre was uppermost in the minds of the presidential clique. Echeverría had to be seen to be accepting the hard line of President Díaz Ordaz in order to guarantee his support, but he also needed to take some distance from him, such as observing a minute's silence for the victims of Tlatelolco in November 1969, an action that also upset the armed forces, in particular General Barragán. He concludes: "Díaz Ordaz may never have tried to replace Echeverría, but not through lack of desire. Echeverría may not have overstepped his bounds in his urge to take center stage, renew the system, and break with his predecessor, but only by a hairbreadth. Marcelino García Barragán may not have tried to unseat Echeverría as PRI candidate, but his irritation reached critical levels."[31] Whatever the process that led to his election, it was clear that, once in office, he would need to make a break with the past, at least on the level of rhetoric. After all, as Minister of Interior, he was directly implicated in the massacre at Tlatelolco.

The different reactions to what the acerbic historian and critic, Daniel Cosío Villegas, in a famous book published in 1974, would call Echeverría's "personal style of government" would divide the intellectual community. What Cosío later saw as the bombast and empty rhetoric of Echeverría was certainly a new style compared with the rather taciturn Díaz Ordaz. Indeed, in the first months of the Echeverría presidency, Cosío was inclined, like many, from his weekly column in *Excélsior*, to give him the benefit of the doubt. He was certainly very industrious, presenting thirty-two new bills to Congress in the first three months of his office. Cosío remarked: "At that moment (8 January 1971), I allowed myself to express the doubt that perhaps our new Leader had confused the term *sexenio* with semester, because he was acting as if his term of office was coming to an end on 31 May 1971 and not on 30 November 1976."[32] It was a good joke that stuck, and it would not have displeased the president. More problematic was the presentiment that became clearer over the following years, that the president talked a great deal, but was not much interested in dialogue: "nobody believed that there was a true dialogue between the President and the citizenry, there was only a monologue."[33] But in the early days it did seem that this president who was happy to don a *guayabera*, and whose wife was anxious to display the regional dresses of Mexico to the world—it was at this time that the traditionally dressed waitresses in Sanborns became known as *estercitas,* after the president's wife María Esther Zuno[34]—brought a new, more popular and open style to governance.

The first major test of the new president's real distance from the policies of the earlier regime came with the events of 10 June 1971, Corpus Christi Day, when a paramilitary group, *los halcones* (the falcons), carrying long sticks and electric prods, as well as a variety of other weapons, attacked a student demonstration. *La Cultura en México* carried a vivid first-hand account of the attack written by two young intellectuals who would in later years line up at different ends of the political spectrum, Héctor Aguilar Camín and Enrique Krauze, written on 14 June, while Sergio Sarmiento also gathered first-hand reports from students who had been assaulted.[35] Sarmiento, writing three days after the event, says that official reports are of a dispute between student groups, and that casualties are put at 9 deaths, while student reports talk of between 80 and 120 deaths and hundreds wounded. He also declares that the mayor of Mexico City has denied the existence of a group known as the *halcones* while student groups talked of the group as a paramilitary organization, operating under the protection of the police and armed forces that had been sent out to control the demonstration. The journal also carries a vivid photo of charging, baton-wielding young men, running unchecked through a police blockade.

The need to explain the attack in the face of mounting criticism became the first test for the new regime of Luis Echeverría. That evening Echeverría declared that he was not responsible and that the attack had been organized by "other forces," the old regime of Díaz Orzaz presumably, to destabilize his government and weaken his own position. He declared to Jacobo Zabludovsky on the *24 Hours* news programme that he would seek out the perpetrators. According to José Agustín's account, Zabludovsky also interviewed Octavio Paz and Carlos Fuentes that evening, and they supported the president's actions.[36] Yet the *halcones* seemed mysteriously to have disappeared and the leader of the pro-government CTM, Fidel Velázquez, was reported to have said that "the *halcones* do not exist because I cannot see them." A few days later on 15 June, Echeverría dismissed the chief of police in Mexico City, Rogelio Flores Curiel, and the mayor of the capital, Alfonso Martínez Domínguez. Nevertheless, the investigation, in contrast to this seemingly decisive action, limped along inconsequentially.

Toward *Plural*

This then was the political climate surrounding the return of Octavio Paz to Mexico after an absence of ten years. He came back to nothing in Mexico, after a diplomatic career of some twenty-five years. For that reason, he had agreed to teach in Harvard from the autumn of 1971, giving the prestigious Charles Eliot Norton lectures. He had met Julio Scherer at a dinner organized by Jaime García Terrés,[37] and Scherer would now approach him to be the editor of a weekly journal attached to *Excélsior*. Paz declined this offer, thinking that this would involve him too much in mainstream journalism.[38] Instead he offered to edit a monthly cultural magazine, which Scherer accepted. Paz came up with the name *Plural*. It is clear that Paz saw his appointment as a personal decision by Scherer, not one that would necessarily have the support of the Scherer associates in *Excélsior*. As the magazine project developed, he remarked, "Scherer's friends thought that we were old fashioned liberals and that it had been a mistake to give us the magazine. The cooperativists in *Excélsior* thought that we were Communist intellectuals. Scherer always defended us."[39]

Why Scherer should be looking to start up a magazine at this time is open to speculation. Perhaps having Mexico's major cultural figure working within *Excélsior* was the major attraction. The star historian, Daniel Cosío Villegas, was already sending in weekly contributions to the newspaper; having Paz as well would really be returning Mexico to the glorious days of the turn of the century and beyond, when the best writers contributed essays and chronicles to newspapers. There would also be the desire to dispute the leadership of the intellectual field with *Siempre!* and *La Cultura en México*, a space that Fernando Benítez and the editor of *Siempre!*, José Pagés Llergo, had controlled for so long. Indeed, as the preparations were being made for the first edition of *Plural*, *La Cultura en México* was celebrating its five hundredth issue in early September 1971, with a stellar line-up of writers: Octavio Paz himself, Carlos Fuentes, Augusto Monterroso, Gastón García Cantú, Carlos Monsiváis, and Gabriel Zaid, with lavish illustrations from José Luis Cuevas. It also took time out in an editorial to congratulate itself on being the leader in the field: "Perhaps we might venture to say that some of the most progressive aspects of contemporary Mexican journalism originated in these pages. And it is the case that some of the most important

books of the decade—poetry and fiction, but mainly political
and cultural essays—originally appeared as contributions to this
Supplement. And, lastly, we would like to insist that we have been
able to express our opinions with absolute freedom thanks to José
Pagés Llergo who, as a friend and a journalist, has supported us
throughout, without any restrictions."[40] Interestingly, however, in
the next issue of *La Cultura,* the editorial states that the *suplemento*
would be moving to a revolving editorship, among six people.

It was certainly the case, however, that a strong bond would grow
up between Paz and Scherer. Some of the best interviews Paz ever
gave were with Scherer, a clear demonstration of the warmth and
trust between them, and Scherer himself—who proved the sincerity
of his liberal principles by also sustaining a close friendship with
García Márquez, a long-time Mexico City resident—has often commented with affection about their friendship. In a recent appreciation
of Paz and *Plural*, he pointed out that when Paz returned to Mexico,
he was cold shouldered by the cultural and academic establishment,
and that not even UNAM was prepared to offer him a job. Scherer,
"convinced that Paz was a genius," offered him employment. For
Scherer, the time was right for the breadth of Paz's vision: "As Octavio
has always said, we went round and round thinking of a name for the
magazine. Plurality in the country was a pressing need at the time.
Lies were eating away at the foundations of society . . . The mask was
of our own making. Suddenly, as always happens, Octavio, convinced
that he had solved the problem, said '*Plural.*' "[41]

The preparations for the magazine seem to have begun in the
second half of July when a large mailing went out to some of the most
distinguished names in modern culture, most if not all of whom were
personal contacts of Octavio Paz. Paz had asked the poet and experienced editor Tomás Segovia to act as managing editor, and Segovia
signed most of the letters that went out in the second half of July
1971. The format of the letter was roughly identical. For example,
Paz explains the project to Claude Lévi-Strauss in a letter dated 23
July 1971. He writes that he is preparing the first issues of *Plural* that
will be published in Mexico as a monthly magazine. The magazine
would seek to express Latin American culture as well as being a source
of information and criticism of literary, artistic and political activity
throughout the world: "A la fois véhicule de la littérature, la pensée et
l'art, et examen de la réalité contemporaine, *Plural* tentera aussi
d'explorer les points de liaison entre la science et la littérature, l'art
et les sciences humaines o sociales."[42] A Latin American journal,
therefore, and one that looked actively to engage with international

debates and trends in culture and politics: not strictly a literary magazine, but one covering a range of disciplines. It was a magazine with significant financial backing: Lévi-Strauss is offered US$ 250 for an article, a very respectable amount in terms of international publishing. Also, the magazine was scheduled to appear in a very short time frame: the contributors are given about six weeks to provide copy, with a deadline of 15 September, for a journal to appear sometime in October.

From an analysis of these early letters, it seems clear that Paz found it easier to attract his international contacts rather than to establish a stable group of Mexican contributors: this was perhaps only natural given his long absence from Mexico but is still noteworthy. That said, the international list was truly impressive. Within a few weeks there were hand written or typed responses from Europe and North America from, Claude Lévi-Strauss, John Cage, Noam Chomsky, Paul Goodman, Roman Jakobson, Henri Michaux, Dore Ashton, Harold Rosenberg, George Steiner, Roland Barthes, Michel Foucault, Pierre Klossowski, Charles Tomlinson, Juan Goytisolo, and many others, while the first Latin American writers to reply were the exiled Cubans Severo Sarduy and Guillermo Cabrera Infante, the Argentines José Bianco, Damián Bayón, and Roberto Juarroz, the Peruvians Blanca Varela and Julio Ortega, and the Brazilian Haroldo de Campos. There is very little correspondence with Mexican writers since, presumably, all the invitations were made on the phone or through informal channels. One begins to get a sense of how the *Plural* editor and his managing editor perceived the achievements and weak points of the magazine once Paz was in Harvard, writing back regularly to Tomás Segovia, as we shall see in greater detail below. One clear weakness that Paz saw in the first two issues of *Plural* and in the discussions leading up to their publication were, as he mentioned in a letter to Segovia on 16 November, the lack of articles on contemporary literary, artistic, and political issues. From the outset Paz was looking for a group of Mexican critics and for a series of critics based in different international centers—Buenos Aires, Paris, London, Madrid, or Barcelona—who would send regular updates on cultural movements in different countries. He was anxious, for example, to woo Monsiváis, at least part-time, away from *La Cultura en México*. Those critics that see the development of Mexican intellectual life in terms of crude polarities—say Paz versus Monsiváis—might be surprised to see the following exhortation from Paz to Segovia: "We must get on to Monsiváis again and ask him to send us an article every two months—on whatever he likes, but emphasizing our interest (and the public's interest) in his political texts. Not theory: his chronicles and satirical pieces." (Paz to Segovia, 16 November 1971.)

Overall, the correspondence with Tomás Segovia is very illuminating as to the overall shape and direction of the magazine. In a letter dated "Thursday 9" (9 December 1971), Segovia responds to a critical letter from Paz complaining about aspects of issue 2. There is also a phone call mentioned: it was one of the luxuries of working in a newspaper that Paz could maintain very regular phone contact with the editorial team while he was out of the country for extended periods as a visiting professor in the United States. I shall just refer to the general theoretical points that Segovia makes. He first of all questions the intended readership for the magazine. Paz, he states, has been sending him reactions to the first issues of the magazine from his friends in the United States and Europe. In Segovia's opinion, this is missing the point. "What we are looking to produce is not a Mexican magazine for New York and Europe, but a magazine, of international quality, for Latin America." He argues that while recognition in New York and Europe is gratifying, it is not the main reason for publishing the magazine. The viewpoint and interests of Mexico-based writers and readers would, of necessity, be very different to the opinions of London poets like Charles Tomlinson (a close friend of Paz). According to Segovia, the print run for issue 2 of *Plural* is twenty five thousand copies, a very large figure for Mexico, greater than the circulation figures for pin-up magazines. Instead of feeling nervous that *Plural* would never have the print run, say, of the *New York Review of Books*, Segovia argues, one might ask if the *NYRB* has larger circulation figures than *Playboy*? Also, Segovia adds, why try to reproduce, or feel guilty about not producing the *NYRB* or the *TLS* in a country with very different academic and literary organizations, where there is not a tradition of university based professors submitting on a regular basis well-crafted scholarly articles? Segovia is conscious that *Plural* is a somewhat different enterprise to the usual literary or cultural magazine in Mexico or in Latin America: 'We are publishing *Plural*: a periodical which is of a higher standard than any journal, but which is not a journal: and we are printing twenty five thousand copies." In his use of the terms *periódico* (periodical) and *revista* (journal), Segovia is stressing that *Plural* is different in scope to the usual pattern of "little magazines" in the subcontinent, with their small print runs and often artisan approach to publication.

A somewhat chastened Paz (though in his correspondence he never remains chastened for long) replies from Harvard on 16 December, giving his own definition of the magazine. He points out that he is

not trying to criticize Segovia, and that the c riticisms he had outlined are in truth directed at himself. He is not trying to turn *Plural*
into a London or New York magazine and he feels that *Plural* is in no
way inferior to the *TLS* , the *NYRB* or to French publications of the
same ilk. Indeed, despite the lack of an academic critical tradition in
Mexico, Paz feels that *Plural* is perhaps even more wide ranging, open
and genuinely universal than its metropolitan counterparts. This
echoes the sentiment famously expressed by Borges in his essay "The
Argentine Writer and Tradition," that being on the "periphery"
makes one more universal, open to all traditions, rather than being
caught in a more self-enclosed and self-regarding metropolitan viewpoint. Paz is happy with the early results: "*Plural* is already the best
magazine in the Spanish language and one of the good international
magazines." His criticisms, he stresses, referred to the presentation of
the material rather than the material itself, though he does agree that
in future issues they should all work to give the magazine a clearer
sense of direction, of scope and orientation.

An analysis of the first two issues of the magazine can put into
context this slight argument over principles between the two main
instigators of the magazine. Office space was made available for *Plural*
in the *Excélsior* offices and the initial staff was Paz, Segovia, and a
secretary/administrator, Sonia Levy. The design of the magazine was
in the hands of Vicente Rojo, the most respected graphic designer of
the time, who was responsible for the "look" of a number of journals
and newspapers in Mexico, and Kazuya Sakai, the Japanese-Argentine
artist, who now lived in Mexico. He was known to Paz more particularly through his translations of Japanese literature. (*La Cultura en
México* had recently published an essay by Paz on "La tradición del
haiku," illustrated by Sakai).[43] It seemed that the *Plural* team was left
somewhat to its own devices within the larger organization of
Excélsior, although Paz always had the ear of Scherer, who had
assigned a link person from inside the newspaper, Pedro Alvarez de
Villar. Indeed one of the recurring complaints from *Plural*—expressed
in internal memoranda—was that the new magazine was not marketed very clearly as part of *Excélsior*'s overall publicity drive and that
they had to find many of their own distribution networks, particularly abroad. Indeed something as simple as distribution figures, the
print run of the magazine, remained a mystery to the editor and successive managing editors. Tomás Segovia, as we have seen, talked of a
print run of twenty-five thousand for issue 2. In a letter to Paz dated
17 October 1973, the then managing editor, Sakai, spoke of issue 25:
"The *Excélsior* people are quite happy—and so they should be—with

this issue: it seems that, despite the gloomy predictions based on the previous issue, that it has sold extremely well. They have upped the print run by 1,500, so that it is now at 21,500." Later in this letter Sakai is predicting that, with proper marketing, they could double these numbers, though that was clearly wishful thinking. However, the memory of other participants puts the circulation figures much lower.[44]

The tone in the internal memoranda is of a small group trying to force a large and mainly reluctant—outside Scherer—organization to help them get into bookshops, attract advertising, increase subscription lists, and the like. But there is never any sense that the magazine might be in financial difficulties or that unless a target figure were reached the magazine might be taken out of circulation. The resources of *Excélsior* were available, though the erratic nature of the typesetters would have Paz almost apopleptic with rage at the number of errors creeping into the magazine. Julio Cortázar was similarly irritated to find that his short story that was the lead in issue 2 had an error in the pagination, though he tries to make a joke of it: "So you'll see that many readers will think that I am conducting strange literary experiments writing new 'Model Kits.'" (Cortázar to Segovia, Paris, 3 December 1971). He does not want *Plural* to add to his reputation as an avant garde writer: he just wants the story to be ordered consecutively, not page three put before page two! The careful, "artisan" approach to literature and publishing that had been Paz's experience and preference up to this time was difficult to enforce and oversee in a larger organization, especially when he was out of the country for so many months at a time.

Paz was in Mexico for the launch of the first issue of the magazine, but from late October until the summer of 1972 he was at Harvard sending a stream of advice by mail and racking up the *Excélsior* phone bill by having the Mexico City office ring him in the United States on frequent occasions. What can we learn about the scope and intentions of the magazine from the first two issues? Issue 1 appeared in large format, in the style of the *New York Times Book Review*, and without a front cover. The title read: "*Plural*, Crítica y Literatura" ("Criticism and Literature"), while underneath was the line, "Revista mensual de *Excélsior*" ("Monthly Magazine of *Excélsior*"). The text throughout is illustrated with vignettes by José Luis Cuevas. The lead article, starting on the front page, is "The Time of Myth" by Claude Lévi-Strauss, which the magazine declares as a scoop, since it has "not been previously published in Spanish." It is followed by an article by Henri Michaux on "Ideograms in China," while later in the issue, the New York based critic Harold Rosenberg offers an article on the "art object" in contemporary aesthetics.

All these international critics and intellectuals are friends of Paz and have thus responded quickly to invitations sent out to them in the last third of July. Paz knows them personally, and knows their recent work, so he or Segovia can ask for something specific or else ask what the writers are working on and would like to publish. All three articles also illustrate aspects of Paz's interests: his engagement with structuralism, structural anthropology and the work of Lévi-Strauss in particular;[45] his passion for Eastern culture and for pictorial poetry (and his longstanding friendship with the surrealist poet, painter, and critic, Michaux); and his interest in certain aspects of modern art. Rosenberg could speak for all the contributors outside Mexico when he sent a handwritten note to Segovia on 17 August: "My best to Octavio Paz. Please tell him I'm happy to see him in action with *Plural*." The name of Elena Poniatowska is printed under that of Michaux on the title page. In her memoir on Paz written shortly after his death, Poniatowska remembers her article as being on abortion.[46] In fact, that article was to appear almost a year later in issue 12 (September 1972). For the first issue, Poniatowska wrote on Avándaro, the Mexican Woodstock, that had taken place in September 1971 and, to the surprise and nervousness of the government, had attracted young people in very large numbers.

Poniatowska—who had known Paz since the early fifties—was now very much in the public eye due to her book on Tlatelolco, *La noche de Tlatelolco* (later translated and published as *Massacre in Mexico,* with an introduction by Octavio Paz), which had been published earlier that year by the publishing house Era. She had also been asked to write a book about "Corpus Christi Day," which she declined because, as she put it, she did not want to be seen as "a professional widow."[47] She had not been to Avándaro—"the boys came to my house"—but she managed a series of lively and evocative interviews on the rock festival that had been greeted with almost universal opprobrium in the official press. With her article, *Plural* is flirting with the field of popular urban culture, a music terrain that was really the domain of such magazines as *Piedra Rodante*, the Mexican offshoot of *Rolling Stone* (which was shut down in 1972 after publishing only eight issues) or the area of cultural critics such as Carlos Monsiváis. This domain of youth culture would not be much revisited in *Plural*, apart from Paz's abiding interest in manifestations of "Dionysian culture," which is the term that he had initially used to describe the student movement. Nor, as we will see in later chapters, would other aspects of counterculture, such as the so-called "literatura de la onda"[48]—Parménides García Saldaña, Héctor Manjarrez, Gustavo Sainz, Federico Arana, and José Agustín—be much represented. National rock music itself—both concerts and distribution networks for records—came under attack post-Avándaro because, in the words of Zolov, the government both feared rock as an "organizing tool" and because, "rock was no longer simply a metaphor of modernity but had become a metaphor for community as well. Rock music, especially native rock music, suggested the possibility of reorganizing national consciousness among youth in such a way that the state was not only mocked but left out of the picture altogether."[49]

Ramón Xirau—the editor of *Diálogos*—contributes an article on José Lezama Lima, the great baroque novelist, whose work was currently being ignored by the revolutionary regime in Cuba. With this article, *Plural* is pointing toward at least three different areas: contact with one of the most established literary critics in Mexico, a longstanding friend of Paz; an exploration of one of the key texts of modern Latin American literature; and, by implication, support for a poet caught up in the backlash of the Padilla affair and also marginalized by the regime due to his homosexuality. The poetry of the Argentine Roberto Juarroz—at this time very much a poet's poet—also figures prominently. The question of the "modernity" of Latin American literature is the subject of a round table debate between Paz, Fuentes, García Ponce, Sainz, and the poet Montes de Oca. Paz had given a series of lectures on "Tradition and Rebellion in Modern Poetry" at El Colegio Nacional in August and September 1971 and the round table was a discussion of his ideas. Paz gives himself the final word, stressing the utopian, radical nature of literature:

> On numerous occasions we have referred to language as a body and to the body as language. Speaking of the traditions that form us, Carlos Fuentes told us that among the European ships that reached America in the sixteenth century, one transported to our shores the tradition of rebellion and justice: the ship of fools, the ship of Erasmus and Campanella. The ship of the body: the tradition of poetry made flesh and of an egalitarian and libertarian utopia. The West implanted in America its rational discourse but at the center of this discourse, poetry and utopia installed...its other coherence. This delirious, corporeal world now interrupts the linear discourse of history. Now is the time of the savage, the black, the chicano, the madman, the child, the lover, the woman, the homosexual, the persecuted—the time of man tortured by the social machine...We live at the end of one modernity and at the beginning of another (issue 1, p.30).

The historian Gastón García Cantú publishes an essay similarly pointing to the "utopian" aspects of progressive movements within the Mexican Church.

On a different colored paper, there is a "literary supplement," a feature that would remain constant throughout the publication of the magazine. In this first issue, we find, "Kenko: el libro de ocio" ("The Book of Leisure"), edited and translated for the first time from Japanese into Spanish by Kazuya Sakai. From the outset, therefore, the reader would be aware that "universal" literature did not merely equate to Europe and North America, but ranged across history and space, to a detailed analysis of a classic fourteenth-century text by a Buddhist monk, Kenko. Sakai paints a vivid picture of the culture of the time and points out how Kenko adapted the Buddhist principle of negation to his discovery of the essence of beauty: "Nobody, not even the Buddhists, find the impermanence of things agreeable, much less discover beauty in this state of affairs. Kenko insists that beauty is found in what is fleeting, unstable, imperfect, incomplete and irregular. This idea would later become one of the fundamental aesthetic principles of Japanese culture" (issue 1, p.17). The contents of these literary supplements, as we shall see, was a somewhat eclectic choice, reflecting the interests of different writers that became associated with the magazine, but most particularly those of Octavio Paz.

By the second issue, published in November, the magazine would begin to find a more definite structure, although it was clear from Paz's correspondence that the demanding editor found running a magazine at a distance to be difficult, and that the decisions of others failed to live up to his high standards. He sent a flood of advice and suggestions to Segovia: apart from phone calls, he wrote to Segovia a seven page single spaced letter on 14 November and other shorter letters on 15, 19, and 20 November. The letter of 14 November contained a brief introductory paragraph when Paz apologizes to Segovia for the fact that they are condemned to talk just about *Plural* and, for that reason, there will never be time to talk about the beauties of Cambridge, or about, "Dore Ashton and Adja Yunkers, and an art work that Joseph Cornell gave us, the Tamayo exhibition…John Cage and a curious dinner the other evening in his house with John Lennon and Lennon's little Japanese lady." After that throwaway introduction to the cream of the East Coast avant garde, the letter becomes a memorandum of concerns and suggestions about the magazine. Its main preoccupations focus initially on distribution: the first issue, according to Paz, had not been seen outside Mexico, and he suggested distribution outlets in the United States and Spain and

Latin America that Juan Goytisolo had provided based on his experiences when editing *Libre*. Other preoccupations were the lack of critical articles and the need to find young people who could write well about cultural and political topics. Perhaps, Paz asks, there might be young political scientists in the Colegio de México, who could write about Mexican politics, "but not in that horrible, frozen Anglo Spanish that they have learned in Columbia University or in Princeton." Cuba remained a sensitive issue and even the forthright Paz thought that some circumspection might be necessary: "We have to *gain the right to criticize Cuba* (the parts that should be criticized), by first criticizing other Latin American regimes, beginning with Mexico." Paz is constantly aware of distribution questions since it takes an eternity, in his opinion, for the second issue of *Plural* to reach him, despite a number of reminders.

When the issue did finally arrive, the form rather than the content became the subject of a rather bitter complaint in a letter of 6 December to Segovia. It is worth glossing the letter in some detail because it gives a particular insight into Paz's concerns and interests. He raises two main objections: the use of explanatory notes and the overelaborate layout of the magazine itself: the cover, the illustrations and the "typography." One feature that would later disappear, at the insistence of Paz, were the introductory notes on contributors. Paz opposed such introductory statements, which either tried to explain the author's intentions or else praise him or her. He also heartily disliked abstracting certain sentences from the main text and highlighting them in bold, to give the reader clues to the most important parts of the argument. Such things, for Paz, are "journalistic" devices that have no place in publications such as *Plural*. The question of who are the ideal *Plural* readers and how much they should be directed or encouraged is thus an underlying concern from the outset, and Paz wanted to aim high rather than low. Paz was also outspoken in his dislike of the magazine layout, finding it overly aesthetic and self-consciously virtuoso, with too many triangles, cubes, and colors. Instead, he suggests, there should be more sobriety and less color, with the illustrations not overpowering the text. He is also opposed to reproducing works of art as cover designs.

Turning his attention to the content, he agrees that the magazine is now beginning to take shape, with only the new section "Letras, letrillas, letrones"—which was intended as a area for local news, events in the world of culture and politics, literary gossip, short extracts of information taken from other journals or written by the *Plural* staff themselves—failing to convince him because it lacked any spark and humor and also because there was very little Latin American and Mexican news. It is clear that for Paz this section had to be humorous and ludic, that the world of the polemic is, in part, in the words of Adolfo Castañon, "a game, and the winner is the first person to raise a smile."[50] It was clear that a long interview with Lukács, translated from the *New Left Review*, was not everybody's idea of fun. Among the comments on Latin American literature in this section, prominence was given to Pablo Neruda winning the Nobel Prize for Literature. But Segovia, in Paz's view, had been ill-advised to reproduce José Emilio Pacheco's favorable comments on Neruda. Is it true, Paz asks, that Neruda was a Picasso of poetry? Is it true that his time as consul was in "the most inhospitable places in the world?" "I lived in those places, in Ceylon to be precise, in the same town—it was paradise." Neruda would remain one of Paz's bêtes noires: they had fallen out in the forties and, even though there had been a partial reconciliation, some two decades later at a brief meeting in London in the sixties, Paz would never miss an opportunity to point out Neruda's weaknesses. One would have to look to other journals to find uniformly enthusiastic coverage of Neruda's Nobel Prize.

Paz is also irritated that the notes on Paul Goodman state that his article had already been published in *Earth* magazine. Paz makes it clear that the policy of the magazine can only be to publish articles that have not yet been published in Spanish, since it would be impossible to expect international contributors to write original essays for *Plural* alone. The quality of the magazine's international coverage and contributors would depend both on the quality of personal contacts, but also on the way in which Paz and others could comb the press for the most important articles of the day. And there was no better place for Paz than the reading rooms in Harvard to scan both periodicals and journals. Segovia would write a spirited defense of this issue some three days later (for once the post must have been expeditious), but such robust exchanges must have been tiring, and the work itself exhausting, and it would perhaps come as no surprise that Segovia only stayed in the job as managing editor for one year.

The better balance that both Paz and Segovia refer to in issue 2 is demonstrated in the contents. A more detailed analysis of individual articles will follow in subsequent chapters, but a brief content analysis gives a sense of the overall shape. This issue opts for an illustrated cover, rather than the rather somber text of issue 1. It is a recent painting by the Mexico-based British artist Brian Nissen that Paz clearly found much too busy and striking. The magazine would continue to have illustrated covers, trying to find a happy medium between illustration and text, but the designs would increasingly become more abstract, following the artistic development of Kazuya Sakai who gradually took over the design features of the magazine. There is a lead short story by Julio Cortázar, "Verano" ("Summer"), set in urban Argentina: a text, that we have noted, was not as avant garde in terms of its structure as *Plural* had tried to make it. The introductory notes maligned by Paz inform the reader that Cortázar has returned to his first love, the short story, and to the sources of his inspiration, city dwelling Argentines, "the sweet and horrible world of the family: these are the Ithaca of his great novelistic odysseys" (p.5). The short story is complemented by poems from the Venezuelan Guillermo Sucre. This is followed by an article by Daniel Cosío Villegas on the presidential system and on the power of the presidency in particular. Once again the readers are left in no doubt as to the importance of Cosío: "At the head of 'Fondo' or, later, the Colegio de México, Don Daniel (as we all call him) never interrupted his work as an historian and as a polemicist. For many years he was almost alone in saying things that others kept quiet about: today he is a precursor" (p.8). And the sentence that the editors use to highlight from Cosío's text refers to the Mexican system for choosing a new president: "It seems like magic that in only eight months a man can go from complete political obscurity to having an almost absolute power over a country" (p.10).

An article by Roger Mounier—thus echoing the work of Mounier and Maritain in the well-established cultural journal *L'Esprit*—is put alongside an article by Paul Goodman entitled "Confusion and Disorder." In a piece published by Susan Sontag in *Plural* some issues later, Sontag would highlight the importance of Goodman: "I admired his bravery...the honorable way that he talked about his homosexuality...I liked it when he spoke about himself and mingled his own sad sexual desires with his desire for political freedom. Like André Breton, with whom there are many points of contact, Paul Goodman was a 'connoisseur' of freedom, happiness and pleasure. I learned a lot about these three things by reading him."[51]

There is an interview with the Uruguayan writer Juan Carlos Onetti, followed by an article by Paz on Fourier, eroticism, and contemporary US society, a comparison between Fourier's utopian view of society organized as "harmony," where all erotic and gastronomic desires are met, and the rather more mundane "reality" of contemporary life. Paz has his article under the heading of "Corriente alterna" ("Alternating Current"), the title of an earlier book of essays and it seems likely, from the correspondence, that he was thinking of having a regular column under this heading. The artist Cuevas sends an illustrated letter from San Francisco, a reminder that the magazine would look increasingly to embrace contemporary art.

In other contributions, we find the beginnings of what would be become a fairly well-established inner group. Paz's old friend and experienced magazine editor José Bianco writes an article from Buenos Aires to commemorate the centenary of Proust, in which he mentions Proust's enlightened views on homosexuality as well as analyzing the narrative structure of *A la recherche*. Salvador Elizondo continues his exploration on the nature of *writing* that would soon become systematized in his book, *El grafógrafo*, while Gabriel Zaid offers a series of pithy observations under the title "short essays." His lead "essay" is on the "art of the insult," which is what Paz is looking to establish in the "Letras, letrillas, letrones" section of the magazine. Zaid would reveal himself as an expert in the art of insult, directed at state power, at incompetent economists, and at misguided writers and intellectuals. He would always look to follow his own advice: "There is no more cruel insult than the truth. Against a bullet of truth there is no possible defense" (p.38). Both of these writers would become regular contributors to the magazine, and Gabriel Zaid would be given a permanent column that would become one of the mainstays of the magazine. Damián Bayón, the Argentine art critic based in Paris writes on baroque art in Mexico: he would become another regular columnist in the magazine. The literary supplement, edited and translated by Ulalume González de León, the Uruguayan poet, is on Lewis Carroll and *The Hunting of the Snark*. González de León would similarly become a regular translator for the magazine and her poetry would be published on occasion.

It was in issue 2 that the section entitled "Letras, letrillas, letrones" was introduced. Underneath this title, we find a dictionary definition from the *Diccionario de la Real Academia Española*. *Letrilla* is described as a "poetic . . . festive or satirical composition," while *Letrón* is an "edict in bold print . . . that was pinned on the doors of churches and in other places to show the names of those that had been excommunicated." The intention here is clearly to have a less serious engagement with aspects of culture, a place to be opinionated or humorous or both, a place where one could speak somewhat on the margins of the great debates. We can agree with Paz that the first attempt at putting together this section was rather uneven. There are some easy jokes at the expense of "celebrations" to commemorate forty years of Mexican sound cinema: "Mexican cinema this month celebrated forty years of the bad use of the word cinema" (p.43). There is an overlong interview with Lukács and mention of the activities of Luis Buñuel and Octavio Paz, as well as commentaries of the award of the Nobel Prize for Literature to Pablo Neruda: a critical account by Claude Roy taken from *Le Nouvel Observateur* and a much more positive assessment by José Emilio Pacheco. Snippets of statements about black power in the United States and also on Mishima speaks to a section that was promising, but had yet to find sufficient variety of extracts and a defining tone.

Interestingly, there was very little on politics and culture in Mexico. This was an aspect of the magazine's coverage that would take some time to build up: to create a forum for commentary and to attract a group of readers and writers. In an optimistic mood, Segovia wrote to Paz on 14 January 1972 about the need to create a "literary space" in Mexico through the magazine: "We have had writers of quality for some time, but what is beginning to emerge is something else: the discussion, circulation and socialization of creative works: what the French call 'monnayer.'"

How this "literary space" opened up is the subject of the following chapters. In issue 1 the words *Crítica* (criticism) and *Literatura* (literature) accompany the title *Plural*. In issue 23, the word *Arte* is added, and from that point the magazine would proclaim itself as focusing on *Crítica*, *Arte*, and *Literatura*. The following chapters follow the divisions outlined by the magazine itself, since these were an accurate reflection of both its general vision and its specific contents. However the weight of critical essays in the magazine necessitates two chapters, which fall naturally into a discussion of politics in the first instance and then of culture broadly defined.

Chapter 3

Politics in *Plural*, 1971–1976

Developments in Mexico

On 30 November 1971 Paz wrote to Tomás Segovia about an article that he had just read in the *New York Times* that discussed the clashes between the government and guerrilla groups in Mexico. In the early months of the Echeverría regime, his self-styled "democratic opening" was being tested by groups who felt that the most appropriate response to government repression post-1968 was armed resistance.[1] Similar groups begin to emerge throughout Latin America at this time, most visibly in Argentina and Uruguay and on the fringes of the Popular Unity government in Chile. In his letter, Paz makes a number of points that help us understand his political thinking at the time.

After wondering who might be the appropriate person to write an article on this violence—and not coming up with a name—Paz sketches how such an article should read. This revealing paragraph is worth analyzing in some detail. Paz writes that, at the present time, the political situation in Mexico is not focused on democratization, but rather on physical confrontation. The different groups are not speaking to each other, but rather exchanging blows. He feels that the "ideology" of the guerrilla groups is one of the reasons for the intensification of the violence. In principle, for Paz, as he argued in *Posdata*, the ideas underpinning guerrilla warfare are false and inoperable, as the recent history of Latin America has shown in cruel detail. In terms of tactics, he is surprised that guerrilla groups in Mexico still cling to an ideology that rejects legal political action, while the whole trend in the rest of Latin America is toward working for change through democratic institutions, as can be seen in Uruguay and Chile. Even Fidel Castro, in his recent visit to Chile, seems to admit that the Chilean road to socialism is viable. Yet, for Paz, in Mexico, it is the government that should bear the greatest responsibility for the violence. It is still the government that is locking people up for political reasons and then denying that there are any political prisoners, while at the same time trying to stifle guerrilla activity by use of state violence. Paz deplores the use of isolated violent action since—though it might seem to have some short-term success—it will never be effective unless it has popular support, or unless the ruling order is on the point of collapse internally, as was the case in Batista's Cuba. For Paz, neither possibility is on the horizon for Mexico. In these conditions, Paz fears that the "Mexican political spring," that began a year earlier, might be about to come to an end. The door might be left open for a military takeover or, at least, increasing military influence over the government. The alternative, for him, is clear: either "violence" or "democratization." He then asks Segovia who could write this article. The answer was, of course, he himself.

Paz, as we shall see, addressed the issue of political violence in a series of articles published in *Plural* in June and July 1973 and August 1974. It is certainly the case that after Tlatelolco and *Posdata*, Paz would increasingly write on contemporary political issues. *Plural* would offer a forum for these deliberations. Most of these essays Paz would later collect in *El ogro filantrópico (The Philanthropic Ogre)* published in 1978. We can divide these interests into four main concerns: the relationship between the writer and the state, that "philanthropic ogre," as he would define the state in a famous article published in *Vuelta* in August 1978; broader concerns about the evolution and legacy of the Mexican revolution; commentaries on the most significant international events of the time, such as the coup in Chile; and an abiding interest in exposing the nature of abuses in the Soviet Union, in particular the Gulag.

The new presidential term of Echeverría, it appeared, seemed to contain elements of the ogre and also the philanthropist. The ogre could appear in different forms, the killings of Corpus Christi Day being the most brutal and also the most symbolic: surely here was a repetition of Tlatelolco, that it was the same ogre, albeit now clad in *guayaberas*, talking of alliances in the third world. And philanthropy was there in excess; Echeverría would lavish money on different cultural and educational projects. He surrounded himself with young, technocratic *universitarios*—what became known as the *efebocracia* or "youthocracy"—and he looked to promote different initiatives in the intellectual and cultural spheres. He released a number of political prisoners still in jail following the post Tlatelolco repression. He spanned the international stage looking to establish Mexico as a leader in third world debates. He reestablished diplomatic relations with Cuba in the face of strong U.S. opposition. But, beyond these overt demonstrations of a new policy and a new style, for many, the president appeared as a genuine campaigner looking to address the abuses of the system and to articulate an independent foreign policy.

The debate about the new president and the writer's responsibility would become a central topic in the early issues of *Plural*. By the middle of 1972, two of Mexico's most respected intellectual figures, Fernando Benítez and Carlos Fuentes, had given their conditional support to Echeverría. In a book of political commentary, *Tiempo mexicano* ("Mexican Time"), published in 1971, Fuentes had asserted that Echeverría seemed to be adopting more progressive policies than those of his predecessor, and voicing his fear that Mexico could be subjected to a "fascist" dictatorship.[2] Soon after bringing this book to a close, Fuentes declared that it would be a "historic crime" to leave Echeverría isolated.[3] This remark, made to a journalist in New York at a time when Echeverría was visiting the United States (and impressing a number of U.S. liberals in a meeting that he had with intellectuals during his trip) caused an uproar, as a short note in *Plural* (issue 10, July 1972) observed. The note, clearly written by Paz, states that the topic is too important to be dealt with in a hasty manner, and it declares that Fuentes will soon be clarifying his position in one or more articles to be published in *Plural*. The columnist states that *Plural* is proud to be hosting an open forum where different ideas can be exchanged (p.39).

Two months later Fuentes would indeed justify his position in a lengthy, main feature article in *Plural* entitled "Opciones críticas en el verano de nuestro descontento" ("Critical options in the summer of our discontent").[4] He seeks to clarify his position: "To leave the current President of the Republic isolated would imply, for me, not taking part in a critical fashion in our public life" (p.3). Fuentes begins by painting a broad picture of the crisis of capitalist development in Mexico and the unacceptable social cost in terms of poverty and lack of income redistribution. He argues that some sort of socialist solution must be found between or outside the military industrial complex of the United States and the bureaucratic autocracy of the Soviet Union, although in both countries he sees the necessary seeds for change in terms of the democratic impulses of their people, in the "new life styles" in the United States, for example, people, "loving, writing, painting, singing, filming, reclaiming the rights of blacks, women and chicanos, and organizing politically to achieve those goals" (p.6). But for Mexico, the fear is the reelection of Nixon and his henchman Henry Kissinger. If the "imperial project" of the United States continues unchecked, then there is no possibility of any autonomous development. For that reason he supports Echeverría taking an independent line in foreign affairs: "I am happy to join in the applause with which Salvador Allende, Fidel Castro, Alvarado Velazco, Michael Harrington, John Womack, Arthur Miller and George McGovern have greeted the President of Mexico" (p.6). In order to achieve a form of independent development, Fuentes continues, the nation state must play the leading role to avoid "Brazilianization" (the U.S. economic and political penetration of that country). "Mexico will not be free without a strong national state; but the national state will not be strong without free citizens" (p.7). Ah, there's the rub, to adapt Shakespeare, like Fuentes, for how, many were arguing, can one call of freedoms after Corpus Christi Day?

Once again Fuentes offers his justification: "I can repeat here the explanation that I have given myself of these events: that on 10 June 1971, all the reactionary forces of Mexico conspired to lay a trap for Echeverría, to stigmatize the new regime as progressive, to discredit the difficult and qualified democratic option with which the new president was looking to come out of the deep crisis of 1968" (p.8). He admits, however, that, with regard to this argument, "almost nobody will pay heed to it" (p.8) But he repeats energetically, that the alternatives are much worse: "The neofascist Mexican right is a club of 'yellow' quislings; their aggressive behavior is aimed at weakening the country and establishing a dictatorship that is submissive to US dictates" (p.8). To combat this possible development, Fuentes offers a four-point plan: 1) To pursue an independent foreign policy; 2) The need to destroy the "emissaries of the past"; 3) To effect radical income redistribution; and 4) To rely on local popular organizations of self-management to carry out these measures. All these four points would need the intervention of a strong Mexican state under Echeverría.

Maarten van Delden has explored how Fuentes looked to reconcile the apparent contradiction of supporting Echeverría while at the same time attacking the "personalist and antidemocratic nature of the Mexican political system" and praising "the idea of local self government, which he regards as deeply rooted in the Mexican cultural tradition."[5] Fuentes does this by arguing that Echeverría is a democratizing force, but also that developments in civil society can lead to a positive strengthening of the nation state. In these conditions, for

Fuentes, the only crime is "abstention." In this debate, writers and intellectuals have a duty to intervene and their actions, their writings do make a difference. In a list of intellectuals and artists looking to express their concerns, he includes the essays of Daniel Cosío Villegas and Ricardo Garibay in *Excélsior* and the "declarations" of Octavio Paz in *Plural*, "who, through the daring and freedom of their ideas, shake up the complacency of the majority and open up many possibilities for intelligent reflection" (p.9). The writer's role is that of a critic, and in the case of contemporary Mexico, "true criticism" has a practical purpose, of preventing an extreme right wing coup. Fuentes's own actions supported his critical approach. On 11 February, some months before penning this article, he had turned down the Premio de Literatura Mazatlán awarded for his book of essays *Tiempo Mexicano* because of police brutality and intervention in the University of Sinaloa.

In the next month's issue of the magazine, Gabriel Zaid wrote an "open letter" to Fuentes, a direct rebuttal of his arguments in typical trenchant and clinical fashion.[6] He states that the most important thing in Mexico at the present time is that public life should be really public. He paints a picture of Mexican politics using the striking image of the *tenebra,* a murky penumbral private space where most of public life is conducted. The writer's role is to fight through the *tenebra* toward clarity. In that task, Zaid argues that Fuentes is wrong to use his international prestige to reinforce the executive instead of reinforcing independence in the face of the executive. The fundamental loyalty of people who publish must be with their readers/public (throughout the article Zaid plays with the different means of the words *publicar* and *público*: to publish and to make public; to have readers and to have a public space). Speaking out in favor of the executive power, in however well intentioned a manner, is a sure way of undermining the independence of writers and journalists. Zaid ends by throwing down the gauntlet to Fuentes: "If you are a friend of Echeverría, why don't you offer him in private the best help that anyone can give him: convince him that Corpus is not a mere hair in the soup of a Policy of Openness, but the public proof of whether he believes that we can become democratic or whether he believes, like Don Porfirio, that we are still not ready for democracy."[7]

A month later, *Plural* would host a discussion entitled "México 1972: los escritores y la política" ("Mexico 1972: Writers and Politics," *Plural* 13, October 1972). In his intervention, the writer José Emilio Pacheco wrote that the attitudes of Benítez and Fuentes in supporting the president had caused consternation among writers and intellectuals.

For Pacheco, "the support for the Echeverría regime, however conditional and critical it might be, of some of our best friends and companions, has caused a crisis in the relationship of *all* Mexican writers with a very important sector of the public," in particular the students who had suffered the aggressions in 1968 and 1971. Many people, he continues, had thought that Paz's *moral* stance against the massacre would turn into a political project, and when this did not happen, the stage was set for the current crisis that was exacerbated by writers entering into a dialogue with the president in the belief that that they finally had access to power, and that they would be listened to, rather than writing in a void. The effect, for Pacheco, was to have readers turn against writers: "The practical effect of this dialogue has been the emergence of an offensive against the group that dominated Mexican literature in the past decade, not from the state but from a significant proportion of their readers who have made them prestigious figures."[8] Pacheco thus offers a defense of Fuentes, who, he considers, has always had the best interests of Mexico in mind, but also takes his distance from the Fuentes position, by showing a healthy skepticism toward the promises of Echeverría.

The group assembled by Paz to contribute to the discussion on the writer and politics—Paz himself, Gabriel Zaid, Jaime García Terrés, Luis Villoro, Tomás Segovia, Carlos Monsiváis, José Emilio Pacheco, Juan García Ponce, and Carlos Fuentes—had points of agreement, but also many areas of divergence. Most explicitly agreed with Paz's opening sentence, paraphrasing Marx that: "An open secret is blowing through Mexico: the political system that has ruled us for more than forty years is collapsing"(p.21). Almost all expressed the same desire as Paz, written in italics, that there was a solution to the crisis: "*The solution can be found in the establishment of a popular, independent and democratic movement that would bring together all the oppressed and dissident people in Mexico in a minimal common programme*" (p.22), some form of democratic socialism. Paz does not develop, however, how this movement might emerge in any concrete form. His focus was on the role of the writer with respect to politics and power.

Paz proclaimed, in italics once again for emphasis, that there was a difference between being a citizen and a writer. As a writer, "*my duty is to maintain my marginality with respect to the State, parties, ideologies and society itself. Against power and its abuses, against the seduction of authority, against the fascination of orthodoxy. Not taking up a seat as the adviser to the Prince, or a seat in the chapter of the Doctors of the revolutionary Sacred Texts*" (p.22). This position, argued with subtlety in each case, was largely shared by Zaid, García Terrés, Segovia, and García Ponce: that the main responsibility of the writer was to the independence of thought. As Zaid put it, "One might say that Cosío Villegas was wiser than the 'seven wise men' in that he concentrated on cultural projects. All of these projects show a faith in endeavors that are appropriate to intellectual life: imagination, research, laying foundations, criticism, public communication." In this respect, for Zaid, the Fondo de Cultura Económica had done more to democratize the country than the Partido Popular Socialista and the PAN, while at this moment, *Excélsior* was more a force for democracy than all the political parties put together. Fuentes, by contrast, reiterated his position outlined in his earlier article that it was the duty of the writer, in certain circumstances, to behave as a *citizen* and support or condemn political initiatives. He mildly rebukes Zaid for his critical article published in the previous issue of *Plural* countering Zaid's accusations about his Manichaen analysis of politics, and alluding pointedly to Zaid's own Catholic beliefs: "What of his *total* condemnation of the current President because he was Secretary of State under Díaz Ordaz? Does this not smack of the unpleasant Christian notion of original sin, the fall without any chance of redemption and the expulsion from paradise?" (p.28). Fuentes most likely interpreted the position of Zaid and others as a "liberal" opposition to Echeverría: that his critics were not so much opposed to relations with the state, but rather with a state that had left-wing inclinations. Such a distinction is never, however, made explicit: indeed every time the word liberal was mentioned with regard to *Plural,* it was greeted with derision from within the magazine, as we shall see below. Van Delden sums up Fuentes's position clearly: "To opt for Echeverría, as Fuentes did in the 1970s, is to opt for the state, and to opt for the state is to acknowledge that a socialist revolution is merely a utopian dream, and that the nation's first priority must be to avoid a fascist takeover."[9] It was this logic that allowed him to accept an Ambassadorship in France in 1975.

While Pacheco and Monsiváis concurred with the Paz proposition that the writer should not engage directly with the state and should seek to work within the terrain of ideas and the intellect, both agreed that ideas themselves could be "transformative" within the public arena. As Pacheco wrote: "Despite its terrible limitations, our profession has a social dignity and importance because it deals with words and only through the exact use of words can we aspire to understand ourselves and the world. And understanding the world leads to an immediate desire to change the world" (p.27). Monsiváis also stated that his work as a writer and journalist was to support the "democratic impulse" of such movements as the Student Movement and independent peasant groups. He saw the present government as the "most recent branch of the Great Capitalist Development Store" that is the institutionalized Mexican revolution, with the "democratic opening" as being the latest autumn promotion (p.24).

The limits of the debate were thus fairly clearly demarcated and, as Jaime Sánchez Susarrey points out in his engaging study of intellectual debates in Mexico,[10] Monsiváis had already begun to take a more explicit position in opposition to "liberal" intellectuals, in the pages of *La Cultura en México*. A special issue of that *suplemento* (issue 548, 9 August, 1972), contained articles by Enrique Krauze, Héctor Aguilar Camín, Héctor Manjarrez, and Carlos Pereira all of which articulated the views of Gramsci's "organic" intellectual, looking to support the popular struggle against dependency and underdevelopment. Paz felt that he was being personally slighted in this set of articles and used the space of "Letras, letrillas, letrones" to laugh away his critics, whom he accuses of producing a mélange of outmoded ideas worthy of Zhdanov or the Falangist movement. In a memorable boutade he talks of Enrique Krauze—later a close associate of Paz—and Aguilar Camín, who cowrote one article in *La Cultura* as both, "intellectual Siamese twins" and as having "half a brain in two bodies." All these columnists, for Paz (although the article is unsigned) are not workers or peasants or guerrilla fighters: "they are bourgeois young people who write in a cultural weekly supplement—with a great number of quotations and very little syntax, but with a certain freedom."[11] Paz would return to the attack in the following issue ("Otro coscarrón," *Plural* 12, September 1972). This exchange showed a clear fissure or fault line within the intellectual sphere, a fissure that would grow wider as the magazine became more explicit about its targets.

Plural showed itself to be relatively "pluralist" in the round table debate about politics and power, seemingly not endorsing any particular point of view, though, as the months went by and the journal acquired a more settled shape, it took up a position that was certainly questioning of government policies and the president himself. For a time, Carlos Fuentes remained a central figure for the magazine, irrespective of his pro-government positions. In fact, Paz openly defended Fuentes, when he was admitted to the Colegio Nacional: Fuentes's inaugural lecture was published in *Plural* 14, the month after the writers and politics debate. In his introduction to Fuentes, Paz extends a metaphor developed in *Posdata* in the "critique of the pyramid," and depicts Mexico as a country of cannibals, salivating after human flesh, with the critics forever sharpening and plunging in their knives: "With a few exceptions we do not have critics but rather sacrificers...The literary gangs periodically celebrate ritual feasts during which they metaphorically devour their enemies. Generally those enemies are the friends and idols of yesterday."[12] He was clearly including himself as another "idol" now being profaned in these quasi-religious ceremonies of destruction. In a later note in the same issue of the magazine, Paz talks about the "lucubrations of claustrophobic Mexican intellectuals," who are incapable of analyzing the impact of international relations on Mexico (p.39). In this same issue Paz is willing to acknowledge some of Echeverría's attempts at fashioning a "democratic opening."

Paz's analysis of Mexico and international affairs would be a dominant voice in the magazine, although internal correspondence revealed that he was always looking to increase the participation of other commentators within Mexico. One notable columnist who appeared on occasion at first and more frequently in later issues of the magazine was the historian Daniel Cosío Villegas, who had, from the late sixties, appeared in *Excélsior* as a witty and incisive critic of government policies in his regular weekly column on page six of the newspaper. Historian Enrique Krauze estimated that Cosío published in *Excélsior* more than two hundred articles on Mexican politics in a seven year period.[13] He was particularly attentive to the new presidency of Echeverría. At first he shared the opinion that the energetic president was looking to democratize the system. He mentions in an article published in *Plural* in April 1972 that the election of the intellectual figure Jesús Reyes Heroles revealed "a desire in the president to change and improve national public life."[14] Yet as the months went by, so he began to see more and more to criticize in the president's measures and also in his "personal style" of government. His book, *El sistema político mexicano* ("The Mexican Political System"), the subject of a *faux* controversy between Cosío and the young historian at the Colegio de México, Rafael Segovia,[15] in which Segovia accuses him of being too idealist, looked in critical terms at the centralization of power of the president and the party. After this book, he began work on his study of Echeverría's presidential style.

Echeverría would try on a number of occasions to win over or at least come to an agreement with the old dissident, and Cosío's memoirs contain many amusing anecdotes about lunches in his house and the president's residence. Yet, it is also clear from this memoir account that Cosío saw himself at the mercy of the government "dirty tricks" department when he ventured his more outspoken criticism. For example, a libelous pamphlet entitled, *Danny, el sobrino de Tío Sam* ("Danny, Uncle Sam's Nephew"), with a print run of some fifty thousand copies began to circulate, and everyone assumed it to be government sponsored. Cosío also became aware of an intrusive police interest in his conversations. Exasperated, he wrote a formal complaint: "I then wrote a few lines to Fausto Zapata (Echeverría's personal secretary) to ask him to tell the president first that I was cancelling the invitation I sent him to lunch at my house; second, that I would stop writing in *Excélsior* and *Plural*; and third, that I would begin the necessary preparations to leave the country and settle abroad for an indefinite period."[16]

At about the time of this confrontation, Cosío published in *Plural*—issue 31, April 1974—an article on the relationship between the press, the government and intellectuals. He saw 1968 as being a parting of the ways, the break-up of the relatively "happy coexistence" between government and the press that had led to a situation in which, "Mexican intellectuals are not used to considering as a normal part of their profession the need to comment critically on public events in their own country."[17] Two things had changed since 1968. The first was that the government of Echeverría openly sought dialogue, "to criticize and to criticize himself, to parade himself and his co-workers in the public gaze."(p.62). The second was that—without openly naming him or his newspaper—Julio Scherer had taken over *Excélsior* and forged a new, independent, style: "The directorship and administration of one of the oldest and most eminent newspapers in the country, fell into the hands of a group of professional young journalists who set out to give it a new lease of life. And among the different means to achieve this end, they proposed three things: to invite new columnists that they promised to support and promote; to give them greater freedom to express their feelings and ideas; and to pay them better" (p.63). Yet *Excélsior* seemed to be something of a lone voice in a country where too many people, including high ranking officials in the government, did not like the government being criticized and—here Cosío seems to refer directly to his own experiences—organized, "unjustified attacks on independent writers, making use of public funds to pay for the mercenary pens of other writers" (p.62). Seemingly prescient in view of later events, Cosío argued that if the president allowed such attacks to continue, then his whole *sexenio* might be condemned by posterity: "the fear is that in the end very little will remain of all this effort by the president" (p.63).

In this period Cosío met Echeverría for the last time, just before the publication of *El estilo personal*, at a lunch at Cosío's house. Here Cosío had invited a small number of journalists and intellectuals, including Julio Scherer and Octavio Paz, to discuss with Echeverría and some of his advisers the issue of the relationship between the press, the intellectuals, and the government. According to Cosío, Echeverría was not looking to discuss ideas, "but to pontificate—his old vice."[18] He attacked Paz for being a critic of the government, despite having been a government official all his life, and also threw barbed comments at Scherer and Víctor Urquidi. Scherer remembers that Echeverría could not see, "essential differences between intellectuals in power and intellectuals who were critics," even when Cosío pointed out to him that the latter were free, while the former were not.[19] Scherer asked Paz to recall his memories of that day and Paz remembered that he had argued that he was not sure whether intellectuals in the government could really call themselves intellectuals: "In the first place, *giving orders* is very different to *thinking*: the first is the sphere of government, the second the sphere of the intellectual. Intellectuals in power cease to be intellectuals; although they remain cultured, intelligent and even upright, by taking on the privileges and responsibilities of power, they replace criticism with ideology."[20] It was clear that, despite the later conviviality of the evening, Echeverría remained deaf to such arguments.

The parting of the ways would come some weeks later when Cosío's *El estilo personal* was published. Even though Cosío gave due weight to some of the successes of the government, he offered a trenchant critique of foreign policy and the president's demagogic style. The book would be remembered for the lapidary phrase that the president was not physically or mentally suited for dialogue, but only for monologue. He could preach but not converse.[21] Cosío had offered the president a right to reply within his book, but no response came. By this time, *Plural* had asked Cosío to write a monthly column for the magazine, entitled *Compuerta* ("Sluice gate"). The first of these articles appeared in issue 25, October 1973, and others would be published—though not on a monthly basis—after that time, until his death in March 1976. In *Plural* 55 (April 1976), Enrique Krauze—no longer the subject of Paz's *boutades* about his brain size—and Octavio Paz wrote appreciations of his life and work. Paz called him the "moralist" of contemporary Mexico and praised his "lucidity" and his "irony": "His final articles appeared in *Plural*. We will endeavor to remain faithful to his memory, by being faithful to his example: we will always defend the freedom and independence of writers."[22]

Another regular columnist in *Plural*, the poet and essayist Gabriel Zaid, offered from late 1973 (issue 25, October 1973) a monthly critique of different aspects of Mexican political and cultural life. We have seen how he challenged Fuentes to rethink his adherence to Echeverría and this antipathy to those intellectuals who supported state power was made explicit in a savage poem published in the June 1973 issue of the magazine. He brought his training as a systems analyst to expose mercilessly the creaking pyramid system of Mexican government and patronage as well as question the orthodoxies of economic theory, in particular the growth of state-owned corporations under Echeverría. The logic of a mathematician, the humor and commitment of an engaged social commentator, and the stylistic fluency of a poet combine in these quirky, acerbic, engaging essays that Zaid initially saw as experiments with the genre of the essay, but that were read, he argued, more for their content than for the originality of the form.[23] Paz wrote to Sakai expressing his appreciation of Zaid's work, its ability to rethink old categories. He remarks to Sakai that Zaid is the only person in Mexico—and probably in Latin America—who has dared to propose a model of development different to those of neo-classical economists and, in Paz's terms (pseudo) Marxists: "Both groups must find what Zaid says sacrilegious: he attacks equally both the dogmas of neo-capitalism and those of (pseudo) socialism." (Cambridge, Mass., 30 November 1973). In a more recent assessment of Zaid's work, Mauricio Tenorio Trillo remarks that in the seventies, one aspect of Zaid's writing was as an economic essayist who exposed "the whole ideological and corrupt racket of a statist 'economy' run by experts; at that moment Zaid did not believe in the centralist, corrupt and authoritarian Mexican state as a means of income redistribution: he saw a clear relationship between the rise in inequality and the increase in taxes."[24]

On the topic of culture and power in Mexico, Zaid wrote a review of Cosío's *El estilo personal* commenting favorably not just on the critique of the president, the presidential system, and the pyramid of power, but also on the style of writing that could equally apply to his own work: "It is a literary essay on a political and historical topic: a personal, intelligent and well written essay."[25] Zaid was always very conscious of the craft of essay writing, whether he was writing on politics, economics, or literature. Indeed, he once remarked that, "the essay form is so difficult that mediocre writers should not write essays, they should limit themselves to academic work."[26]

The antics of the president and his cohort of intellectuals and academics would never be far from Zaid's sights. In August 1974, he commented caustically on the hundred intellectuals joining Echeverría on his state visit to Argentina.[27] Some months later, in February 1976, along with Octavio Paz, he ridiculed the writers paying court to the president in waiting, José López Portillo, recounting with amused detachment, a rumor that the president's sister Margarita was being considered for the presidency of the writers association because, in López Portillo's "reported" phrase: "That Mayo...is good at writing!"[28] In the event it would be the film world that would receive the attention of Margarita López Portillo in the next presidential term. In a lead article published in April 1975, Zaid pointed out that Echeverría's policy was based on integrating dissidence rather than repressing it. But he argued that all this relentless self criticism was mere gestural politics, because on fundamental issues like bringing to justice those responsible for the Corpus Christi Day killings, the president was resolutely silent. The only course to take in this situation was to write for the "reading public" rather than the "Great Reader and Judge and Legislator and Elector."[29] In September 1975, as the *destape* or unveiling of the new president was about to occur, Zaid famously compared the running of the Mexican state to the running of a major corporation. As in business, the true electors of Mexican politicians are their superiors and within the pyramid of power, everyone refers to the Big Boss. In a *tour de force* final statement, he sees the PRI as having managed to create a strong central business, with, "vertical negotiations instead of horizontal negotiations, the buying and selling of aspirations within a framework of obedience; an inversion of loyalties and clients to favor the integration of a great Common Market of obedience, where the possibility of being independent becomes a form of merchandise; an option that you pay not to take. All this has become the great national business: the most modern enterprise that Mexico has come up with."[30]

At the same time, *Plural* was conscious that it was attempting to open a debate on Mexican political and cultural institutions, often through Zaid's articles. In a short statement entitled "Denuncias sin respuestas" (September 1975), *Plural* argued that it had spent the last six months criticizing developments in the cultural field, without receiving any response: "We are thus left with two unfortunate conclusions. That official cultural organizations remain in the hands of mediocre or incompetent people...And that the State, which proclaims to the world a policy of openness, stubbornly pays no heed to the real specialists and instead supports ideologues."[31] One such critical article was Zaid's "La regañada al INBAL" (*Plural* 45, June 1975), in which he once again ridiculed the president for suggesting that the Instituto Nacional de Bellas Artes y Literatura was an ineffective organization because artists and intellectuals were too individualistic.

Paz's own views on Mexican history were equally trenchant, if not aimed so squarely at the figure of the president. The magazine prints a number of articles by him on Mexican politics. Outside his own interests in the topic, he was also very conscious that articles on Mexico were something that the public was interested in, and that they should be given their "pound of flesh." (Letter, Paz to Segovia, Cambridge, Mass., 26 March 1972). It was also clear that the editors in *Excélsior* were anxious to see articles on contemporary issues. Segovia remarked in a letter to Paz on 12 January 1972 that there was pressure on them from inside the office. Talking about the upcoming issue 5, he remarks: "Pedro has just told me that they (the managing editors of *Excélsior*) think that it is essential to have something 'meaty' on Mexico." (Segovia to Paz, Mexico 12 January 1972). But Paz realized from the outset that the magazine would have to work to win over contributors whose natural home was *La Cultura en México* to comment of Mexican issues in particular. In an earlier letter to Segovia, he talked about the weakness of the "Letras, letrillas, letrones" section and added that he got upset when he read through the literary supplements of *Siempre!* from mid-October to mid-February: "A lot of what we have *not* been able to do, they have done—and with less resources than us … In any event it is a lively review, up to date with what is happening in Mexico and in the world, a review that gives the sense of a group at work" (Paz to Segovia, Cambridge, Mass., 10 February 1972). That sense of a group in *Plural* would develop over time, but from the outset Paz felt that he would need to cover a number of political issues himself.

Paz's essays spanned both general historical issues and more specific political commentary. In the February 1972 issue, Paz published a letter to Adolfo Gilly, the imprisoned political activist (he had been jailed in 1966 for his part in guerrilla movements in Guatemala): an extensive critique of his recently published book, *La revolución interrumpida*. In it, Paz declares his general ideas for the future of Mexico: a need to return to the tradition of Cárdenas and the need to consolidate the "three great conquests—still alive but disfigured—of the Mexican Revolution: the *ejido,* decentralized public enterprises and trade unions."[32] He agrees with Gilly that a "great popular alliance" is both necessary and still "*possible*" (p.16, Paz's emphasis). It was a question of bridging the gap between the two Mexicos, the developed and the underdeveloped through peaceful political rather than violent means: "terrorist violence is not a language it is a cry" (p.17). It was necessary to analyze and also reform the particular power of the Mexican "Party" and the political bureaucracy. The choice was between an, "independent popular alliance or authoritarian violence" (p.17). Paz would make the same arguments in a round table discussion at Harvard on 15 November 1971, alongside Albert Hirschman, Frederick Turner, and John Womack, which was translated and published in the following issue of *Plural* in March 1972. Once again he argued that the "the immediate goal continues to be *democratization*."[33] The way of achieving this remained, for him, an *independent* popular movement, rather than working from inside the government and the party for change. It is not clear in these writings how this popular movement might be consolidated in the actual political situation, though on occasion he would mention favorably the political coalition that Demetrio Vallejo and Heberto Castillo were looking to form. In a note in "Letras, letrillas, letrones" commenting on a lecture by José Revueltas, Paz (once again unsigned) concurred with Revueltas about the need to create a democratic movement outside the traditional political parties that could offer a real alternative to the PRI: "That is why we are sympathetic to the efforts that Demetrio Vallejo and Heberto Castillo are making in this respect. Despite its obvious limitations, their work is *healthy*."[34]

Paz, as mentioned above, would keep a close eye on manifestations of political violence. In the first of his articles on this topic, "Entre Viriato y Fántomas," in the "Letras, letrillas, letrones" section—the other two, "Los doctores montoneros" and "El plagio, la plaga y la llaga" would be published in July 1973 and September 1974—he addressed three of his constant preoccupations: the futility and danger of unjustifiable *guerrilla* violence; the need for the state to stop intervening in a heavy handed fashion in the universities; and the overall poverty of the university system. All three were interlocking problems for Paz. Because of the overall poverty of "political imagination" the universities had lost sight of the democratic principles of 1968 and were now flirting with "Guevarist Blanquism." They gave intellectual justification to middle-class students and intellectuals to organize kidnapping and other acts of guerrilla violence that would lead just to isolation and defeat. Such actions would also make the state more predisposed to acting with repressive violence and away from the intended path of "self criticism and liberalization: The criticism of antigovernment violence is half the story. The other half is a criticism of government violence."[35]

The university would be a constant source of concern to Paz. The "Letras, letrillas, letrones" section would contain a number of references to university politics. Indeed in the next column after the open letter of Gabriel Zaid to Carlos Fuentes, in issue 12, there is the first of a series of commentaries on the university beginning with a discussion of the occupation of the Rector's offices by masked groups of disaffected students "à la Sierra Maestra" (*Plural* 12). The response of the different university groups, for *Plural* (and it is certainly Paz writing here) is confused and far from what was needed: a "democratic mobilization" in defense of university freedoms. Instead there was a lot of university posturing, "a revolutionary farce written and directed by a perverse but amusing reactionary sketch writer" (p.54). Even the beleaguered Rector, the distinguished sociologist Pablo González Casanova, was not let off the hook. In another of the *bons mots* associate with the "Letras, letrillas, letrones" section, González Casanova was seen as having an "astronomical theory" of student unrest: "Attributing the events in the university to the crisis of world capitalism is like explaining the history of humanity by the position of the planet earth in the solar system. It is not false: it is remote" (p.54). For *Plural*, the fault lies in a bloated, underfunded university system, where too may unqualified students are chasing too few resources.

Following the month's intervention of the Rectory offices—the organizers were allowed to escape without reprisals—the university union went on strike and Pablo González Casanova was now being put under pressure by the Sindicato de Trabajadores y Empleados (STEUNAM) over wages and union rights. *Plural* declared that González Casanova was being bullied by the unions who were being myopically supported by left-wing student groups within the university. The columnist asks: "Will Pablo González Casanova suffer the fate of many of his predecessors in the Rector's office and will his name be added to the list of distinguished Mexicans—the most recent case has been the illustrious Dr Ignacio Chávez—who have been sacrificed through demagogy, intrigue and stupidity?"[36] The answer was, yes, because the rector resigned on 16 November 1972, after a long and bruising strike called by the STEUNAM. In the following issue of the magazine, "Letras, letrillas, letrones" once again surveys events in the university and ridicules the ideas in vogue among student and university circles that disturbances in the university had either been caused by imperialist forces or right-wing agitators. The columnist—almost certainly Paz again since he or she repeats the phrase that the Mexican right do not have ideas but just interests, a well known Paz leitmotif—wonders at the paucity of thought: "The abuse of revolutionary vocabulary also reveals that the ideas of the left have become gaseous and loutish, and by signifying everything to everyone, they end up signifying nothing."[37] This is a parody of left-wing thought that has always, throughout history, been associated with "critical thought." The analysis puts the blame at the poverty of such thought at ineffectual left-wing groups such as the Communist party who seek in the university some vestige of power denied them in the political arena. Ultimately the source of the problem is the monopoly of power of the official party that closes off all spaces where open political debate might take place.

A few years later, when the president visited UNAM on 14 March 1975 and was greeted by uproar and the occasional missile, Paz wrote a satire glossing a "debate" that might have taken place within Pedro Calderón de la Barca famous Golden Age play *La vida es sueño* (*Life's a Dream*), which deals with the responsibilities of a monarch and his subjects. Here, the "innocent" Clotaldo asks a number of pertinent questions about the Echeverría regime and the response of intellectuals, while the "advisers," Astolfo and Basilio debated the pros and cons of radicalism, violence, state intervention, and the like. All the excuses for student violence are mercilessly ridiculed, and in the end Clotaldo remarks: "The fact that the opposition has expressed itself in such a low and irrational form is lamentable. If no sense of agreement can be found, is it feasible that a political plurality might be developed?"[38]

Paz did make an attempt to bring some independent young university teachers to the pages of *Plural* to give a more measured critique of the contemporary political situation, which Paz described in the July 1973 issue as a political desert, due to the absence of critical thought and self criticism. *Plural* published an "Overview of the Situation in Mexico" by Rafael Segovia, Mario Ojeda, and Carlos Bazdresch. Such a measured critique, for Paz, would be an effective counterweight to the more extreme aspects of political commentary. Speaking in the light of the recent military coup in Uruguay, he argues angrily: "We condemn those who from the safety of university or newspaper offices, vitriolic doctors with their mouths slavering with anger, bless the Tupamaros, here and there, with truncated phrases from revolutionary tracts."[39] While the articles from these young scholars were a useful overview of current politics, such analysis would not become an integral part of the magazine, but rather occasional interventions. Rafael Segovia, the director of the Centro de Estudios Internacionales in the Colegio de México, who worked closely with Cosío Villegas, would publish several articles over the years and other young scholars would also appear. One article that was often remarked upon not necessarily for the quality of its argument, but rather for the subsequent fame, or notoriety of its author, was the future president Carlos Salinas de Gortari's thoughts on dependency.[40] But *Plural* was never a magazine that would be based in the academic community: Zaid's comments about those who can write, write essays, while those who cannot write work in academia, was a view shared by many in the magazine.

Plural would also bring out supplements linked to contemporary problems, though there is a gap between their original intentions, as expressed in internal memoranda, of having a number of supplements each year dedicated to contemporary issues and the eventual practice. After the first year, where there were special supplements on "La crisis de las sociedades industriales" ("The Crisis of Industrial Societies"), with Galbraith and others (January 1972), "La sobrevivencia de la especie humana," ("The Survival of the Human Species," April 1972), "Hacia una política de la población en México" ("Toward a Policy for Population Control in Mexico," September 1972) and the supplement on writers and politics already analyzed (September 1972), this interest tailed off. It would always be much easier for the personnel in *Plural*, with their range of contacts, to produce a supplement on contemporary poetry rather than rather than, say, the issue on population and population control, edited by Víctor L. Urquidi. This said, in the area of population control, the magazine could point to one article by Elena Poniatowska on the issue of abortion (issue 12, September) and several articles by Octavio Paz.[41] Poniatowska would later remark: "Octavio already had a great awareness of the demands of feminism and the subject of abortion was central to him; one had to argue for it to be made legal."[42] There was not however, a regular discussion of social issues in contemporary Mexico.

The recurring issues, as we have seen, are the presidential system in Mexico, and the foibles of the president himself, ideological debates over certain key issues, such as the university and inappropriate guerrilla violence, and the responsibility of the writer or intellectual in the political arena. These interests focused on Mexico, but would also be mapped onto the complex arena of international affairs. It is here that what would emerge as a sustained attack on certain aspects of the creed of revolutionary nationalism would emerge in sharp focus, especially in the debates over Cuba and the Soviet Union.

International Affairs

Plural's comments on international affairs should be seen within the context of the active foreign policy of the Echeverría regime. The political scientist Mario Ojeda summed up Echeverría's foreign affairs policy in the July 1973 issue of the magazine: "the ties with the Chilean socialist government of Salvador Allende, the unfreezing of relations with Cuba and the recent visits of President Echeverría to Moscow and Peking: this more independent foreign policy is designed to legitimate the regime, in the face of criticism from the left."[43] His foreign policy was seen as audacious at the time, since it caused diplomatic difficulties with the United States. The fact that Mexico now recognized Cuba diplomatically and allowed regular flights there, in direct opposition to the U.S. embargo and blockade, was a source of national pride for many in Mexico. Let us look in greater detail at *Plural*'s view of two countries, Cuba and Chile, before widening out the debate.

Cuba, as we have seen, became something of a touchstone for intellectuals in Latin America, especially after the Padilla affair. The disillusionment with Cuba was a gradual affair, despite the vehemence of the comments in the Padilla debate. It was also not the case that political differences over Cuba, and other issues, would necessarily cause splits in what had been long friendships. Perhaps the most vocal defender of Cuba and many other radical causes was Julio Cortázar. Yet, as we will see in the following chapters, he remained a contributor to *Plural*. His memories of a friendship with Paz could stretch back over twenty years, to different locations throughout the world. In a letter to Paz, dated 25 October 1973, Cortázar could move from the immediacy of political action over Chile and his novel, *Libro de Manuel* (*A Manual for Manuel*), about guerrilla cells in Argentina, to a more timeless world of memory and delight: "I finally read the travel journal of Basho along with your beautiful commentary and it was like being back with you and Marie-José in the pretty garden of your house in Delhi, talking about poetry and breathing the perfumes of the night air. Do you remember the time that we had a sort of improvised hai-ku and we had such a good time? I always follow you closely, as far as I can, I read your beautiful poems in *Plural* and I remember how much you taught me in India and I remember our agreements and our disagreements, both equally stimulating." (Cortázar to Paz, Paris, 25 October 1973).

Not everyone shared the openness of Cortázar's response to difference and dissent. Cuba was a very delicate issue. Even Paz, as we have seen, acknowledged that one had to "gain the right to criticize Cuba" in a letter to Tomás Segovia dated 16 November 1971, at the outset of the magazine's publication. Paz is clearly chafing under what he clearly sees as a form of self-censorship. In this letter he expresses concern at "our" attitude toward Cuba and he is not sure that he is right not to express this criticism, not just of the cultural policies of the regime, which he sees as "monstrous," but also of the disastrous state of the economy and the progressive militarization of the country: "In any event, as I have said many times, Castro is a caudillo in the Spanish mold. But perhaps it might not be appropriate to mention this topic in the first issues." Paz thinks that he can gain this right to criticize the regime by first criticizing other Latin American regimes, beginning with Mexico (Paz to Segovia, 16 November 1971). Segovia's reply to his deliberations, on 12 January 1972, chimes with his analysis: Segovia argues that they should not begin to criticize Cuba "without having first shown or interest in and love of the country. I don't know how we will do that, but I don't think it is impossible." In correspondences dated 10 and 13 February 1972 between Paz and Segovia, there is a discussion about whether to refute declarations made in *Excélsior* by the Cuban critic Roberto Fernández Retamar, but this is not followed up.

While the magazine would never seek to take up Segovia's "solution," Paz's critique, rather than being overtly directed at Cuba itself, tends to be incorporated initially into his denunciation of Soviet policy, in particular on the issue of the "Gulag." In an article by the prominent U.S. writer and journalist for the *New York Times*, I.F. Stone on the imprisonment of dissidents in Soviet mental institutions, we find mention of an explicit link between Cuba and the Soviet Union. Stone argues that, "many of the characteristics of Stalinism reappear in China under Mao and in Cuba under Castro."[44] Two years later *Plural* brought out a special issue, dedicated to Solzhenitsyn, which contained Paz's own analysis of the Soviet system, alongside articles by Irving Howe and Roy Medvedev. Paz begins the article by recalling a time twenty years earlier, when he had published a dossier of David Rousset's work denouncing the concentration camps in the Soviet Union (published in *Sur* in March 1951). In this dossier, he remarks, he had fallen into the trap of saying that the camps were a blemish on the Soviet system, but not an inherent part of the system. He now knows that the camps were an institution of "preventive terror," integral to the system. Already in the fifties, by making such a denunciation, he had been denounced by what he called "progressive" intellectuals. The campaign against him, he adds, still continues: "The adjectives change, but not the vituperation: I have been called at different times, cosmopolitan, formalist, Trotskyist, a CIA agent, a 'liberal intellectual' and even a structuralist serving the bourgeoisie!"[45] Here, Paz first of all defends Solzhenitsyn and his book *The Gulag Archipelago* against the campaign of defamation in the Soviet Union and abroad. While disagreeing with many of Solzhenitsyn's ideas—he was, after all an orthodox Catholic and a strong nationalist—Paz applauds his moral integrity and feels this moral rather than "intellectual" affinity with him. This leads to a brief analysis of the development of Marxist-Leninism and to the conclusion that the Leninist party of professional revolutionaries, "always turns into a caste, as soon as they reach power." Revolutionary parties become ruthless bureaucracies. "The phenomenon is repeated everywhere: the dictatorship of the Communist Party over society, the dictatorship of the Central Committee over the Communist Party, the dictatorship of the revolutionary Caesar over the Central Committee. The Caesar might be called Brezhnev, Mao or Fidel: the process is the same" (p.22).

To reject this system does not imply, for Paz, any justification of U.S. imperialism, racism, or atomic bombs, or any blindness to the injustices of the capitalist system, although he did not dedicate much time to exploring the nature of U.S. imperialism. Closer to home, "What is happening amongst us is injustifiable, be it the imprisonment of Onetti, the murders in Chile or the tortures in Brazil. But it is also not possible to close our eyes to the fate of Russian, Czech, Chinese or Cuban dissidents" (p.22). Paz would return to the topic of Solzhenitsyn in *Plural* in December 1975 reiterating many of the same points, and reaffirming his support while castigating the Russian for his lack of knowledge of world affairs outside the United States/USSR power division.[46] Paz had also tried to organize a survey of writers' opinions some two months before the special issue of 1974 appeared, entitled, "Spanish American writers and the repressive Soviet system." The text of his survey can be found in the *Plural* archive dated 2 January 1974 as part of a letter to Kazuya Sakai. The preamble assumes that nobody can remain indifferent to Solzhenitsyn's book and asks three questions: whether the repressive system described by Solzhenitsyn is an integral part of the Soviet system, or a "deformation"; whether the repressive system is inherent in Marxist-Leninism, or just a Russian characteristic; and whether it is possible to distinguish between the Soviet and the Nazi systems of repression. Paz wanted this questionnaire to be sent to leading Latin American writers and to a group of Mexican intellectuals.

The questionnaire was never sent and it is clear from a letter from Sakai to Paz, dated 8 January 1974, that both Sakai and other staff in *Excélsior* (the link man Pedro Alvarez del Villar) had been opposed to it and that they had had a major row with Paz over the phone from Cambridge (Mass). In his letter Sakai is very apologetic, but also justifies his opposition to sending out a questionnaire about a book before this book is published in its entirety in a language other than Russian. But it is also clear that Sakai saw the phrasing of the questionnaire as being too provocative in the current climate. He writes that he is not looking to shield Paz from attacks, but that he does know, "the public opinion that is forming around *Plural* and around you. If it's good or bad, I don't really care just as long as we do not unnecessarily increase the number of our enemies." (Sakai to Paz, Mexico, 8 January 1974). For whatever reason, Paz accepted being overruled on this matter, but a note in handwritten in the margin of the Sakai letter shows what he really thought of this matter. (I am not sure, since my copy is a photocopy that Paz gave me, if this comment in the margin was written for my benefit or soon after the event itself, for posterity.) The letter, the note says, "refers to a Questionnaire (that was not sent out—to the disgrace or shame of those that opposed it)." I have also not been able to ascertain whether or not Paz wrote his article quoted above (March 1974) after the questionnaire debacle. If he did—and the article does indeed answer all the questions laid out in his survey and there is no reference in the correspondence to Paz having written an article before January—then it was a good way of cocking a snook at those who counseled prudence.

While there remained no overtly critical articles on Cuba in the main body of the magazine, its questioning of the regime and its upholding of the right to dissidence can be seen in its publication of essays—which will be analyzed in the following chapters—by some of the major dissenting voices, Guillermo Cabrera Infante (and also the somewhat less overtly political Severo Sarduy). It also reviewed "dissenting" books. Mario Vargas Llosa and Emir Rodríguez Monegal reviewed *Persona non grata*, the Chilean writer Jorge Edwards' account of his time in the diplomatic service in Cuba at the time leading up to the Padilla affair. The Vargas Llosa article is particularly interesting because we can measure with some accuracy his still only gradual disenchantment with Cuba. In the first place, Vargas Llosa argues that Edwards has impeccable left-wing credentials—he had long supported the Cuban revolution and he was chosen personally by Salvador Allende to represent the newly elected Unidad Popular government in Cuba—and that he has been very brave to break, "a sacrosanct taboo for a left wing intellectual: that the Cuban Revolution is untouchable and that it cannot be openly criticized, for any critic is immediately branded as being complicitous with reactionary forces."[47] He states—a reading that is probably more apposite to himself than to Edwards' text—that Edwards' criticisms come from his "support" of the revolution and socialism and of the benefits that it has brought to Cuba, "which are much greater than any prejudicial aspects" (p.74). It was a risk to publish a book at a moment when it seemed that the right was gaining power throughout Latin America, with totalitarian regimes in Brazil, Bolivia, and Uruguay: would this criticism from the left give arms to the right? Vargas Llosa's response is very clear: "the very existence of the book is a daring proposal: that the Latin American left should break its secret circle, its support of ritual truths and secret dogmas, and air in a civilized manner the differences that exist within its ranks" (p.75). The best way of giving strength to the enemy would be if thinking on the left were to become fossilized.

Edwards' book deals with the climate of fear and repression in Cuba in the early seventies. (Indeed some commentators have argued that it was Edwards' very open involvement with dissident opinion that helped to trigger the crisis that erupted in the Padilla affair.) Vargas Llosa gives reasons for this state of paranoia: the country was suffering a severe economic crisis and subject to constant sabotage from the United States, and so "idealism" and "spontaneity" had to give way to "realism" and "bureaucratic organization." This new severity affected all sectors but since Edwards' friends were writers, he talked about the intellectual community. The book demonstrates the way in which free thinkers were being made to serve the state: "the bureaucrat replaced the writer as the main protagonist of literary life" (p.76). There were, of course, major benefits for writers to toe the official line: as in Cuba, in the case of his own country, Peru, writers were being wooed with grants and other forms of recognition to support the policies of the state. Dissenting voices would be dealt with severely, as happened in the case of Padilla. Vargas Llosa deplores this state of affairs and hopes that now that conditions are less governed by a siege mentality, liberties will return. He ends the review with a very personal confession: that the revolution had been the most significant political event in his life, the first tangible proof that socialism could be a possibility in Latin America. But he had gradually become aware that while such regimes might bring about income redistribution, they could not guarantee intellectual freedom. Yet this system remained for him the lesser of the evils: "For that reason, despite the true horror that police states and dogmatism inspire in me, if I had to choose one system or the other, I would clench my teeth and go on saying, 'I'm with socialism'. But I say it now without the hopes, the joy and the optimism that for years the word socialism inspired in me, thanks exclusively to Cuba" (p.77). This review was a clear example of what Paz meant by earning the right to criticize Cuba, but the criticism remained circumspect, as we have seen, especially since the magazine's publication coincided with a wave of military dictatorships spreading throughout the Southern Cone. The 1964 coup in Brazil led to a more extreme dictatorship between 1968 and 1971. In Bolivia General Hugo Banzer ruled with repressive severity between 1971 and 1978. In Uruguay, the military overthrew one of Latin America's most stable democracies in 1973. Later the same year the armed forces under General Pinochet ended Chile's three year experiment of democratic revolutionary change. In Argentina, after the death of Perón in 1974, the country was torn by near civil war, a violence that was extended and systematized when the military took power in 1976. Of all these events, it was the military coup in Chile that received the most attention in *Plural*.

   Plural's attention focused on Chile in the aftermath of the coup. Octavio Paz wrote an article published in the "Letras, letrillas, letrones" section in *Plural* 25 (October 1974). He sent it from Harvard and in an accompanying letter to Sakai and José de la Colina, dated 28 September 1973 he wrote that he could not write a brief, impersonal note, because "Chile is a problem that touches me and causes me pain ... But I'd like to make clear that these are my opinions, not an editorial position (the only option for *Plural* is the plurality of opinion that it would look to express)" (Paz to Sakai and de la Colina, Cambridge, Mass., 28 September 1973).

   Paz's article begins with a memorable paragraph hurling his disgust at the developments within Latin America and in the international arena. Brazil, Bolivia, Uruguay, and now Chile have fallen to military coups. In a line worthy of the best tradition of Latin American protest literature—and, though Paz might not welcome the comparison, with distinct echoes of Neruda at his most invective, in his Spanish civil war poetry and in parts of the *Canto General*—Paz remarks: "The continent has become suffocating. Shadows on shadows, blood on blood, corpses on corpses: Latin America is becoming an enormous and barbarous monument made out of the ruins of ideas and the bones of its victims. A grotesque and ferocious spectacle: at the top of the monument a tribunal of uniformed and medaled pygmies gesticulate, deliberate, excommunicate and shoot the skeptics."[48] The grotesque horror permeates the whole international horizon: "While Nixon washes his hands stained by Watergate in the bloody wash bowl that Kissinger hands to him, while Brezhnev opens new psychiatric hospitals for incurable dissidents, while Chou en Lai fêtes Pompidou in Peking and alerts western Europeans to the 'Russian peril,' our little Latin American generals are at it again" (p.49). There is a long list of "destroyed democracies": Greece, Czechoslovakia, Uruguay, Chile. In Prague, Russian tanks, in Santiago generals armed and trained by the Pentagon: the one acting in the name of Marxism, the other in the name of anti-Marxism. This is Paz's most explicit condemnation of U.S. imperialism, and its complicity with right-wing regimes in Latin America, contained anywhere within the magazine.

After his poetic invective, Paz warns that protest is not enough, that it must be accompanied by an analysis of what Paz sees not just as a great tragedy, but also as a great defeat. For Paz, the left is faced with formidable enemies: U.S. imperialism, oligarchic interests, the military, and the former conservative parties. But it also has to deal with its own internal divisions, the relative weakness of its forces and the "the geometric and absolute nature of its programs." The radicalism of "extremist" groups such as the MIR in Chile also hindered the road to socialism. Paz does not wish to see the defeat of Allende as the definitive defeat of any democratic road to socialism. In fact, he argues, along with the *Le Monde* correspondent, Maurice Duverger, whom he quotes, that the Popular Unity policies should have been less rather than more radical, they should have tried to bring the middle class sectors along with them, rather than alienating them. The whole experiment raises the question as to whether socialism is achievable in an underdeveloped, dependent country, a possibility that, in Paz's analysis, Marx and Engels would have denied. This is an important point for Paz, for throughout this period he would refer to himself as a socialist, despite his detractors trying increasingly to paint him into the opposing camp. Was, by extension, a form of democratic socialism possible in Mexico, and through what means? Paz also attempts an early analysis of the Chilean regime within the wider Latin American context: "A strange triangle: there is the Chilean military regime and the Brazilian regime, and the extraordinary ambiguity of Peronism. The failure of traditional political ideologies . . . are the immediate cause of these *bizarre* regimes, in the meaning that Baudelaire gave to that word: singular in its horror" (p.50). More remote causes, for Paz, date back to the tradition of *caudillismo* after the Independence period. He ends the article with an exhortation to come up with appropriate political solution for Latin America and asks that *Plural* serve as a forum for these debates. Paz is not offering prescriptions for the way ahead, but rather inviting discussion.

Three other short articles deal with Chile in the same issue. José de la Colina, the then managing editor, continues the same tone of indignation. There is a note on the funeral of Pablo Neruda that glosses an article in *Le Monde*. We learn that Neruda's funeral, on 25 September was the first public demonstration of resistance within Chile. There were shouts from the funeral cortege of "Compañero Pablo Neruda, presente" and "Compañero Salvador Allende, presente" and the "International" was sung despite the overwhelming presence of the army with their tanks and machine guns. By contrast, Alejandro Rossi's "Manual del Distraído" ironically warns against reducing the Chilean experience to that of hero worship and reminds us that the lessons of the Chilean experience are far from clear and that, in effect the Chilean economy had been in ruins and the government chaotic.[49] Here Rossi, in the first of what would become a regular column, chooses to question the most sacred of sacred cows.

Plural did not have the debate about Chile that Paz had invited, but references to the coup recurred. Two issues later, Paz would gloss the reactions of the *Le Monde* correspondent in Italy to the coup. Instead of stating that Allende should have armed the people, the columnist Jacques Nabecourt notes that the Italian Communist party had come up with a completely different analysis: in order to venture down the road to socialism it was necessary to include not just socialists and left-wing groups but also the middle classes and the Christian Democrats.[50] This clear, realistic political analysis was one that Paz clearly approved of. He was drawn to independent thought—be it the more open nature of Italian political thought or the Venezuelan MAS—at a time when Brezhnev was lambasting the Communist Parties of Western Europe and in Latin America for their deviations.

Events in Uruguay and Argentina would also be charted in the magazine. In March 1974, a year after the Uruguay coup, *Plural* noted that five writers, including Juan Carlos Onetti, had been imprisoned and that the cultural journal *Marcha* continued to publish under very reduced circumstances.[51] Some two years later, in a comprehensive analysis of cultural censorship in Uruguay, the magazine reported that the cultural journal *Marcha* had been forced to close in November 1974 and that its editor Carlos Quijano had gone into exile in Mexico.[52] One exile from the military persecution and from *Marcha* was the critic Angel Rama, who would write on several occasions for *Plural*.

Argentina was the country in Latin America closest to *Plural* in terms of literary affinities, as we shall see in the next chapter. But its political developments—the collapse of the military regime, the return of Perón in 1973, after eighteen years in exile, the brief rule of Perón, and, following his death, the presidency of Isabel Perón and her sinister henchman López Rega, the spiraling violence between right-wing death groups and the guerrilla groups—left Paz and others increasingly mystified and alarmed. In a letter to his editor at Sudamericana, Enrique Pezzoni, in July 1973 (just after the return of Perón to Argentina), Paz states that he does not understand how Argentines continue to believe in Perón and how it is even more mystifying that many intellectuals who were former critics of Perón now discover that he has revolutionary virtues. This does not mean that Paz has any time for the oligarchy in Argentina or the military. He is particularly alarmed that there is a Trotskyist terror group operating: "Trotsky always criticized terrorism—which was very different to revolutionary terror and would have been scandalized by this resurrection of Blanquism in Latin America. The Guevarist archetype is spreading: a proletarian revolution without the proletariat." (Paz to Enrique Pezzoni, 10 July 1973 (no.106/73).

Argentina seemed to be conforming to Paz's worst fears. The magazine would comment on what seemed like a slide toward violence. In issue 13, October 1972, it published an account of the murder of sixteen *guerrilleros* by the military in Trelew in August 1972, following a mass break-out of the Rawson prison camp. Under the brief presidency of Perón, it noted that there was an increase in "intellectual repression and political violence" in Argentina that included the seizure by the police of novels by gay writers (the bookshop was accused of "mariconazos").[53] With the death of Perón violence spiraled and in October 1975, the magazine published a long and very lucid interview with the critic H. Alsina Thevenet on the Argentine crisis, with details of the many writers and artists persecuted and forced into exile by right-wing death squads such as the AAA (the Alianza Anticomunista Argentina) ("La crisis argentina," *Plural* 49, October 1975). *Plural* would be suffering its own censorship at the time when details would be emerging about the military coup in Argentina at the end of March 1976: it took some time for there to be concrete news about the extensive repression of the coup, by which time (July 1976), the last issue of Paz's *Plural* was to appear.

What of events north of the Mexican border? It was in the final issue of *Plural* under his editorship that Paz was to publish his only major article in this 1971–1976 period on the United States entitled

"El espejo indiscreto" ("The Indiscrete Mirror"). This was published to coincide with the two hundredth anniversary of U.S. Independence. In it Paz talks of the shadow of a giant that covers the whole conti- nent, a giant that can be both generous and bloodthirsty. For a Mexican to travel in the United States is to venture into the giant's castle and "traverse its chambers full of horrors and marvels. But there is a difference: the Beast's Castle is surprising because it is archaic: the United States surprises us because of its newness. Our present is always a little bit behind the true present while their present is always a little bit ahead. Their present already has the future inscribed in it, while our present is still tied to the past."[54] The United States is both desire and threat: the desire to emulate the modern, democratic principles of that country, and the threat of imperialism. The essay is structured around a comparison between the United States and Mexico and in it Paz reiterates his long held view that the differences arise in the United States being marked by the Reformation and Mexico by the Counterreformation. While most of the article maps a general overview of two hundred years of comparative history, there are some comments on contemporary issues in the United States, the loss of confidence in its aims and methods, the growth of income inequality and the disastrous effects of the U.S. economic system on the third world, the growth of a political bureaucracy with its methods of surveillance, and the swings between isolationism and intervention on the world stage.

While Paz would also contribute comments on international affairs regularly to the "Letras, letrillas, letrones" section, it is fair to say that in these five years between 1971–1976, his attention was much more drawn to events in the Soviet Union, than in the country where he was living for protracted periods of time. His time in the United States and his visibility as an internationally celebrated poet and critic meant that he was in touch with the major figures of the U.S. liberal intelligentsia. Most of the articles covering international affairs in *Plural* would be drawn from these liberal groups and their publications in different East Coast journals. This had not been Paz's original intention, as he wrote to Segovia on 4 June 1972, after he had been in Massachusetts for some seven months. He is still con- cerned at how difficult it is to get hold of good, or at least decorous articles of criticism on contemporary Mexican, Latin American and world affairs: "I think that *for now* we will have to keep on reprinting articles that have appeared in foreign journals, in the hope that, one day, people writing in Spanish will decide to think for themselves and *say* what they think." In the interim, while these new writers were emerging—and they were to emerge only sporadically in the years of *Plural*—he would continue to ask permissions to republish significant articles on contemporary politics and society. "When we publish them, we won't prevent people inside and outside carrying on saying that *Plural* is exquisite and esoteric—but they'll have to bite their tongue" (Paz to Segovia, Cambridge, Mass., 4 June 1972). The "inside" here most likely refers to the editorial staff in the *Excélsior* offices. Later in the letter Paz complains that issue 7 of *Plural* was given hardly any coverage in the main newspaper. It was also Paz's constant preoccupation that there was no concerted policy to distribute *Plural* outside Mexico (and even within the country). Here he argues that *Excélsior*'s lack of interest was not only losing them six or seven thousand readers in Spanish America, but was also distorting the magazine's original focus, since it had been conceived from the outset as a "Latin American journal."

A few weeks after that letter, *Plural* published in issue 10 two of the articles that Paz mentions, I.F. Stone's article on Nixon's foreign policy (from the *NYRB*) and Jim Peck's "Why China turned West" (first published in *Ramparts* magazine). Stone was a journalist and critic, a regular contributor to the *NYRB*, and *Plural* would publish a number of his articles, in particular on abuses in the Soviet Union. Paz could also find eminent contributors in the Faculty Club at Harvard or in private dinner parties around the university. Paz approached the internationally regarded economist, John K. Galbraith, in mid-November 1971 at a dinner and he agreed to offer Paz the Spanish language rights of his latest article (and his subsequent debate with Mendes France and Roger Garaudy) on "the crisis of industrial societies." This intervention was published as a special supplement in *Plural* in January 1972 (issue 4). Galbraith also appears in issue 18, March 1973, a lecture on "economists and power" delivered when he was president of the American Society of Economists. Galbraith, of course, could be seen as emblematic of the political figure that the magazine would be comfortable with: a man who had been close to the Kennedys throughout, who would represent a clear liberal credo. *Plural* also published Noam Chomsky's Bertrand Russell Memorial Lecture, "Interpret/Change the World" in issue 3, December 1971—Chomsky, of course, was just down the road from Harvard at M.I.T.—and would publish another article by him in January 1975 (an interview initially published in *Black Robe*). In a later appreciation of the work of *Plural*, Gabriel Zaid would remark that it was common practice in Mexico to read an interesting article from abroad and then pirate a translation, without

ever communicating with the author or with the journal that published the article. For Zaid, such behavior, "implied that we were
invisible with respect to creators from abroad, incapable of dialogue
with the creative centers. I remember some strange comments on
foreign contributors that I did not understand until I realized that
for many it was inconceivable that Claude Lévi-Strauss or John
Kenneth Galbraith were contributors to *Plural* (instead of remote
eminences that could be pirated); it was inconceivable, for example
that Galbraith would send an article with a hand written note saying
something like: 'Come on Octavio. Pay me a bit more.' "[55] Another
long article that Paz had sent across with his 4 June 1972 letter was
by the distinguished Harvard professor of politics and sociology,
Daniel Bell, who had recently acquired recognition for theorizing
(and coining the phrase of) the "post-industrial society" that *Plural*
would eventually publish in April and May 1974. Bell would later
publish an article on the end of U.S. exceptionalism in *Plural* 58, the
last issue under Paz's editorship. The coverage north of the border
thus tends to come through major articles by luminary East Coast
intellectuals, and through snippets in "Letras, letrillas, letrones."

What does emerge consistently in the magazine is what Paz signaled as the "central question" of our time: "What is the true historical nature of the regime that in Russia and in other countries has
usurped the name of socialism?"[56] This central preoccupation can be
seen in the publication of a number of articles on abuses in the Soviet
Union, often by dissident writers. There is also some exploration of
Maoism, and more general essays on the vicissitudes of Marxist
thought. We have already discussed Paz's analysis of Solzhenitsyn and
the Gulag (It seems quite possible that this issue was produced in reaction to the news that Solzhenitsyn had been deported from the USSR
in early February 1974). In that same issue—issue 30, March 1974—
there is an article by Roy Medvedev, "On the Gulag"—which offers a
critical account of Solzhenitsyn, agreeing with a number of points
about the Gulag, but arguing that Lenin's errors did not negate the
whole Bolshevik project. An article by Irving Howe, the editor of
Dissent magazine, explored whether the Hungarian Marxist critic,
Lukács, was right to describe Solzhenitsyn as a true "social realist
writer." For Howe and for Paz socialist realism was very much a dogmatic and bureaucratic offshoot of Stalinism, while Solzhenitsyn himself was very much in the Slavic/Christian tradition of a Tolstoy or a
Dostoievsky. Another Russian writer that Paz positioned as ideologi-
cally mid-way between Solzhenitsyn and Medvedev was the liberal
mathematician and physicist, André Sakharov, the subject of an article

by I.F. Stone in *Plural* 26 (November 1973). Here Stone points out when faced with the economic slow down of the Soviet Union in comparison to the United States, Sakharov had argued the need for détente and democratization in three "open" memoranda that he wrote in 1968, 1970, and 1971. But contrary to his hopes, the seeming détente between Nixon and Brezhnev was not leading toward democratization and liberalization, but rather toward an extension of the old practices of bureaucratization of working practices and the suppression of dissent. Two years later, when Sakharov won the Nobel Peace Prize, *Plural* published his acceptance speech in which he declared that he loved his country but that he felt it his duty to point out its negative traits: "This is very important for international relations and for understanding within the country, since criticism is silenced by Soviet or Rusophile propaganda."[57] In the same issue of *Plural*, issue 26, there was an interview with Solzhenitsyn originally published in *Le Monde* in which he speaks out against the state's attempt to cow him. This was at the time when excerpts from *The Gulag Archipelago* were just appearing in French, having been banned in the Soviet Union. The autobiography of Nadezda Mandelstam, widow of the poet Osip Madelstam, who died in the Gulag in 1938, was published in two parts in 1970 and 1974. *Plural* published an extract in July 1972, which deals with his imprisonment and death in the Gulag. She speaks of how she had preserved and circulated her husband's work, but points out that now the Russian state was attempting to recuperate and take over his publications claiming all the rights over his work.[58] A poem by Mandelstam against Stalin would also be included in the "writers and politics" issue 13 (October 1972), as well as a later review by the poet Joseph Brodsky of Mandelstam's *Hope Abandoned*.[59]

Issue 10, July 1972, which contains Mandelstam's "testament," also includes the most thorough coverage of Chinese politics that the magazine was to offer: an article by Stone on Nixon's foreign policy with regard to the Soviet Union and China and an extensive article by Jim Peck on why China was opening up to the West (*Plural* 10, July 1972). Later, Etiemble would send an article, "Maoísmo o neo-confucionismo" that was published in issue 29, (February 1974). In it Etiemble argued that Mao should be seen in the tradition of Chinese emperors, especially Ts'in Che Huang-Li who in 221 AD reunified and centralized the territory of China, and that Mao was as inaccessible as those monarchs in his lofty and remote appeal to virtue.

Plural would also publish the work of dissident former Marxist critics on issues of political theory. Two important figures in this regard are Kostas Papaioannou, the philosopher who had become a friend of Paz in the forties in Paris.[60] Leszek Kolakowski, the Polish dissident forced into exile in the United Kingdom in 1968, would also offer a series of heterodox views.[61] It was such writers who gave Paz and *Plural* the theoretical justification for the reassessment of Marxism as a political project, although most of the coverage, as we have seen, was denunciatory.

The political analysis in *Plural*, therefore, was consistent across a range of national and international issues. In Mexico, the prism through which to read the political situation was through the PRI and the power of the president. Events in Latin American and the rest of the world were viewed through the prism of Soviet "totalitarianism" and the need to explore the abuses of the Soviet system. This is not a Manichaean Cold War position: there is no easy alignment with economic or political policies of the United States that are criticized, albeit less systematically than those of the Soviet Union. In the same way, within Mexico, there was not a clear alternative position to the PRI developed, but rather a constant reiteration of the need for democratic reform and for curtailing the power of the president and his court. What was consistent was an implied argument that Mexico could progress without needing to maintain the rhetoric of revolutionary nationalism. What *Plural* was arguing was that such nationalism and the political systems that supported it was entering into decline; the legitimacy of the USSR was in free-fall; the ideological argument that state-led communism was the only panacea was untenable; the Gulag was real; Castro was a tyrant; the dictatorships in Latin America must be overcome by some sort of democratic alternative; the dialogue with the United States could be maintained without political guilt or feelings of inadequacy; the left had lost the subtlety of its thinking.

The political criticism in *Plural* is not based, in the main, within the academy. It is found in essays, in notes in "Letras, letrillas, letrones" and it is given coherence by the energy and passion of Paz's vision and essays by Cosío Villegas and Zaid, amongst others. It was an outlook that could put into debate both Fuentes's defense of a state-led political system which, with all its faults, had guaranteed Mexico a degree of stability, while all around democratic regimes were falling prey to military dictatorship, and also Zaid's devastating criticism of presidential power. Of course, the magazine was never seen as a political journal per se. The term "crítica," criticism, covered a whole range of issues, from the Gulag to contemporary art. Indeed some of Paz's most cited authors, such as Fourier, would imagine a political future that was deeply imbued with a utopian, "poetic" vision.[62] *Plural* would look to explore the ways in which politics and art might become melded. The following chapter will outline the main parameters of cultural criticism within the journal.

Chapter 4

Cultural Criticism in *Plural*: Literature and Art

On 19 November 1973, Paz wrote to Sakai expressing his enthusiasm for the quality of contributors and for the balance of issue 26: "The truth is that it is difficult to find another magazine publishing such good quality articles. I really don't understand the attitude of Mexican writers: they should be fighting to publish in *Plural*" (Paz to Sakai, Cambridge, Mass., 19 November 1973).

What is in this issue? On the cover, between the word *Plural* and the number 26, both in bold red, are the words *Crítica, Arte, Literatura* (Criticism, Art, Literature). The magazine had used this form of words on its cover since issue 23, August 1973, and would retain it until issue 58. In the next issue of *Plural*, December 1973, *Plural* would begin to publish a regular monthly—usually four-page, color-illustrated—"artistic supplement," and the first subject would be the work of Sakai himself (explored in an essay by Jorge Alberto Manrique). The bright cover, with Sakai's now trademark circles and swirls announces Paz's essay "el ocaso de las vanguardias" ("The Decline of the Vanguard Movements," later published in book form as *The Children of the Mire*). Inscribed within Sakai's circular design are the announcements of Stone on Sakharov, poems by Juan David, Georges Bataille, "Madame Edwarda," and Roland Barthes on "the third sense" (the work of Eisenstein). Beneath the color illustration, there are references to Mario Vargas Llosa on Enrique Congrains, Fernando del Paso on Italian futurism, an extract from a novel by José Balza, and the aforementioned interview with Solzhenitsyn. Inside one also finds poems by Henri Michaux translated by Paz himself and an essay by Cioran on Michaux. Georges Bataille is the subject of the "literary supplement" introduced and translated by Salvador

Elizondo. In addition there is a biting essay by Cosío Villegas in his "Compuerta" column, regular features by Rossi and Zaid, book reviews and the "Letras, letrillas, letrones" section. Paz concludes his letter by observing that perhaps there should have been fewer French writers and only one article on the Soviet Union, but apart from these "peccadillos," he thought the issue was "magnificent." The issue is indeed a balance between *Crítica, Arte*, and *Literatura*, with the greatest emphasis on *Crítica*. There is also a blend of Mexican (Paz himself, Elizondo, Cosío, Rossi, del Paso, Zaid, plus regular reviewers such as José de la Colina, Ignacio Solares, and Ramón Xirau), Latin American (David is Colombian and Balza is Brazilian, Sakai is Argentine-Japanese, Vargas Llosa is Peruvian) and world-wide contributors (the French Bataille and Barthes, the Belgian Michaux, and the Paris-based Cioran, the Russian Solzhenitsyn, and the U.S. scholar Stone). Paz thought that at this moment no Spanish language journal, and very few journals in the world, could put together an issue of this range and quality.

In this chapter, we will analyze cultural criticism, in particular the two areas that dominated the magazine, literature and art. Chapter five will explore literature, the publication of poetry and works of fiction. These of course are somewhat artificial divisions and the different overlapping areas will tend to meld even though the chapter divisions might look to keep them apart. For one thing, an individual contributor could be a novelist or a poet, a literary critic and an art critic. The exemplary case here is Octavio Paz himself and *Plural* is very much shaped by his interests, passions, and contacts. Jason Wilson reminds us of the advice that he gave to the poet Alejandra Pizarnik when faced with the solitary moment of writing a poem: "Octavio Paz...advised her to write essays (*Diarios*, p.495). That is, reading and criticizing a book would wake up her response and would lead to a poem. This technique was his own strategy and he accompanied all his poems with critical essays that overlapped, so that they can be read together."[1] These overlapping strands of Paz's interests between a poem and art or cultural or political criticism, are traced between chapters 3 and 5 of this book. The same procedure can be noted in other writers such as Mario Vargas Llosa, whose rethinking of the social function of literature can be seen in both his fictional work and his essays on literature in this period. Indeed it is interesting how often *Plural* would use novelists or poets as literary or cultural critics, especially Latin American writers.

There are two points that should be noted here. It was a feature, in particular of the boom writers, that they were their own best critics and helped to map their own and each others' position within the development of national and continental literatures. It was also the case that Paz and others thought that the contribution of the writers in Latin America far outstripped the ability of critics to understand them and write criticism at a level worthy of them. In this situation it was natural to have writers comment on other writers. No other Latin American writer of the twentieth century was better prepared or qualified to lead such an enterprise as Paz himself: he was one of the finest poets of the era and also one of the greatest essayists, not just as a *pensador* or purveyor of ideas, but also as a literary critic and historian, and an art critic. As a long-term (perhaps life time) member of the international avant garde, Paz always believed that there should be no barriers between different areas of specialization or intellectual endeavor and that specialization, taken too far, was a dehumanizing phenomenon.

In terms of mapping the field, it is also appropriate to sub-divide the different contributions coming from Mexico, Latin America, and the rest of the world. Since Paz always argued that *Plural* was a Latin American magazine, it here that we should have our first sub-division.

Latin America

On several occasions Paz called *Plural* a *revista hispanoamericana* (Spanish American magazine) and pointed how difficult it was to find good criticism in the Spanish language. In a letter to Segovia dated 4 June 1972, he states that *Plural* is a Spanish American journal and should be distributed throughout the continent and in Spain. He adds that the magazine covers both "criticism" and "literature," which means that it can be a challenging reading process. It is not an "exquisite" magazine but rather a rigorous journal which, he argues, offends lazy readers. He is conscious that in its first issues, the journal has not covered contemporary literary, artistic, and political reality, but he is sure that this gap will soon be filled. Once again he blames not the orientation of the magazine, but rather the dearth of good essayists in Hispanic culture, and particularly in Mexico. "There is no criticism because we have not been taught either to think or to say what we think. We swing between silence and insult because we are moved by fear and by envy" (Paz to Segovia, Cambridge, Mass., 4 June 1972).

It was certainly the intention of the magazine to receive regular contributions from across the world, and there was an attempt to enlist correspondents in Latin America to write regular columns on the culture and politics of specific regions. This idea never really came to fruition, despite some isolated examples. Instead, the Latin American coverage would be somewhat more piecemeal, and would come from three main sources: Latin American writers and critics in Latin America, those in Paris, and those based in the United States (who had often taken up teaching posts in the newly emerging area of Latin American Studies). Out of all the countries of the subcontinent, *Plural* had the closest contact, perhaps significantly, with Argentina. This came initially from Paz's contacts with the *Sur* group, as we have seen, especially with its long-standing managing editor, José Bianco. *Sur* had ceased regular publication in August 1970 and to some extent *Plural* would continue and extend its working of building bridges between the cultures, albeit in a much more dynamic way: *Sur* by 1970 had run its course. Both magazines relied greatly on the range of cultural contacts of their editors: those of Victoria Ocampo were unsurpassed in the 1930s, but she had not managed to keep pace or have sympathy with many movements in the sixties. Paz, by contrast was effortlessly up to date, and equally at home among writers and in academic gatherings. But he would still rely on the friends that he had made back in the forties, in particular José Bianco, for his access to Argentine writers. And while he saw himself in the *Sur* tradition, he thought that *Plural* was a much livelier and more diverse journal.[2]

Plural's Argentine contacts came from three main sources: Paz himself, the Argentine-Japanese painter and critic, Kazuya Sakai, and in the final issues, from the Uruguayan, Danubio Torres Fierro, who had come to Mexico when the military coup in Uruguay censored the work of such publications as *Marcha*. The work of Sakai would become increasingly influential from late in 1972 when he took over as managing editor from Segovia who had taken up a temporary post at Princeton. He was responsible, in particular, for developing coverage on art and oriental literatures, but he also had a say across the magazine itself and was not, as he wrote, perhaps partly in jest, to Cabrera Infante, a mere "invention of Octavio Paz": "Just in case [in English in the original], I am male, Japanese-Argentine, educated in Tokyo, a painter and an orientalist (Japanese literature and theater) and I now write from time to time chronicles on art and jazz. The rest you know." (Letter, Kazuya Sakai to Guillermo Cabrera Infante, Mexico, 18 March 1975).

Paz's friendship with Bianco led him to ask his advice as to coverage from Argentina. Paz asks him to write a regular "letter from Argentina" column and also wants him to comment on Peronism in its latest manifestation. Paz also points out that they have as yet not been able to publish an article on Chile, "because we have not yet found a Latin American with the capacity and also the desire to write something for us" (Octavio Paz to José Bianco (no place mentioned), 8 December 1972). The ever-cautious Bianco did not want to take on such a regular commitment, but was persuaded, together with Enrique Pezzoni and Edgardo Cozarinsky, to prepare a special issue of the magazine on Argentina. In the event, despite a long correspondence, and even a handwritten proposed table of contents from Bianco, this special issue did not materialize (there is no correspondence as to why this occurred). It is likely that the increasingly polarized and violent political situation in Argentina was making choosing an even-handed, nonpartisan group of contributors rather more difficult, added to the sheer amount of work involved. Bianco would be the conduit for contributions from a group that included Adolfo Bioy Casares, Silvina Ocampo, Juan José Hernández, and the essayist María Rosa Oliver (one of the founding members of *Sur* in the early thirties), and he was also linked by friendship to the essayist and publisher Enrique Pezzoni and the then critic and short story writer Edgardo Cozarinsky, who later went on to become a filmmaker and writer in Paris.

Criticism on and from the *Sur* group came mainly from a series of interviews conducted by Danubio Torres Fierro. The interview format had been used infrequently in the magazine, but here it systematically covers a group of writers often famed for their reticence. The main interviews are with the novelist Ernesto Sábato (February 1975); the poet and short story writer Silvina Ocampo (November 1975); the editor and critic Victoria Ocampo (December 1975); José Bianco himself (January 1976); the short story writer and novelist Adolfo Bioy Casares (April 1976), and the poet Alberto Girri (July 1976).[3] The interview format perhaps gained its greatest exposure in Latin America with *Primera Plana*, which sought to give mass exposure (and celebrity status) to writers and artists, in particular, of the boom. There were also key books of the period such as Luis Harss's, *Los nuestros* (*Into the Mainstream*) and Rita Guibert's *Siete voces* (*Seven Voices*) that continued the work of the "star" interview, sometimes with mixed results. Paz revealed in a letter to Guillermo Cabrera Infante that he was not averse to the interview format, depending on the quality of the person being interviewed. Rita Guibert, he writes, has just sent him *Siete voces* that he found tedious in parts: "But your interview dazzled me, lit me up. A vivacious, vibrant, clairvoyant, vindicatory, virile voice. A violent viola. Look, you've got me doing it." (Octavio Paz to Guillermo Cabrera Infante, no place specified, 10 December 1972).

This Argentine group of writers, however, had not received the same critical attention in terms of the world of the market place and the boom, and Torres Fierro's skilful questioning elicited many interesting comments from them. Taken together, they offer a series of illuminating snapshots of cultural life in Buenos Aires in the twentieth century. The missing name from this group was, of course, Jorge Luis Borges, but he had been the subject of an earlier interview in *Plural* in August 1974.[4] The interviews serve as introductions to these writers' work, which would be published elsewhere in the magazine. Of this group, only José Bianco would publish work of criticism in *Plural* with any regularity, including two essays on Proust (the first to coincide with the Proust centenary).[5] Bianco's friends María Rosa Oliver and Edgardo Cozarinsky would also publish on occasion.

Another Argentine writer, Julio Cortázar would write a moving homage to the Chilean poet Pablo Neruda published in March 1974. In it he traced the impact of Neruda's poetry on his generation growing up in Argentina and throughout Latin America, from the publication of *Veinte poemas de amor* (*Twenty Love Poems*) in the 1920s to the final act of defiance in 1973, *Incitación al nixoncidio y alabanza de la revolución chilena.* (*A Call for the Destruction of Nixon and Praise for the Chilean Revolution*). He focuses in particular on the *Canto General*: "That immense work is an anachronistic monstrosity (I said this once to Pablo and he gave me one of his long slow glances, like a beached shark), and that is a proof that not only is Latin America outside European historical time, but that it has the perfect right, and indeed the most pressing obligation, to be so."[6] In the light of current events in Chile, Uruguay, and Bolivia, the *Canto General* seems to Cortázar to have a pressing immediacy, verifying "the implacable prophecy and the invincible hope of one of the most lucid men of our time." The article ends with Cortázar's memories of Neruda in Isla Negra, in declining health, and argues that his death is the "final protest poem." In words echoing the final broadcast of Salvador Allende only hours before his death, Cortázar concludes: "I know that one day we will return to Isla Negra, that his people will go through that door and will find in every stone, in every leaf of every tree and in every seabird cry, the always living poetry of a man who loved them deeply."[7]

The publication of this article in *Plural*—in particular in an issue dedicated to the abuses of Stalinism—showed that Paz was finding space to pay certain dues to a man with whom he had such an ambivalent relationship for almost four decades. He surely could not refuse such a lyrical obituary from such a close friend as Cortázar. Although it is interesting to note that in an earlier article in the same edition, Paz is still blaming Neruda for whipping up a negative campaign against him in Mexico in the early forties.[8] As he made clear in many articles and in his private correspondence, Paz considered Neruda to be a poet capable of splendid, but also very uneven work. Also, Paz considered the political poetry to be "immoral," as he explained in a letter to the Argentine poet and critic Saúl Yurkievich some months before Neruda's death. Commenting on Yurkievich's own work on Neruda and other Latin American poets, he argues that his own critical account of the work of Neruda would have to face up to the problem of his Stalinism: "Of course, this was a tragic error, but the roots of this error lie in intellectual and moral confusion that also affects his poetry" (Octavio Paz to Saúl Yurkievich, México, D.F., 4 December 1972).

The most frequent contributor to *Plural* from among the Latin American writers was Mario Vargas Llosa. He had not been an immediate first choice for the magazine—a further example of the distance of Paz from the world of the boom—and indeed it is Vargas Llosa who approaches Paz with his first contribution to the magazine, an extract from his novel *Pantaleón y las visitadoras* (*Captain Pantoja and the Special Service*, published in issue 21, June 1973). In quite a circumspect letter dated 17 February 1973, Vargas Llosa remarks that he has been reading Julio Ortega's copies of *Plural* since he cannot get hold of it in Barcelona and he praises the magazine for its vitality and for finding "the correct line in terms of cultural and more specifically literary issues, and in terms of political matters, and I wish the magazine a long life because the truth is that there are now very few worthy forums in the Spanish language." (Mario Vargas Llosa to Octavio Paz, Barcelona, 17 February 1973). By this time, as Vargas Llosa's most incisive critic, Efraín Kristal, points out, he had suffered a critical backlash in intellectual circles for his stance over Padilla: "Within months of the day he drafted the letter protesting Padilla's confession, Vargas Llosa's image changed from the novelist committed to leftist causes to the bourgeois defender of reactionary thinking. And, ironically, Vargas Llosa continued for years to justify the moral and political superiority of the political regime that had humiliated him."[9] We have already seen in the previous chapter that in December 1974, in his review of Jorge Edwards's *Persona non grata,* Vargas Llosa was still defending socialist alternatives, while "biting his tongue."

The year 1975 would prove to be a significant turning point in Vargas Llosa's thinking about politics, revolution, and the social function of literature. This can be seen in two essays that he published in *Plural*: an article on Flaubert's *Madame Bovary* and an appreciation of Albert Camus. The article on Camus—"Albert Camus y la moral de los límites" ("Albert Camus and the Morality of Limits"), *Plural* 51, December 1975—marks Vargas Llosa's final distancing from Sartre and his rereading of Camus who, as a young man, he had viewed with a certain impatience at what he considered to be Camus's "intellectual lyricism." It was in Peru a few months earlier, in the aftermath of a terrorist attack in Lima, that he had reopened *The Rebel*, Camus's essay on violence in history, and had been astonished at the lucidity and contemporary relevance of his work. Vargas Llosa found that his own developing ideas chimed with those of Camus in a number of key areas. What does it mean, Vargas Llosa asks, to call Camus a democrat, a liberal, a reformist, all of these terms that, "have come to define at best, political naiveté and at worst, to signify the hypocritical masks of reactionaries and exploiters. It is more useful to try to define what these terms meant to Camus. Basically, he completely rejected totalitarianism as a social system in which the human being is no longer an end and becomes an instrument. The morality of limits is a state in which the antagonism between means and end disappears, in which the means justify the ends and not vice versa. The theme of totalitarianism, of authoritarian power, the extremes of madness that can be reached when man violated the morality of limits, obsessed Camus throughout his life."[10] Such systems, for Camus, are based on violence—"all the tragedy of humankind began the day that it became admissible to kill in the name of an idea" (p.15)—and on conformity. Camus's rejection of revolutionary violence struck a chord with Vargas Llosa, as did his views on, "the relationship between the creator and the principles that govern society." Agreeing with Camus's views that the artist must be a recalcitrant, Vargas Llosa argues that it is the duty of the artist and the intellectual to maintain freedom of thought in the face of the blandishments and also the pressures of the state, to proclaim that freedom "is the main condition of their existence" and that it is necessary "to remind those in power, at every moment and by every means at their disposal, of the morality of limits." This was perhaps not so beguiling for young people, "as those prophets of adventure and apocalyptic denial such as Che Guevara or Frantz Fanon," but this did not make Camus's message any less true or any less important (p.12).

While Vargas Llosa could find an echo for his own concerns regarding Communist states, revolutionary violence and the role of the writer in society in Camus, it was in his analysis of Flaubert that he began to reassess the function of literature. We now see, as Efraín Kristal, points out, that "the leitmotifs of his essays on the political commitment of the writer reappear without socialist implications."[11] In his essay on Madame Bovary, he still asserts that his favorite novels cause certain emotions in him—"my admiration for some rebellious gesture, my anger at some stupidity or injustice, my fascination with situations charged with excessive emotion"[12]—but these emotions are not allied to a conviction that literature must be politically revolutionary and thus instill in the reader the necessity for social change. Instead he volunteers the idea that literature can act as some sort of compensatory fantasy, a way of living out and working through difficulties encountered in real life. He gives the rather dramatic example of a moment in his life when he had considered committing suicide and Emma Bovary came to his rescue. "I remember reading about her suicide in those days, embracing the novel in the same way that others, in similar circumstances, might have taken refuge in religion, or drink or drugs, and finding consolation and equilibrium in those terrifying pages, a hatred of chaos and a desire for life. Fictitious suffering neutralized the suffering that I was experiencing."[13] He would remark to Danubio Torres Fierro, some months after this article on Flaubert, that literature is always a permanent testimony of dissatisfaction with life as it is, and an act of insubordination against existence, but he qualifies this remark by saying that existence must be defined in the broadest possible terms, not merely in terms of politics. He also confesses that he is caught in a sort of political limbo, equally alienated from right and left.[14]

Vargas Llosa's reading of Camus and Flaubert is also linked to his appreciation of *Plural*'s quirky, original, anti-utopian intelligence, Gabriel Zaid. By the time of his review of Zaid's *Cómo leer en bicicleta,* which is mainly a compendium of Zaid's articles published in *Plural,* Vargas Llosa is supporting Zaid's standpoint: "This point of view is uncommon in a writer of our times: a liberal outlook."[15] Zaid's work is refreshing for Vargas Llosa, in particular in an age where the two axioms of "third world intellectuals" are that all the faults in society are due to U.S. imperialism and that the only cure for cultural underdevelopment is revolutionary social change: "The respect for these axioms (both of which are false) has meant that many Latin American intellectuals exempt themselves from thinking and merely gloss, with infinite variants, certain abstractions that they express through a sociological rhetoric which is almost always mind numbing."[16] Vargas Llosa's articles in the magazine are perhaps the clearest statement of what we might term *Plural*'s "outlook," which questioned certainties or received ideas concerning politics, nationalism, revolution, and the social function of the writer and of literature itself. It is absolutely appropriate that Vargas Llosa dedicated his essay on Camus to Octavio Paz.

Contributions from other Latin American writers are more episodic. *Plural* publishes several essays by the Cuban Severo Sarduy that are in a category that the magazine describes in its index as "poetic prose/prose" as opposed to literary criticism: "Gran Mandala de las divinidades irritadas y detentoras del saber" and "Big Bang."[17] Sarduy would also review the latest novel of Juan Goytisolo, *Juan Sin Tierra (Juan the Landless)* in issue 48, where he would focus on the experience that he shared with Goytisolo, that of being on what he calls the "periphery" or the "nomadic state": "*Periphery, nomadic state*: the work of Goytisolo, its extraordinary centrifugal force, can be found in the resonance between those two terms, in the points of tension: always directed outwards, to the exterior that beckons, far from the sedentary group and their codes, far from the despot and his administrative machine."[18] The despot here is both literal, Franco/Castro, but also the strictures of the realist text. Sarduy connects to the criticism of Roland Barthes and also works the publishing house De Seuil that publishes translations of Latin American writers. But there is no sense that through Sarduy a certain poststructuralist approach to literary criticism is being privileged in the magazine: his are intervention of a well-known writer, rather than an example of a literary school. The magazine can adopt a "pluralist" tone by publishing both Sarduy and Vargas Llosa, opposite ends of a literary-critical spectrum. Overall, Vargas Llosa is perhaps a more comfortable critical fit within the magazine with his concentration on good writing rather than on literary theoretical experimentation. There was, for example, a certain incompatibility between Paz and the poststructuralists, with their critique of universals. A significant gap, for example, separates Paz's *El mono grámatico* (*The Monkey Grammarian*) published in 1974, from Sarduy's playful *Cobra* (1972), even though Paz was anxious to point out how much Sarduy had learned from Paz's own meditations on Eastern philosophy. In a letter to Tomás Segovia, dated 12 February 1972, Paz suggests, with Rodríguez Monegal's approval, that Monegal's survey essay on the boom, published in *Plural,* should contain the following added sentence: "The essays of Paz, addressed not to Mexican issues but rather to Eastern topics, are also present in Severo Sarduy's *Cobra,* although, of course, admirably transfigured" (Paz to Segovia, Cambridge, Mass., 12 February 1972). Vargas Llosa, for his part, confessed to Danubio Torres Fierro that he was diametrically opposed to Sarduy's views on literature as extreme literary experimentation, a play of forms. He also pointed out that he could only ever understand about 20 percent of what Sarduy writes or talks about.[19]

Guillermo Cabrera Infante discusses his work and Cuban literature in an interview with Alex Zisman ("30 respuestas para Alex Zisman," issue 31, April 1974, p.58). We are some years away, however, from Cabrera's tirades against the Cuban government and its cultural policies that would later be published in *Vuelta* in the late seventies and beyond. This perhaps reflected the general circumspection about dealing with the issue of Cuba. The magazine published Cabrera and Sarduy, the two best known Cuban writers living abroad, and studiously ignored such critics as the main cultural critic from inside the regime, Roberto Fernández Retamar, who could write for *La Cultura en México*. Thus "revolutionary" Cuban literature—*pace*—some mention of Alejo Carpentier and Lezama Lima—and *Casa de las Américas* are what Althusserians at the time, such as Pierre Macherey, used to call "structuring absences" in the magazine, as indeed was the structural Marxism of Althusser or Poulantzas, that found more favor in *La Cultura en México* or in Argentine journals such as *Crisis* or *Los Libros*. *Plural* was marking out a space that was not subject to the political correctness or the revolutionary enthusiasm of other journals. We remember, for example, that Cortázar had threatened to resign from the magazine *Libre* if Cabrera were to become a contributor. Cabrera Infante's regard for the magazine is expressed in a letter to Kazuya Sakai on 22 February 1975: "*Plural* seems to me (and I say it everywhere) not just the best magazine currently being published in the Spanish speaking world, but one of the best there has ever been, including the *Revista de Occidente*" (Guillermo Cabrera Infante to Kazuya Sakai, London, 22 February 1975).

If *Plural* could call itself a Latin American journal, this claim depended quite heavily, in the case of Brazil, on Paz's friendship with the de Campos brothers, Augusto and Haroldo, and his interest in particular in the Brazilian concrete poetry movement. The de Campos brothers introduce and select concrete poetry in the "literary supplement" of issue 8 of the magazine, as we shall explore in the next chapter. Haroldo de Campos would also introduce other Brazilian writers, including the famous Brazilian modernist novel *Macunaima* by Mário de Andrade, in issue 27. Haroldo de Campo is the main Brazilian contributor, but Brazil would always be mentioned in the surveys of Latin American literature and art, published by, amongst others, Emir Rodríguez Monegal and Damián Bayón.

The magazine forged links with Latin American critics who were now based in the United States, helping to develop the curriculum in contemporary Latin American literature. The best known of these was Emir Rodríguez Monegal, the former editor of *Mundo Nuevo*, a magazine that, as we have seen in chapter one, had helped to promote the development of the boom. It is therefore entirely appropriate that the major contribution of Rodríguez Monegal was a series of long articles on the new novelists and the boom in Latin American fiction published over four issues of the magazine in 1972, a slightly modified version of which he published in book form that same year.[20] This offered perhaps the first systematic guide to a field that was constantly developing, although Gerald Martin has argued that Rodríguez Monegal has a great, unacknowledged debt, with the literary criticism of Carlos Fuentes throughout the sixties.[21] It was Fuentes, as can be seen his book, *La nueva novela hispanoamericana* ("The New Spanish American Novel"), first published in 1969, and in a series of articles published in different journals, who was the most active disseminator of the new narrative from Latin America. In the seventies, however, Fuentes would become increasingly distanced from Monegal's interpretations of modern Latin American literature, especially the espousal at Yale of Sarduy as the touchstone for literary experimentation. In the early seventies, however, Paz could be satisfied with Monegal's survey essays. He wrote to Monegal that while he was pleased with his work, there had not been much response from literary critics: "The only thing I am sorry about is that, up to now, very significantly, we have only received letters from Argentina. The rest of the Continent only knows silence and insult." (Paz to Emir Rodríguez Monegal, no place mentioned, 21 July 1972). Rodríguez Monegal was, of course, just down the road from Paz for much of this period, at Yale.

In terms of a "plural" space within the magazine, Paz did find room for both Emir Rodríguez Monegal and his severe critic from the days of *Marcha*, *Mundo Nuevo* and beyond, Angel Rama, who was initially in exile in Venezuela before eventually moving to the United States. One such "insult" to Rodríguez Monegal's interpretation of the boom came in the pages of *Zona Franca* (Venezuela) when Rama pointed out that any discussion of the boom must pay close attention to (mainly negative) effects of market forces. This interesting polemic that involved Rama, Rodríguez Monegal, and Vargas Llosa at the time of the award of the second Rómulo Gallegos prize to García Márquez found Rama decrying both the exclusive club of the boom and the potential detrimental effect of merchandising these stars.[22] Despite this contretemps—or more likely because of this contretemps: this, after all, was a world where García Márquez was now garnering all the prizes and probably needed having his fame punctured from time to time—Rama would be welcome in the pages of *Plural* and he wrote on several issues, including Cortázar's *Libro de Manuel* and Calvino's *Invisible Cities.*

Another critic to make his home within U.S. academia was the Peruvian scholar Julio Ortega, and he was one of the first choices for the magazine and a regular contributor. He edited the literary supplement on the birth centenary of the Peruvian poet Eguren (*Plural* 35, August 1974), which was the only supplement along with the issue on Brazilian concrete poetry dedicated to a Latin American (non-Mexican) cultural topic, despite Paz's best efforts to plan issues from other countries. Other critics include Manuel Durán at Yale and the Venezuelan poet and critic Guillermo Sucre who was teaching at Pittsburgh (which had offered Paz a teaching post in 1969). Sucre had previously edited the revista *Imagen* in Venezuela, and he would point out to Tomás Segovia how good *Plural* was in comparison to other more modest literary journals. Speaking of the first issues he states: "*Plural* is getting better all the time. The last two issues (I have up to issue 6) are splendid...I think that it is the magazine that all of us, in some way, would have liked to have done (*Imagen* is just a pale image of *Plural*)" (Letter, Guillermo Sucre to Tomás Segovia, Silver Spring, 17 April 1972). These critics would be joined by the Paris-based Latin American critics, most notably the poet and critic Saúl Yurkievich who published in all areas of the magazine's interests: poetry, poetry criticism, and art criticism. Other Paris-based critics included Héctor Bianciotti, who worked at the *Quinzaine Littéraire* and with the publishing house Gallimard. He sent one "literary chronicle" from Paris that was published in issue 21. *Plural* was in touch with a number of Argentines in Paris: Cortázar, of course, Yurkievich, the poet Alejandra Pizarnik, the art critic Damián Bayón. It was Paris and its literary groups that still maintained a strong presence in the magazine as we shall see in the next section.

Criticism beyond Latin America

In an essay on Paz's criticism in the 1960s, Anthony Stanton speaks of the dominant interests in this work: "Three fundamental 'encounters' shape this period: a careful reading of Mallarmé, a deep interest in the innovative theories of structuralism and a passionate study of the history and thought of Indian religion and civilization, especially those of Buddhism."[23] If we were to add to this list an engagement with English language cultural critics, mainly through his time at Harvard, and his reading of such magazines as the *NYRB* and the *TLS*, we are close to a list of the dominant strands that can be said to group the non-Latin American contributors. These contributors tend in the main to be Paz's choices and he was drawn to certain critics, certain tendencies.

His engagement with the structuralist anthropology and literary structuralism of the sixties would lead him to write a book on the work of Claude Lévi-Strauss (1967) and it was Lévi-Strauss who provided the lead article for the first issue of the magazine. Paz would argue in a 1985 interview that the magazine's attention to theory and its introduction of such names as Lévi-Strauss brought a new element to Mexican cultural life.[24] *Plural* would also publish Lévi-Strauss's inaugural lecture when he was elected to the Académie Française, along with the introductory presentation by Roger Caillois.[25] Paz's visiting professorships at Harvard would also put him in close personal contact with perhaps the world's leading semiotician, Roman Jakobson, who taught in the department of Slavic Languages and Literatures. His article on the Portuguese writer Pessoa—a close textual analysis demonstrating the application of theory to specific texts—would appear in issues 7 and 8.[26] Jakobson would later suggest another contribution in *Plural*: the *P.S.* from his very recently published *Questions de Poétique*, which, as he pointed out to Paz, "is my creed in questions of poetics with respect to linguistics" (Letter Roman Jakobson to Octavio Paz, Cambridge, Mass., 21 February 1973).[27] Jakobson would also map the development of his field of semiotics in an article published by the magazine in two parts in 1975.[28] The application of semiotics can be seen in isolated essays by Roland Barthes, Gillo Dorfles, and Umberto Eco, though the magazine would not much favor local critics writing as semioticians: it would normally select criticism that was based more on the tradition of the essay than on cutting edge literary theory.[29]

The engagement with North American/English language critics is somewhat sporadic, though Paz mentioned in a letter to Enrique de Rivas in Italy that he had Harry Levin and Dore Ashton signed up as regular correspondents in the United States. (Letter, Paz to Enrique Rivas, Mexico, D.F., 14 October 1972). In the event, Levin, Paz's colleague in the Comparative Literature department at Harvard, would contribute two articles to early editions of the magazine: a lead article on *The Waste Land* and a commentary on Sartre's reading of Flaubert.[30] In an elegant compliment to Paz, Levin wrote of the success of his Norton Lectures: "In order to sustain the kind of impact your Norton Lectures made last year, this year's lecturer will have to be supplemented by well over a hundred musicians and singers" (Letter, Levin to Paz, Cambridge, Mass., 25 September 1972).

Paz did receive one "Crónica literaria desde Londres" ("Literary Chronicle from London"), a survey on contemporary poetry by the British critic Donald Davie, resident in the United States (July 1973). Since Paz was always looking to engage with critics, he supplied his own discussion forum in a letter to Donald Davie. After thanking Davie for his "fine piece of writing," Paz goes on to disagree with most of his article, giving his own opinions on Eliot and Pound, Latin American poetry and surrealist poetry in the United States. He gives Davie an alternative reading of modern poetry over the course of the letter ending by refuting Davie's argument: "I don't think Pound is a realist. He is, as Eliot, an antiromantic. Both of them were nostalgic of an impossible classicism. Eliot had his eyes fixed in Christian Rome, Pound in an imperial order (Mediterranean or Chinese)" (Letter, Paz to Donald Davie, Mexico, D.F., 13 October 1972). Paz blames the "bluntness" of his criticism on his "very imperfect command of English," and asks Davie to contribute a regular two monthly column, but this contribution did not materialize. Perhaps the thought of such elegant rebuttals to each article was somewhat demoralizing, but it does show the extraordinary involvement of Paz in every aspect of the journal. There was also hope initially that Susan Sontag might become a regular contributor, but although she promised to send several articles (Letter, Susan Sontag to Tomás Segovia, 15 November 1972), these were eventually not forthcoming, outside her article on Paul Goodman that, as we have seen, *Plural* published in issue 17. One important critic linked to Paz's fascination with eroticism, explored below, was Norman O. Brown, who published an essay entitled "Dafne o la metamorfosis," which puts together a series of texts exploring the myth of Daphne and Apollo. One particular quotation, from Petrarch, would resonate within the magazine: "Poetry, the creative act, the act of life, the archetypal sexual act. Sexuality is poetry."[31]

It was equally difficult to find regular contributors among European writers. Despite his best efforts, Paz could not maintain regular contact in the magazine with critics in Europe, apart from with his established friends and collaborators such as the Catalan poet and his editor at Seix Barral, Pere Gimferrer, and the Spanish poet and critic Julián Ríos, who brought out a book-length interview with Octavio Paz, *Sólo a dos voces* published in Barcelona in 1973. Gimferrer will be discussed more closely in the next chapter, but for the purposes of this section, he did maintain the most regular contact out of all the putative "foreign" correspondents. He would select, along with Ríos, a special issue on New Spanish Literature published in October 1973, as we will see in chapter 5. Gimferrer would also prepare two further literary supplements translating and introducing the work of two major medieval Catalan figures, the Majorcan philosopher, Ramón Llull (published in December 1972) and the knight and poet, Ausias March (published in February 1976). He would also supply book reviews of contemporary Spanish writers, Juan Benet, Luis Goytisolo, and Vicente Aleixandre, as well as reviewing recent Catalan poets such as Vicente Molina Foix. He would also review Paz's books *Sólo a dos voces* and *El mono gramático*—and comment favorably on the work of Manuel Puig. For his part, Ríos would prepare a supplement close to Paz's heart, and suggested by Paz, on Raymond Roussel (issue 5, February 1972), who had been such an influence on the surrealists, on the work of Duchamp, and certain contemporary U.S. poets such as John Ashbery. Of the Spanish writers, Juan Goytisolo would be on hand in Paris to give advice on magazine distribution (following his recent spell as magazine editor at *Libre*) and to offer extracts from his new work, as well as talking of the difficulties of censorship and exile under Franco. It was he who would write the obituary to Franco in *Plural* in January 1976.[32] But in terms of the sheer volume of contributions and weight of correspondence, Gimferrer was the closest Spanish writer to the enterprise.

Paris was, of course, a focal point for many critics, although the cultural moment there in the early to mid-seventies was not as exciting as in the late forties, when Paz had known "le tout Paris," the writers, the painters, the intellectuals. Even though, unlike say Mario Vargas Llosa, Paz had never been a devotee of Sartre, by the seventies he found this mandarin's statements about current affairs completely misguided and superficial: from Sartre's pronouncements about the revolutionary potential of such groups of the Tupamaros in Uruguay, to his misreading of the Soviet Union and China, and his trivialization of the function of the intellectual. Even though Sartre had come late to the idea that the Soviet Union was a bureaucratic dictatorship, his analysis still lacked substance. For Paz, Sartre had become a "evening suit worker," a "Sunday proletarian," denying his intellectual responsibility that is "precisely to try to know" about issues such as the Soviet Union.[33] The situation of contemporary literature in France was not deeply exciting, as the occasional Paris correspondent, André Dalmas made clear in his "Carta de París. La literatura que se hace en Francia" ("Letter from Paris. Literature in France." *Plural* 8, May

1972). Indeed most of the extensive coverage of French literature would come in the literary supplements. These would concentrate in the main on writers from earlier in the twentieth century, especially those associated with surrealism.

The Romanian-French philosopher, aphorist, and essayist, Emile Cioran published on a number of occasions in *Plural* on a range of topics from Beckett to Michaux. Paz was also familiar enough with writers such as Michel Butor to ask him to prepare an issue on Fourier and also to ask him to reselect his dossier when Paz found it somewhat weak. There was also a section on new French poetry published in the fiftieth anniversary edition of *Plural*. But for the most part, *Plural* offered a space for mainly Mexican critics—with Paz in the forefront—to comment on the influential figures of—mainly French—twentieth century literature, art, and philosophy.

One of the most innovative aspects of the magazine was its treatment of non-European topics, in particular its attention to the East. While Paz would continue to be influenced by his time in India, it was Japan that received the most attention from Paz and in particular, Kazuya Sakai. Paz had long been interested in Japanese literature, since his first diplomatic posting there in 1952, and indeed it was one of his many links with José Bianco and *Sur* to have introduced the Japanese expert Donald Keene to the Argentine magazine and to have written a prologue to Keene's selection of modern Japanese literature that appeared in *Sur* 249 (November/December 1957). Just before taking on the editorship of *Plural*, Paz published an essay on "La tradición del haiku," illustrated by Sakai in *La Cultura en México*. In it he pointed out his long-standing interest in Japanese poetry in particular and reminded his audience that, along with a Japanese colleague, Eikichi Hayashiya, he had published in 1956 the first translation in the West of the poet Basho's *Oku no Hosomichi*, a travel diary to the northern provinces of Japan. This translation was now being reedited by Barral in Barcelona with a new preface by Paz. Here Paz talks of the influence of Japanese culture on the West and remarks: "I think that what we are all looking for in Japanese culture is another style of life, another vision of the world and indeed of the afterlife."[34] It was here that he gave a first intimation of what would later become his collective poem, *Renga*: "A religious pilgrimage and a journey to famous places . . . the expedition of Basho and Sora is at the same time a poetic exercise: each of them is writing a diary littered with poems and in many of the places they visit, the local poets receive them and compose with them those collective poems called *haika no renga*."[35] His own *renga*, cowritten with Jaques Roubaud, Eduardo Sanguinetti, and Charles Tomlinson would be published in *Plural* in March 1972.

But the most important contributor to this field was Kazuya Sakai. Paz would acknowledge that in *Plural*, "we published a series of texts on Japanese culture that were absolutely new to Mexico."[36] He was referring in the main to Sakai's four literary supplements on Japanese culture. Paz's interest in highlighting this new field is shown in his choosing Sakai's translation and selection of Kenko's "El libro del ocio" for the first literary supplement of the magazine. This was followed by Murasaki Shikibu's "La historia de Genji. Capítulo IV/ Rostro del atardecer" (supplement 9, June 1972), an issue that also contained an article by Sakai on the Japanese novel. Six months later Sakai introduced "Las tres Komachi en el teatro Noh" (January 1973), and a year on, "Makura no Sōshi: El libro de la almohada de Sei Shonagon," an issue that contributed to the magazine's abiding interest in erotic literature. Sakai had a blend of talents particularly appropriate to the magazine's overall interests: he was bilingual and a well-regarded translator of Japanese, as well as being an internationally regarded artist, with established contacts with artists and critics throughout the continent and beyond.

High quality translation was, of course, at the heart of the *Plural* project: knowing how and what to translate. The core staff of *Plural*: Paz himself, Tomás Segovia (the managing editor in the first year), José de la Colina, and Sakai were all first-rate translators, and they would be joined by other writers such as Ulalume González de Léon (on Lewis Carroll, E.E. Cummings, etc.), the poet Gerardo Deniz, and Salvador Elizondo. Indeed, several internal memoranda indicate that Paz saw the core group of translators in *Plural* as de la Colina, Gonzàlez de León, Deniz, and Segovia. The range of texts was, of course, determined by the dominant interests of the editor, his staff, and other contributors.

Mexican Critics

From the outset, Paz was looking to establish a regular group of Mexican critics to contribute to the magazine but, as we have seen, many preferred to stay with *La Cultura en México* or with their already established columns in *Excélsior*: the supplements *Diorama de la Cultura* and the *Revista de Revistas*. The magazine began and very much stayed as Paz's magazine reflecting his diverse interests, but gradually a group of Mexican writers became more identified with the journal, a fact reflected in Paz establishing an editorial board in

March 1975. The statement about the Board, signed by Paz and Sakai in the "Letras, letrillas, letrones" section, is entitled "Continuity and Change." The statement is worth transcribing in full:

> From the outset, *Plural* looked to be a place of convergence for independent writers in Mexico. Convergence does not mean uniformity or even agreement, except in a common adherence to autonomy of thought and to a passion for literature conceived not as a sermon but rather as a quest and exploration, of language or of mankind, of the individual or of society. Several writer friends have accepted our invitation and have decided to participate more fully with *Plural*; we have thus formed an editorial board with José de la Colina, Salvador Elizondo, Juan García Ponce, Alejandro Rossi, Tomás Segovia and Gabriel Zaid. The *Contemporáneos* writers called themselves a "group of solitudes"; the editorial board of *Plural* is not a group and nor is it a body of solitudes. We will use an expression of Albert Camus to describe the current situation of Board members: *solitarios/solidarios* [*solitary/solidary*].[37]

In fact certain writers such as Gabriel Zaid and Alejandro Rossi had been contributing regular columns since late 1973, and when the magazine established a regular book review section, in issue 22 (July 1973), this offered space for both the established names and also for emerging younger writers such as Enrique Krauze and Adolfo Castañon. The change of shape of the magazine in issue 26 reducing from large format to a more regular A4 size coincided with this more stable "Mexican" base, with the columnists Cosío, Rossi, and Zaid, along with the book reviewers. The artistic supplement began in December 1973. Indeed by September 1973, Paz was seeing a core group emerging. In a memorandum entitled "Supplements" he wrote a series of suggestions/instructions to Sakai and de la Colina. On the top of the memorandum, in Paz's handwriting, there is inscribed the date of September 1973. In this memo he tells Sakai and de la Colina that they should ask the following writers for contributions: for Mexico, Fuentes, Zaid, Pacheco, Elizondo, García Ponce, Carlos Páramo, Isabel Fraire (poetry), Ulalume González de Léon (short stories or poetry), Poniatowska (chronicles or novels), García Terrés, Villoro, García Cantú. With regard to writers from abroad, he says that they should approach the "more or less frequent contributors" such as Rodríguez Monegal, Rama, Bianco, Vargas Llosa, Sarduy, Cabrera Infante, Goytisolo, "but also ask Mutis (we have never yet approached him), Cobo Borda (a Colombian: an excellent critic), Oviedo (a Peruvian), Cisneros (a Peruvian poet)." Paz adds that, "we should publish young writers quite often," but he asks for suggestions about who these new poets might be. (Internal Memorandum *Plural*, September 1973). Once again back in Harvard, he writes about how good the magazine is in all aspects save that of expressing Mexican literature: "but we all know that this is very difficult and we won't start crying about it again." He is admitting that despite attempts to attract them, popular culture critics such as Monsiváis and writers from the *onda* generation had not been tempted across. There was even an attempt to ask Héctor Manjarrez to work within *Plural* in the early days, but he turned down the offer preferring to stay with *La Cultura en México*. Paz recognizes that there is competition, not just from *La Cultura en México* but even from the other cultural publications within the *Excélsior* group: the *Diorama de la Cultura*, directed by Ignacio Solares, and the *Revista de Revistas* edited by Vicente Leñero. He remarks in 1973: "There are (in)explicable cases such as Pacheco who publishes in *Diorama* exactly what I suggested that he should do (if he wanted) for *Plural*." (Letter Paz to De la Colina and Sakai, Cambridge, Mass., 19 October 1973). Some two years into the publication of the magazine, it was increasingly clear who felt comfortable being inside the magazine, and who remained outside, or those who occupied an intermediate space, like Pacheco, who published on occasion for *Plural*, but kept his regular column in another *Excélsior* publication: *Diorama*. Of the increasingly settled number of writers around the magazine, José de la Colina could remember with nostalgia: "We were a society of friends: like Dr Johnson's tavern."[38] Whereas it might be possible to see the magazine more as a group activity in its last year, with the founding of the management committee, the conviviality and friendship that many of the contributors talk about would be more influential in the magazine *Vuelta*, after 1976, when the group had more time to consolidate.

While for the purpose of our narrative we are treating Paz's criticism of history and politics, art criticism, and general literary and cultural criticism, in separate parts, we must always remember that often all three aspects of this criticism could be present in any particular issue of the magazine, as well as a poem. When I asked Paz as to what he saw as the magazine's main innovations and interests in the cultural field, he talked initially of three main areas: the coverage of art, the interest in "experimentation" (John Cage and others), and the interest in sexuality and eroticism. We might begin this survey of Mexican criticism by looking at the issue of "eroticism."

The first essay that Paz published in his "Corriente Alterna" section of the magazine is on Fourier, in issue 2 (November 1971). It is entitled "mesa y lecho," an article that he would rewrite for publication in book form in *El ogro filantrópico*.[39] In it, Paz, newly settled in the United States, reflects on food and the sexual revolution in the United States, as seen through the prism of Fourier's ideas of his ideal society, Harmony. In Harmony, Paz reminds us, sovereignty is divided between Administration and Religion: "The jurisdiction of Religion is two-fold: love and taste, Eroticism and Gastronomy. Eroticism is the most intense pleasure ... gastronomy the most extensive passion. Whether it be sex or taste, pleasure is not the satisfaction of a need, but rather it becomes an experience in which the body is at once the incarnation of the imaginary, and the revelation of who we are" (p.17). In the light of this ideal definition of erotic love—so close to Paz's own view of the transformative nature of poetry itself, where reality touches desire—both the eating habits and the sexual mores of the United States fall somewhat short of the ideal, even though Paz notices changes in both a Puritan palette and sexual imaginary, what he calls, "the discovery of ambiguity and the exceptional" (p.19). At the end of the article, Paz gives his own definition of eroticism: "Eroticism is always a *going beyond* ... and this *going beyond* is but a moment in a double movement that leads us, from our body, to imagine other bodies and, immediately, to search for the embodiment of these images in a real body. Eroticism is sex and passion, not in brute form, but rather transfigured by imagination: it is ritual, theater" (p.20).

Some months later the magazine published a literary supplement on Fourier edited by Michel Butor, which included André Breton's "Ode à Charles Fourier" (translated by Tomás Segovia), along with a series of articles by Italo Calvino, Pierre Klossowski, and others to celebrate the two hundredth anniversary of Fourier's birth. In an introduction to this issue, Paz asks "Why Fourier?" His answer is in part a reprise of his earlier statements about the erotic, but here seen in a more radical light, as a touchstone with which to judge the contemporary malaise of society: "By preaching *absolute doubt* with respect to conventional ideas, Fourier taught us to trust our body and its impulses ... he teaches us that the shortest route between two bodies is the route of *passionate attraction*." Fourier, in Paz's reading, argues that work is not drudgery, in a Marxist sense, but can be a pleasure. He had also intuited that curbs should be put on industrial progress and demographic increases and that women's rights should be respected: his thinking showed an "indissoluble link between *vision and criticism*, imagination and reality."[40]

This independent, visionary, proto-socialist thinker was very attractive to Paz and this magazine issue traces a lineage of thought from

Fourier to Paz, via André Breton. André Breton, of course, had been greeted with hostility by the orthodox left when he visited Mexico in 1938, because they found his politics to be too libertarian and Trotskyist. Paz now saw himself, Fourier, and Breton to be linked by their hostility of orthodox radical thought to their endeavors: he points out how the Breton poem had been attacked by the likes of Aragon and Sartre for its outdated utopianism. Instead, for Paz, while these critics now seem outmoded, the poem and Fourier's thinking are very contemporary. If Fourier can be criticized, it is perhaps for his optimism with regard to society: "is it possible, viable or even imaginable to have a society without prohibitions and repressions? Here Freud, Sade and Bataille are all agreed: that there is no civilization without repression and, for that reason, the essence of eroticism is transgressive violence."[41] Paz tends to sympathize with Fourier, that the basis of the erotic does not have to be "transgressive violence." Yet he also admits that Georges Bataille's work offers a radical counterbalance to Fourier in his claim that there is no pleasure without transgression of the norms of society and the collective, and that men and women seek in transgression an affirmation of their sovereignty. Paz signaled his interest in Bataille very explicitly at the end of his book-length study of Lévi-Strauss, when he criticized Lévi-Strauss for his lack of interest in the erotic that, for Paz, transcends communication.

   A thorough exploration of Bataille's views on sovereignty, evil, *maudit* writers, and the link between eroticism and death is offered by Salvador Elizondo, in a literary supplement dedicated to Bataille and his story "Madame Edwarda." Elizondo reveals his own fascination with, and debt to, Bataille, when he glosses Bataille's analysis of the photograph of the Chinese man being tortured to death by a thousand cuts. This image was, we remember, the structuring element in Elizondo's most famous novel, *Farabeuf.* Talking of Bataille's book *Les Larmes d'Eros*, Elizondo states that what is particularly impressive is Bataille's analysis of the Chinese victim, an image in which Bataille notes all the essential characteristics of eroticism: "cruelty, violence, the violation of the inside of the human body, the profaning of vital structures…and the mystic ecstasy."[42] In the same vein, Juan García Ponce offered a lead article on "Literatura y pornografía" in issue 15, thus developing an abiding interest that can be seen in the work of García Ponce and Elizondo in the magazine *S.Nob*, albeit presented in a more academic and scholarly fashion. *Plural* would even look at the earliest manifestations of the erotic in Mexico by asking the leading Mexican scholar Miguel Léon-Portilla to prepare a supplement entitled "Aquiauhtzin de Ayapanco: poesía erótica náhuatl" (*Plural* 49, October 1975).

Elizondo's supplement is published in the same issue as Octavio Paz's lead article entitled "El ocaso de la vanguardia," which also deals with the topic of the erotic in literature, in its survey of the development of contemporary poetry.[43] These are the Charles Eliot Norton lectures, published in Spanish as *Los hijos del limo: del romanticismo a la vanguardia* (Barral, Barcelona, 1974). The survey is published in three parts in the journal and in it Paz explores the relationship between the poet and society since romanticism. As Jason Wilson points out, Paz discusses a whole range of issues—religion, tradition, revolutionary politics, and the like—"without aspiring to writing literary history. In these lectures he turned to Wordsworth's stay in France and reaction against the French Revolution. Wordsworth resorted to childhood's 'moments of translucency' to combat the disasters of history and revolutionary despotism."[44] Paz's analysis of *The Prelude* points to poetry as offering a different time to the time of history: the poet turns inward to find a time before time. A critic that Paz had recommended to the magazine, José Miguel Oviedo, offers an interesting analysis of the book, "Octavio Paz y el drama de la modernidad."[45] He quotes Paz's own introduction to the work, which states that he is dealing with the modern tradition of poetry arguing that modernity itself is a tradition. Yet, as Oviedo notes, Paz ranges across definitions of modernity in the arts, including the idea and practice of revolution. Oviedo isolates four main overlapping areas that structure the text: "1. Modernity is synonymous with criticism and is based on change...2. Analogy is a poetic principle...3. Irony is the stuff of modernity...4. The modern conception of time implies the rebellion of the body and of the imagination" (pp.82–83). He salutes Paz's passionate, polemical, and enormously provocative work. Interestingly, the first essay that Paz published in this series is entitled significantly, "Revolución, eros, metaironía" ("Revolution, eros, metairony"), which explores the gaps between "the   linear time of progress and history and the instant time of eroticism..."[46]

The literary supplements published monthly in the magazine can be seen to reflect Paz's literary tastes. What might seem at first sight to be a series of random and eclectic texts share certain characteristics that largely concur with Paz's interests in both the erotic and in literary experimentalism outlined above. We have seen that, at the outset, these supplements were intended at least four times a year to cover Mexican and Latin American culture and politics. This did happen for the first year, when there were different issues on social themes.

After that first year, however, social issues would all but disappear from the supplements. Instead, the dominant interest is in poetry, French poetry in the main, though with references also to Japanese, Chinese, Russian, English, U.S., Spanish, and Brazilian poetry. Some of the French poets discussed were personal friends of Paz from the forties, in particular Benjamin Péret, who Paz first met in exile in Mexico and who introduced him to the surrealist circle around Breton in Paris in the mid-forties. Two other friends from the same period in Paris were the poet René Char and the sociologist and philosopher Roger Caillois. Paz's interest in surrealism—the erotic intersection between love, poetry, and freedom—is reflected in the publication of the anonymous surrealist text *Irene*, published in two parts in *Plural* 17 and 18 (February–March 1973). Paz was one of the three writers to introduce this text. It can also be seen in the surrealist "precursor," Raymond Roussel and his critique of modernity as embodied in machine culture (*Plural* 5, February 1972). Paz was reading poets such as Blaise Cendrars (*Plural* 21, June 1973) and Mayakovsky (*Plural* 6, March 1972) from the late thirties in little magazines in Mexico such as *Crisol*. Valéry was part of his early reading—at the Preparatoria in San Ildefonso—in what Guillermo Sheridan aptly calls the "treasure trove of literary magazines," the major journals of the thirties such as *Contemporáneos*, *Sur*, and the *Revista de Occidente*. Sheridan quotes Paz initial reaction to this treasure-house of literature. He and his fellow students: "went from curiosity to wonderment, from instant illumination to perplexity. These mysteries did not dishearten me, but rather spurred me on."[47] In a sense Paz was trying to transmit in *Plural* that same enthusiasm for reading, for discovering texts that might not always be easy but that could act as a "spur." The introductions to the texts in the supplement offered entry points into this world. The Valéry supplement, which publishes fragments of his notebooks, celebrated the centenary of his birth (*Plural* 3, December 1971).

Paz's rereading of Mallarmé, especially in the sixties, can be seen as the spur to the supplement on "Mallarmé: las tres versiones del fauno" (*Plural* 48, September 1975). With respect to other poets in the sub-continent, he had established contact with the Brazilian poet and critic Haroldo de Campos, whose own experimentation in concrete poetry would also heavily rely on the lessons of Mallarmé. The supplement on concrete poetry presented by the de Campos brothers,—"Poesía concreta: Configuración/Textos," *Plural* 8, May 1972—would bring this important movement to the attention of a Spanish reading audience. Such explorations of Latin American culture in the supplements were, however, rare. There were also supplements on Mexican topics: a selection from the archive of Alfonso Reyes introduced by Tomás Segovia (issue 10, July 1972), and a reappraisal of the work of the *Contemporáneos* poet, Gilberto Owen who, some two decades before Paz, had worked for the Mexican government in New York, and who with Paz had been on the editorial board of *El Hijo Pródigo*. In the main body of the magazine, *Plural* would also dedicate an issue (July 1975) to the history and culture of New Spain.

A more playful account of linguistic experimentation can be found in the supplements on Ramón Gómez de la Serna (the selection entitled "Ramón mismo, ramonismo," entrusted to José de la Colina in issue 29, February 1974), and more particularly in the issues on the English "eccentrics": Lewis Carroll's "The Hunting of the Snark" (*Plural* 2, November 1971), Edward Lear (*Plural* 14, November 1972), and " 'Jabberwocky,' el nonsense y algunas conclusiones sobre la lectura de poesía" (*Plural* 57, June 1976). Most of these supplements are translated by Paz's favorite quartet, Segovia, de la Colina, Deniz, and Ulalume González de León, who are often commissioned to write the explanatory notes and the introductions. It would be misleading to view Paz as the exclusive arbiter of this section. While a number of supplements are suggested by him, he is also taking ideas from a group of contributors and from significant biographical dates such as centenary celebrations (Jarry, issue 27, December 1973). For example, Sakai clearly initiates the Japanese sections, while Gimferrer, as we have seen, offers several supplements based on Catalan writers. Elizondo offers his dominant interests on Bataille and also an appreciation, close to Paz's heart, of Pound and Fenellosa's study of "los caracteres de la escritura china como medio poético" (issue 32, May, 1974). The only exploration of contemporary North American poetry can be found in two supplements on E.E. Cummings, introduced and translated by Ulalume González de León.

Paz is the most frequent contributor to the magazine in all its different facets. Other core staff members of the magazine were also frequent contributors. Sakai was the designer and the main commentator and translator of Japan. He was also interested in jazz and contributed reviews on jazz from early 1974. He covers the great names of jazz, Sonny Rollins, Duke Ellington, Miles Davis, and John Coltrane, and more modern exponents such as Herbie Hancock and Dave Brubeck. He reviews concerts of some of these practitioners in Japan offering interesting insights into the "universality" of jazz. There is also consideration of Latin America's contribution to the form in his study of Gato Barbieri, who Sakai argued gave jazz an "authentic" Latin American inflection.[48] In this, his interests dovetailed with that passionate admirer of jazz, his compatriot Julio Cortázar.

Overall, the two dominant cultural interests in *Plural* are literature and art. Outside these Sakai reviews there are only isolated articles on music such as Lévi-Strauss's analysis of Ravel's "Bolero" and a supplement on the avant garde musical theory of Eric Satie.[49] There is a similar attitude to film. José de la Colina, who was both a film and literary critic, tried to establish his own regular column on cinema. He had been a film critic for many years starting his own magazine, *Nuevo Cine* in the early sixties.[50] The regular column does not come about, but he does write irregularly on movies for the time that he is most closely linked to the magazine, in 1974 and early 1975. The key link between de la Colina and Paz with regard to cinema is Luis Buñuel, who, received Paz's backing for *Los olvidados* when it was shown in Cannes in 1951. Paz quite overstepped his diplomatic bounds—he was sent to Cannes by the Mexican foreign affairs department—when he did everything he could to support the movie that his own government had declared "offensive to Mexican dignity." He organized his surrealist friends to support the movie and himself wrote an appreciation of "the poet Buñuel" that he handed out at the entrance to the cinema.[51] Paz would therefore be glad to see de la Colina's review some twenty years later of Buñuel's *El fantasma de la libertad* (*The Phantom of Liberty*, *Plural* 39, December 1974). De la Colina would later write an important book on Buñuel His reviews in *Plural* showed an attention to the movie greats such as Kurosawa and also on the Mexican directors Gurrola and Arturo Ripstein. Sakai's passion for jazz and de la Colina's reviews of international cinema cannot, however, be seen to constitute a major focus on popular culture. It was to other journals, particularly Monsiváis's columns in *La Cultura en México*, that one must look to find an appreciation of Mexican popular culture, from music to the movies. These columns offer a different way of reading Mexican culture upturning what might be seen as a pyramid of taste that would have, say, Breton at its pinnacle and the Mexican actors Cantinflas or Tin Tan or María Félix a lot further below. Issues of ideology and cultural prestige apart, it would have been very difficult to find space in *Plural* for Monsiváis, as Paz had initially hoped, because a column by Monsiváis would have been subsumed in a very different way of understanding Mexican culture and politics. Even though Paz once wrote a panegyric to the eyes of María Félix in such films as *Enamorada* ("In Love",

1947),[52] he would have found it difficult to sustain a regular interest in, say, the leering contortionist Cantinflas or the crooning of Agustín Lara or the street culture of Mexico City that were the trademarks of Monsiváis's regular columns.

De la Colina was the most consistent book reviewer in the "Libros" section that appeared after two years of publication, covering a range of books published in Spanish, from Victor Serge to Juan García Ponce to Mario Vargas Llosa. Several books were reviewed in each issue, the reviews tending in part to support, quite naturally, the interests of what can be seen as an emerging *Plural* group. For example, all of Paz's books are reviewed mainly from inside the Latin American/Spanish "group": there are reviews on Paz's books by Pere Gimferrer, Ortega, Oviedo, and Juan García Ponce. Ramón Xirau reviews the poetry of Tomás Segovia, Pere Gimferrer, and Saúl Yurkievich; Ortega and Vargas Llosa review Zaid; de la Colina comments on García Ponce twice and also on Vargas Llosa's book on Flaubert; Elizondo reviews the poetry of Arjidis and Montes de Oca; Sarduy reviews Juan Goytisolo; Pacheco reviews Julieta Campos; Manuel Durán reviews Xirau's poetry; Danubio Torres Fierro gives a more extensive coverage of books throughout Latin America as well as covering local writers such as Ignacio Solares and Gustavo Sainz; Guillermo Sucre writes on the Argentine Roberto Juarroz and Homero Arjidis. In this sense the criticism can be said, in part, to comment on the original works of literature published in the magazine, as poems or extracts from novels.

The two regular Mexican columnists, from issue 25, are Gabriel Zaid, with his "Cinta de Moebio," discussed in chapter 3, and Alejandro Rossi's "Manual del distraído." Rossi, a researcher at the Instituto de Investigaciones Filosóficas in Mexico City (born in Italy, brought up Venezuelan, naturalized as Mexican only in the nineties), had brought out a pioneering book on analytical philosophy in 1969, *Lenguaje y significado.* But, as Juan Villoro puts it, "When Octavio Paz invited him to *Plural,* he was not thinking about the expert on philosophy but rather about the brilliant conversationalist that he knew. It was a high quality signing: Rossi became in writing what he already was as a conversationalist."[53] Rossi had been out of the country throughout 1972 and when he returned, Paz asked him to contribute a regular monthly column that in his words, "went up to the final issue of the magazine. The genre I was writing had a very free form, and had nothing to do with academic philosophy. Perhaps they were exercises in style."[54] On another occasion, he described his work as an "exploration of more literary genres."[55] Adolfo Castañon, who joined the magazine as a proofreader in 1975, before also being given book reviews, was one of the many young writers to be engaged by Rossi's style, which Castañon describes as "deceptively short, clear and artful."[56]

Rossi became one of the structuring elements of the magazine, but he also recognized that when the editorial committee did begin to meet, there were many points of contact. He spoke of "certain sense of a catacomb culture," "common literary tastes and preferences," and "a clear outlook on Latin American tradition."[57] Certainly we can chart a set of common literary tastes and preferences along with a sense of belonging and contributing to a tradition of dialogue between Latin American countries and with the wider world. Rossi, for example, was a good friend of José Bianco and the *Sur* group. There is no doubt that there was no other publication in Mexico, or even in Latin America, that could open up to such a degree to major issues and debates, and with such major contributors from across the world. If the remark about a catacomb culture—which was an image of a beleaguered civilizing minority that found favor with *Sur*—might be somewhat overstated in the case of *Plural,* it was clear that their definition of pluralism would not chime with everyone in the field in Mexico itself, that the magazine's questioning of nationalism, revolution, and the social function of the writer, with all that implied in terms of literary models and literary exclusions, would spark a debate, or in Paz's oft repeated phrase, "silence and insult." Some of these tensions can also be seen in the magazine's coverage of art.

Art Criticism in *Plural*

The magazine's interest in art would, as with all other aspects of the magazine, initially take its lead from Octavio Paz. As can be seen by the two volumes in his *Obras Completas* dedicated to art criticism, *Los privilegios de la vista*, Paz has an abiding interest in art and art history: he wrote essays of enormous breadth across a range of different topics and tendencies in modern art. He writes in his introduction to these volumes: "My first notes on art date from 1940; the most recent date from just a few months ago. I never wanted to be systematic or limit myself to this topic or that: I could write a book on Marcel Duchamp and also a poem in honor of my friend, the poet/painter Swaminathan. I wrote motivated by admiration, curiosity, indignation, complicity, surprise."[58]

In the early issues, we see the stamp of Paz on the selection on art, his own interests and his conception of international art. He writes on

Tamayo and on "hombres-bestias-hombres," the monster in paint-ings. The article on Tamayo is a statement about Paz's own concep-tion of, and defense of modern Mexican art (and by analogy, poetry) outside the stranglehold of nationalism. It also marks a friendship dating back to New York in 1945 and Paris in 1949: Paz organized Tamayo's first exhibition in Paris in 1950 and asked Breton and Cassou to write for the catalogue. His first essay on Tamayo dates from 1950. The essay, dated 11 April 1968, is published in issue 7 of *Plural* and reprinted in the collection of essays, *El signo y el garaba-to*.[59] In this essay, Paz first of all recaps his abiding interest in Tamayo and points out that his first reading of the painter, in 1950, was his-torical: he had explored the ways in which Tamayo radically ques-tioned the ideological and didactic art of the muralists and their imitators. Now he concentrates more on the pictorial originality of Tamayo, his critical questioning of objects: "critical painting: a reduc-tion of the object to its essential artistic elements." In pointing to his own reading of Tamayo, Paz explains what art criticism should be: "Let me make clear, once again, that I am not asserting definitions: I am risking approximations. Expressionism, critical purity, a critique of the object, a passion for the material, a conception of color: names, pointing arrows. Reality is other: the paintings of Tamayo. Criticism is not even a translation although it should aspire to this: it is a sum-mary, a guide. And the best criticism is something less: it is an invita-tion to the only act that really counts: the act of seeing."[60] In exploring Tamayo's reading of pre-Columbian sculpture, Paz points out that the rediscovery of Mesoamerican cultures was the result both of the revival of interest in Mexican culture following the Revolution, *and also* the interest of cosmopolitan European artists in the art of other cultures; there is no "national property right" in art, he argues. And Mesoamerican art appealed to modern painters because it offers a "logic of forms, lines and volumes."

Interestingly, the ideological debate about Tamayo that many thought had belonged to an earlier moment of revolutionary nation-alism returned in 1976 when the director of the Museo de Bellas Artes stated that priority would not be given to building a museum to house a donation of paintings—both his own and his collection of international art—which Tamayo was prepared to offer to the Mexican government, because this museum would not have an "eminently popular" function. Artist Manuel Felguérez and critic Juan García Ponce poured scorn on this declaration in *Plural* 56 (May 1976) decrying this vulgar manifestation of state control over culture and the minds of the people. In a statement that covered perhaps not just

Tamayo but also his colleagues in *Plural*, García Ponce states: "It is impossible to keep on mentioning, if only to attack them, words as repulsive as *extranjerizante* (alien imports), 'elitist,' 'antipopular' and others of similar ilk. They only have a place in the mouths of banal and freeloading politicians."[61]

Along with Tamayo, Paz had also written frequently on José Luis Cuevas, who had famously talked about Mexico's "cortina de nopal" and had spent his career looking to rip it down. Cuevas is an acknowledged presence in *Plural*: his vignettes are in issue 1, and there is, as we have seen, a letter from him from San Francisco in issue 2. Once again this is a statement of affiliation: Paz's had been calling Cuevas's work extraordinary for more than a decade. Juan García Ponce, who had an established reputation as a leading art critic in Mexico, with several books on Mexican painting published in the sixties, wrote an artistic supplement on Cuevas published in the magazine in 1976 exploring Cuevas's "marginal" world.[62] Other friends or interests of Paz include the distinguished North American critic Harold Rosenberg—who writes to Segovia saying that he is happy to see Paz "in action with *Plural*." Rosenberg was one of the most vigorous promoters of the New York vanguard artists that, he argued, had saved modernism and wrested power from France as the capital of art, although his writings on the "cultural cold war" are only implicit in the several articles he writes in *Plural*. Another eminent critic and friend of Paz, Dore Ashton, publishes an article in issue 3. She is the partner of Adja Yunkers, one of Paz's favorite expressionist artists, and a critic who Paz often quotes in his own work. It was Ashton, for example, who took Octavio and Marie-José Paz along to meet Joseph Cornell in his studio in Queens in the autumn of 1971. Claude Esteban writes on one of Paz's dominant interests, surrealism in art. These contributors, therefore, are part of the world of Paz's extensive contacts.

In addition, from the earliest issues of the magazine, Paz would have working in the *Plural* offices the painter, Kazuya Sakai, who had already garnered international attention and had his own developed contacts in the art world, especially with Argentine artists and critics. Initially Vicente Rojo, who had been responsible for the art work on most Mexican journals in the sixties, was responsible for the design of the early issues, along with Abel Quezada, but Sakai gradually took over a much more central position in the magazine as managing editor and also as artistic designer imposing his own design on the magazine and by increasing the number of articles on art. By July 1972, for example, Paz is congratulating

Sakai on giving "a shape to the magazine, an attractive shape." He remarks in the same letter that a greater definition should be given to art in the magazine and that he was looking to Sakai to give him "essential" advice (Paz to Sakai, Cambridge, Mass., July, 1972).

Sakai had been born in Argentina in 1927, was educated in Japan between 1934 and 1951 before returning to Buenos Aires. Here he worked as a translator and a painter of delicate abstraction, with echoes of Japanese calligraphy and topography. His work was well received in an expansive moment of post-Peronist culture in Argentina, though in 1963 he traveled north living for a period in the United States before being offered a job to teach Japanese culture at UNAM. His employment with *Plural* coincided with a change in his art that had been moving increasingly toward geometric drawing throughout the sixties. The change, he states, was influenced by an early Japanese master, Ogata Korin (1658–1716): "By transforming certain natural forms into geometric shapes...Korin pays specific attention to the elegant and repeated painting of curves, circles and sumptuous lines that flow without any apparent beginning or end. This aspect of Korin's paintings moved me to begin, a few years back, some exercises with circles, volutes and other repetitions and reiterations."[63] It would be these swirls of color that would become the distinctive covers of *Plural* from around the middle of 1973. Sakai writes to Severo Sarduy on 13 January 1975 pointing out that his new work is affecting his designs for the magazine cover: "If you receive number 39 (December) of our glorious magazine, you will see on the cover something similar to what I am painting in a very large scale." (Sakai to Sarduy, Mexico, 13 January 1975).

From issue 27, December 1973, *Plural* published an artistic supplement within the magazine. The first artist considered was fittingly Sakai himself and it focused on the work that Sakai was exhibiting in Mexico City late in 1973. In a letter to the Argentine critic, Fermín Fevre, Sakai pointed out that the idea was to produce "a series of articles on contemporary artists in Latin America and Spain." (Sakai to Fevre, Mexico, 3 September 1974). Thirty-one supplements would be published before the magazine's demise covering a range of modern painters from Mexico, Latin America, and the wider world, and some classics. It was Sakai's insistence that was to bring about this regular section on art. In a letter to Paz on 17 October 1973, he suggests that they should increase the coverage of art in general, "including survey essays and other brainy things like that, which will be illustrated in color (color, Octavio, attracts a lot of people, even if the paintings are surrealist or abstract)" (Sakai to Paz, Mexico, 17 October 1973).

From the outset there would be features on art. There was a regular column initially entitled "De las artes," later subsumed under the "Letras, letrillas, letrones" section, which would cover national and international exhibitions and other contemporary matters. But interest in this area grows. The clearest demonstration of the increasing importance of art was the second anniversary edition—issue 24—of the magazine dedicated to "Las artes de hoy" ("The Arts Today"). The issue is introduced by a poem by Paz—he would increasingly express his views on art through poetry in the magazine, with later poems on Cornell and Balthus. This is followed by articles from some of the most significant critics of contemporary art of the day: the North Americans Harold Rosenberg and Dore Ashton; the British guru of pop Lawrence Alloway; Gillo Dorfles and Pierre Restany, the promoter of Nouveau Réalisme in the sixties, the French inflection of pop art. Some of these critics already had experience of art in Latin America through the invitation of the Argentine art critic, Jorge Romero Brest, who, when he was the director of the Di Tella Center for Visual Arts in Buenos Aires in the sixties—which became the main center for showcasing Latin American avant garde art in the sixties—invited Restany and Alloway down to Buenos Aires to judge national and international prizes.[64] Jorge Romero Brest was perhaps the best known critic in Latin America, although he was first and foremost a critic and promoter of Argentine art, with links to U.S. galleries, as part of the sixties inter-American networks.[65] As is the case with literature, the strongest links that the magazine has with countries in Latin America is with Argentina. Sakai is Argentine as is the critic Damián Bayón. In addition to Romero Brest, there are articles by the by now "established" *Plural* critics, Juan Acha, Damián Bayón, and Jorge Alberto Manrique. Acha offers a Latin American focus, while Bayón, in an interview, surveys international movements, and Manrique talks about new tendencies in art in Mexico. There is also international coverage: Dorfles on art in Italy, Chalupecky on Czech art, and Borras on art in Catalan regions.

Juan Acha had been an art critic in his native Peru before moving to Mexico in 1971, becoming the "coordinator" of the Museo de Arte Moderno in Mexico City as well as teaching at the Escuela Nacional de Artes Plásticas. Acha was to organize six of *Plural*'s artistic supplements as well as commenting on diverse aspects of the international art world. The Argentine Damián Bayón studied in Paris at the École de Hautes Études and remained based in Paris for most of his life. Bayón would write six supplements and a steady supply of articles and notes within *Plural*. Bayón was the main art critic in the magazine, who moved between Paris, his main base, Latin America and the United States. In the first issues of the magazine, he would provide reports on contemporary Peruvian, Chilean, and Argentine art, as well as an overview of contemporary movements in Paris. As well as providing regular articles and notes, he would keep up a steady correspondence with Sakai in the *Plural* offices. Bayon's work would be systematized in a series of books that offered—in a similar way to Monegal as a literary critic—an archive, a bringing together of disparate material from all over the continent, a broad-ranging survey. It was Bayón, for example, who had written the first ever catalogue for Sakai, for an exhibition in Buenos Aires in 1957. Bayón's work over a twenty-year period at least, began to be system-atized in books at the time of his *Plural* collaborations: *América Latina en sus artes* (UNESCO series) published in Mexico by Siglo XXI in Mexico in 1974 and *Aventura plástica de Hispanoamérica* published by Fondo de Cultura Económica in Mexico in 1974. *Plural*'s coverage of art had in part a didactic function, a desire to map the field: in a letter to Bayón, Sakai talks about Bayón's book with Fondo as establishing the foundations for the study of Latin American art, a pioneering book. Sakai states that he would have preferred a less encyclopedic book, covering fewer, essential, artists and exploring the "social conditions of artistic production." The nexus between Bayón's' *Aventura plástica* and *Plural* is clear: the book is dedicated to Octavio Paz and the illustration on the book cover is one of Sakai's most recent works.

Bayón was one of a small group of critics who was sponsored by North American cultural organizations—such as the Visual Arts Section of the Pan American Union under the directorship of the Cuban José Gómez Sicre[66]—to disseminate knowledge about Latin American art in North America. He would curate with Sakai the exhibition *12 Latin American Artists Today* at the University Art Museum at Austin, Texas, which was cosponsored by *Plural*, the University of Texas at Austin, and different U.S. cultural foundations. The twelve artists were six Mexicans, Felguérez, Rojo, Von Gunten, Toledo, Nissen, and Gerzo; two Argentines, Bonevardi and Tomasello; the Peruvian Szyszlo; the Brazilian Camargo; the Venezuelan Cruz-Díez; and the Colombian Negret. With characteristic modesty, Sakai did not include his own work in this selection but, according to his wife's account, the director of the Austin gallery hung a painting by Sakai in the entrance to the exhibition hall.[67] Accompanying the exhibition was a symposium on Latin American art and culture attended by Tamayo and Szyszlo amongst others.

In an introduction to the exhibition, the director of the Art Collection at Austin, Donald Goodall states that he is happy to leave the selection to *Plural,* given the quality of the magazine's coverage of art and sculpture. This would be the first exhibition in Austin of Latin American art.[68] In a statement accompanying Goodall's introduction, Sakai and Bayón point out that their choices were determined by a need to give certain artists more visibility north of the border. Tamayo and Matta, they argue, are already well known, while younger artists had still to prove themselves. The selection thus focused on avant garde artists considered "mature": between the ages of thirty-five and sixty. Accompanying the article are illustrations of a representative work from each of the chosen artists. In a paragraph that clearly signals the Pan American and internationalist intentions of the organizers, they consider that "these works can be compared to the best poems or novels that the best Latin American writers have been able to produce in the last twenty or thirty years."[69] It is time that these artists, although well known in their own countries, received a wider audience. The implication is clear: instead of being the junior partners of the boom writers in terms of international exposure, artists should claim their rightful place on the world stage. On the next page of the magazine, there is a short article describing the success of the Mexican artist Manuel Felguérez winning the "Gran Premio de Honor" at the XII São Paulo Biennale.

On 22 November Dore Ashton, a long time contributor to the magazine wrote about this exhibition in a letter to Sakai: "As I think back, the most important experience, going through the exhibition, was recognizing strong individual expressions as such. None of that nonsense about 'national characteristics' or 'third world art' or identity as having any bearing on the fact that, for example, Gunther Gerzo makes pictorial illusions that are as real as the hardness of a table, as spacious as a desert, and as convincing as a cube in the hand. Hard and true paintings by a master." In all she thought it important that so many gifted artists could be seen at Austin. "It is important for them, for me, for *Plural.* If you like, you can say I said so!" (Ashton to Sakai, New York, 22 November 1975). They do indeed say that she said so by publishing her letter in *Plural* 52 (January 1976), alongside a number of appreciations of both the exhibition itself and also the accompanying symposium on contemporary Latin American art.

An interesting commentary on the symposium is offered by one of the organizers, Damián Bayón. His own prejudices are made quite clear. He has little sympathy for Marta Traba and her political reading of the contemporary art scene: "For Traba, the drama of Latin

American art is that it permanently suffers the pressures of the centers of authority, where capital resides, and which dictate the orders that must be followed. For her, the only possible antidote is what she proposes to call 'an art of resistance' which chimes with the idea—presented by the Brazilian Aracy Amaral—of an *occupied continent*, a notion that remerged time and again throughout the symposium."[70] Bayón's answer to this definition is to gloss the presentations of the artists Felguérez and Szyszlo, for whom "resistance" meant not to conform to dominant orthodoxies of whatever sort, in particular, conservative governments and *marchands* with their *idées fixes* about "national" art, or those critics who demanded that artist should always be up to date and in search of the "new."

Bayón's defense of his selections for the exhibition can also apply more broadly to the choice of artists that the magazine chose to showcase in its artistic supplements and in articles and notes throughout the magazine. In the supplements there are studies of ten Mexican contemporary artists, seven Argentine, two Venezuelans, two Colombians, two Brazilians, and one Nicaraguan, Peruvian, and Uruguayan painter. It would be difficult to characterize them, outside the broad definition given above by Bayón and Sakai, that the magazine was focusing on artists, sculptors, and architects already with established national reputations, but that deserved to be better known throughout Latin America and in the United States and Europe. They represent different aspects of abstract, geometric, op art, pop art, and conceptual art, along with sculpture, though these are very loose categorizations for a range of different styles. None of these artists can be viewed as *explicitly* socially committed in terms of content, though it would seem too simple to subscribe to the cultural dependency models then in vogue that the magazine subscribed to an aesthetic of "political apoliticism."[71]

How "plural" was the art aesthetic? The most regular contributors were Damián Bayón and Juan Acha, along with Jorge Alberto Manrique, who worked in the Colegio de México and had been involved in magazine publishing editing for a period at the *Revista de la Universidad de México*. There is also the constant presence of Juan García Ponce who had been reviewing modern Mexican painting from the late fifties and whose brother ran arguably the most important private gallery of modern art in Mexico City. His support for modern art had already been seen in two recent books—*9 pintores mexicanos: la aparición de lo invisible* (1968) and *Vicente Rojo* (1971)—and a number of articles. The Argentines Saúl Yurkievich and Fermin Fevre would also contribute occasional essays on art. The overall coverage of art has a very clear didactic and informational focus, unlike the more quirky, though constantly interesting interventions in, say, the literary supplements. The overwhelming majority of the artistic supplements cover a broad range of contemporary artists in Mexico and Latin America: introductory essays with, for the time, quite lavish illustrations in color and in black and white. Alongside this overtly didactic focus, other articles in the main body of the magazine would take up different interests—such as the special edition on Balthus in *Plural* 42, March 1975 or essays on Joseph Cornell in issue 39, December 1974—while the "Letras, letrillas, letrones" section commented on exhibitions and events in Mexico and throughout the world.

The art critic Marta Traba—the bête noir of Damián Bayón—was approached by the magazine. She makes an interesting comment about its contents in a letter to Sakai in 1974. Traba points out some of the potential fault lines in the *Plural* vision of uniformity. She says that she considers *Plural* to be "very beautiful" and "super-aesthetic," with excellent material that for her are as important and distant from her as the contents of any excellent European magazine: "I mean that my problems and research are in areas that are far removed from *Plural*...in particular in the coverage of art, where the general articles are almost always flirting with 'marivaudage.'" (Marta Traba to Sakai, Caracas, 15 February 1974). Despite this, because of what she calls her "adolescent and unconditional admiration for Octavio Paz," she does send an article, with illustrations, on Ana Mercedes Hoyos, which was published immediately as an artistic supplement in *Plural* 30, March 1974. The reference to *marivaudage* is probably addressed at Bayón in particular—they would take opposing views at many international symposia—while later in her letter she lambastes the critic Jorge Romero Brest for talking *galimatías* (gibberish) in his articles for *Plural,* in particular his attempt to survey the field of modern art in blank verse.

Yet outside personal antipathies and animosities between the major critics in the field, Traba is also alluding to the fact that *Plural* seems removed from immediate issues in Latin America. She wrote this criticism before the magazine started publishing regular supplements on art, so perhaps her discrepancies with the coverage on art might have become softened in later years, though interestingly she publishes just the once in *Plural,* which does not tend to support the view that she later approved the magazine's coverage. Her own views of "art of resistance," that had made Bayón nervous at Austin was not based on simple issues of "content." She openly criticized some of the political simplicities of the Mexican mural movement and was equally opposed to the superficial "indigenism" of political Andean art in the early decades of the century. Her own career was within "the belly of the monster," both supported by and reacting to the grants of U.S. institutions. She was very aware that the picture of North American funding of Latin American art was not Manichaean as dependency theorists might like to argue: nobody could deny, for example, that it was the support of the Pan American Union, who offered Cuevas a solo exhibition, that helped to give him an international profile at a very early age. Traba, like *Plural* would support the work of Fernando de Szyszlo and José Luis Cuevas amongst others, and would have agreed with the observation by Mario Vargas Llosa that, "localism and cosmopolitanism are two major areas of frustration in art."[72]

José Luis Cuevas would offer a critical account of art criticism in Latin America, pointing out that he and his good friend Marta Traba felt isolated by what he would term "opportunistic" critics at many symposia throughout the region, including the Austin seminar. He would see the two of them as marginalized by a dominant apolitical orthodoxy that had at its center such critics as Damián Bayón. In a particularly acerbic personal attack, published in *El Sol de México*, he ridiculed the pretensions of "Monsieur Bebe Bayón," who he depicted as a farceur with no knowledge of Mexican and Latin American art. Such crude, knockabout nationalism would not be seen in the pages of *Plural*, which would offer space to Cuevas and Traba as to Bayón.[73]

Obviously we cannot imply that no differences separate Traba from Sakai and Bayón and argue that art criticism in *Plural* was a broad church in every respect. There were clear ideological differences between the two "positions" and Traba was indicating in her letter to Sakai that she found *Plural* insufficiently *engagé* by her own lights. Sakai had a "decorous" view of Latin American modernism and would not be tempted into discussions about "revolutionary art" in say Cuba or Chile, or the mobilizations of radical artists in Argentina, who rejected the gallery system and looked to more direct forms of popular engagement. He was more interested in establishing guidelines: "*Plural* , I think, must *also* have a didactic function and orient the public—inform them. The confusion in the art world is now greater than ever (I think)." (Letter, Sakai to Paz, Mexico, 14 January 1974). While Sakai did not achieve all the aspirations outlined in this letter—he wanted to extend the coverage of the magazine to Eastern art and to different modern art movements—he could certainly feel that in great part he had achieved the goal of mapping the field of

contemporary Latin American art. He must have felt that certain bat-
tles had already been won, that it was not necessary now to revisit the
debates of the 1950s and 1960s in Mexico between "nationalist" and
"cosmopolitan" views of art. But he remarked in surprise in a letter to
Pere Gimferrer in September 1974 that *Plural* was embroiled in a
"struggle among artists, critics, museums and galleries about a very
local, but at the same time universal problem: nationalist, xenopho-
bic, revolutionary (?) muralist, Mexicanist art against *extranjerizante*,
class based and aestheticized art (that is what they call us)." Sakai calls
the opposition "the pseudo-revolutionaries of the outmoded Mexican
school," but he is nervous enough at what he describes as personal
attacks against him to worry if his status as a foreigner in Mexico
might be jeopardized if the government joined in the debate directly.
Once again, *Plural* perceived itself to be caught up in a dispute,
defending certain principles at a moment when there was a revival of
more overtly political discussions about art and the gallery system.

In its criticism, *Plural* opened up new spaces for the discussion of
art and literature. Its art criticism in particular had a very clear Latin
American and didactic function. Its coverage of literature brought a
number of different critical schools and eminent critics into play
achieving a blend of local, Latin American, and international critics.
Whatever the different polemics in the field, the poet and editor
Tomás Segovia could look back on this time as a "plural" moment in
Mexican cultural history, a time before polemics and rancor became
defining characteristics of the eighties and nineties:

> In arts and letters there was at that time a slight and partial consensus
> that I bring to mind with nostalgia. My generation had grown up in
> Mexico in a strongly ideological, very dogmatic, nationalist moment.
> A group of our teachers had resisted this ideology with difficulty: the
> *Contemporáneos* group. We felt ourselves to be their inheritors and,
> supported by the example of Octavio Paz, who acted as a bridge
> between them and us, we began to break through these constraints. I
> think that *Plural* was one of those battle grounds...[for a] freer, more
> universal, more lucid and more critical literature.[74]

Chapter 5

Literary "Creation"

In every issue, *Plural* published original works of literature, what the magazine referred to in its indexes and elsewhere as "Creation." While there is some attempt to keep a balance between poetry and fiction, it was clear that the dominant interests of the editor Paz (and of the first managing editor Tomás Segovia) were in poetry. It is on the community of poets therefore, that we first focus our attention.

While a considerable amount of the work published is originally in the Spanish language, there is a constant need to translate texts. The group around the magazine is as much a community of translators as it is a community of poets or critics. It would be Paz who would offer a theory of the process in a book published in 1971, *Traducción: literatura y literalidad*.[1] In the first line of this study, Paz states that language itself is already a translation: "To learn to speak is to learn to translate; when children ask their mother the meaning of this or that word, what they are really asking is that she translate the word into her and their language" (p.7). Every society repeats this childhood experience when faced with the language of another social grouping, and the strangeness and consternation of being faced with another language becomes also a doubt about the language that we ourselves speak. "Language loses its universality and is revealed as a plurality of tongues, all of them strange and unintelligible to each other" (p.7). While in the past, for Paz, translation could dissolve this doubt by positing a "universal" society in which people would say the same thing in different languages, the modern era has broken down and destroyed this security, by revealing the "variety and heterogeneity of different civilizations" (p.9).

This awareness of difference in the modern world should perhaps make translators feel discouraged, but in fact, the reverse has happened and there is now an ever-increasing move to translation. Paz unravels this apparent paradox: "At one extreme, the world is presented as a collection of heterogeneities; at the other extreme as a superimposition of texts, each one slightly different to the previous one: translations of translations of translations. Each text is unique and, at the same time, it is the translation of another text. No text is entirely original because language itself, in its essence, is already a translation: firstly of the non-verbal world and later because every sign and every sentence is the translation of another sign and another sentence" (p.9). This allows the possibility for translation which, for Paz, must always avoid being literal and become instead a literary operation, for "translation implies a transformation of the original," a verbal object that reproduces the original through, in Jakobson's analysis, metonymy and metaphor (p.10). Paz finds the idea that poetry is untranslatable "repugnant" (p.11). Translation is very difficult, he argues, as difficult as writing original works, but not impossible, and the translator should try to produce a poem that is analogous, but not identical, to the original poem. He quotes Valéry approvingly: "The ideal of poetic translation, as once Valéry defined it better than anyone, is to produce with different means analogous effects" (p.16).

Critics have further explored Paz's theory and practice of translation that he mapped out succinctly in the essay quoted above written the year before *Plural* first appeared.[2] These ideas inform the work of the different translators in *Plural*: the complex but essential task of literary translation as a way of building bridges between different linguistic communities. In an early issue of *Plural*, the magazine's very accomplished and extremely overworked translator, Tomás Segovia, would give his own account of the difficulties faced by translating poetry as opposed to prose: "For example: for the translator of an article on cardiology, the fact that the Spanish word *corazón* has three syllables, while the English word *heart* and the French word *coeur* has just one does not present any major problem. For the translator of poetry, by contrast, this chance, arbitrary and insignificant circumstance is a major conundrum."[3] In the event, Segovia concurs with Paz that poetry can be translated. In a later issue of the journal, Salvador Elizondo was to remark that all the members of the Management Committee of *Plural* were "passionate" about the craft of translation and all were engaged in translation on a regular basis.[4] It is perhaps significant that the first poem Paz published in the magazine was an exercise in translation, a communal work by poets in four different languages.

Poetry

Paz and his Poetic World

As with all other aspects of the magazine, Paz's poetry is a major structuring element. The first poem that Paz publishes in the magazine is the collaborative work *Renga* along with Jaques Roubaud, Edoardo Sanguinetti, and Charles Tomlinson. This is published in the same issue as Paz's round-table discussion on contemporary Mexico with Womack and Turner at Harvard (*Plural* 6, March 1972). In some ways this poem mirrors the overall strategy of *Plural:* a poetic experiment—based on a traditional Japanese form—linking poets across the world.

In fact, Paz makes it very clear that the twentieth century is the century of translations and that he himself is dedicated to this enterprise: "For us, translation is transmutation, metaphor: a change and a break; it is therefore a way of ensuring the continuity of our past by transforming it into a dialogue with other civilizations."[5] In this spirit, the *renga* is a poetic practice that chimes with an experimental attitude toward poetry as well as aspiring to a collective notion of poetry, away from the romantic view of literature as the original work of an exceptional author. Paz explores the affinities and differences between the *renga* and surrealist poetry. He then describes the process of joint creation, by four poets in four different languages: "Let me add and emphasize this point: it is in four languages and a single language: the language of contemporary poetry."[6] For Paz, it makes no sense to talk about "national" poetry, there is instead contemporary poetry written in all the languages of the West. Thus there is a diversity of languages within a community of poetic language. The poetic exercise consists of the poets writing a series of poems together, in their own language, with a translation into another language on the other side of the page. As Jason Wilson explains: "The revised rules of this Western *renga* led to using sonnets, chance associations and four languages. The experiment was dedicated to André Breton, who invented several games (like *le cadaver exquis*) to break down the differences between poets and allow chance, shock and surprise to enter a text."[7] This playful poem thus marked out a space in the magazine that would be concerned with literary experimentation as well forging links across languages.

If we compare Paz's vast output of essays, prose poems (in particular *El mono gramático* (*The Monkey Grammarian*), written in 1970 and published in 1974, and poems written in the period of *Plural,* we find that he is not looking to swamp the magazine with his own work. Most of the work published chimes with areas being explored within the journal. For example, several of the poems published in *Plural* are commentaries on artists who are being analyzed in the magazine: on the photographer Manuel Alvarez Bravo (issue 11), Robert Motherwell (issue 15), Joseph Cornell (issue 39), and Balthus (issue 42). If we look at the issue on the photographer Manuel Alvarez Bravo, we find Paz's poem published alongside an appreciation of the photographer by André Breton, a letter from the famous U.S. photographer Edward Weston—the mentor of Tina Modotti—addressed to Alvarez Bravo, in which he speaks of being "stimulated to enthusiasm" by his work, and an appreciation by Xavier Villaurrutia. This choice again speaks to *Plural*'s interest in cross cultural links, with Paz in dialogue with his surrealist mentor, Breton, a modernist American photographer, a key member of the *Contemporáneos* group and, of course, Mexico's best known photographer. The issue is also illustrated with several photos by Alvarez Bravo himself. In this context, Paz offers a reading of different images, the titles named within the poem capturing in words the moment in which "Manuel" can photograph or name "the imperceptible cleft" between image and language, where the "arrow of his eye" can hit the target of the "instant" capturing the face of every day events that we never see.[8] Paz would later slightly rewrite this poem and reprint it in what would be the final issue of the magazine, issue 58.

This period also offers a space for memory, occasioned by the "vuelta" or return to Mexico in 1971 as in the poem "Nocturno de San Ildefonso" (issue 36) reveals. This young poet, as we saw in our analysis of the poem in chapter one, is caught up in the agitation of those years, because the young aspired to "good" and to putting the world to rights. In a world of youthful political commitment, the young man discovers a poetic vocation, and that poetry cannot offer historical certainties or political solutions. Poetry is seen as a "hanging bridge between history and truth," it is a way to see "the stillness in movement," for history is the "journey itself."[9] In a poem published six month earlier in the special edition on the Gulag, "Aunque es de noche" ("Even though it is night," issue 30), Paz continues in an autobiographical vein speaking of his early inability to face up to the nature of political evil, an evil that feeds on such neglect: for, "evil is emptiness/replete." He also repeats the idea that writing can somehow offers a consolation and a way out of the horrors of Stalin and other twentieth-century atrocities, because through writing and reading one reaches out to another: "I am yours, the truth of Writing."[10]

If Paz is abstemious in the number of his own poems published, his friendships and tastes certainly determine to a great extent the selection of poets published, in particular, outside Mexico. In Latin America there are the Brazilian concrete poets Haroldo and Augusto de Campos; from Argentina Alejandra Pizarnik (based in Paris), whose work Paz had appreciated for many years, Alberto Girri and Roberto Juarroz; the Peruvian Blanca Varela, who Paz had first known in Paris in the mid-forties; the Venezuelan critic and poet Guillermo Sucre, and the Argentine critic and poet based in Paris, Saúl Yurkievich. Sarduy also offers his poetry and prose poems from that period, in particular "Big Bang." Personal contact also facilitates the publishing of the poetry of the Catalan Pere Gimferrer and Julián Ríos, as well as Goytisolo's "prose poems." Paz was conscious that there was still much work to be done in having Latin American poetry more widely distributed and understood. He writes in a letter to the critic Donald Davie that when Davie discusses the impact of Latin American poetry in the United States, he just mentions Neruda and Vallejo, but he fails to notice Nicanor Parra, Paz himself, and very important Brazilian poets. Paz asks if Davie has seen the anthology of Brazilian poetry edited by Elizabeth Bishop. "Do you believe really that the 'act of creative imagination' is located now in the 'minority' languages? In the case of the Hispanic world, the best Catalan poet (in my opinion), Pedro Gimferrer, writes indistinctly in Spanish and Catalan" (Letter, Paz to Donald Davie, Mexico, D.F., 13 October 1972). Of course, Paz's own reading of Latin American poetry was selective. One does not find in *Plural*, for example, the work of Pablo Neruda, Ernesto Cardenal, Nicolás Guillén, all the poets of the Cuban revolution (though they do review poets inside Cuba not favored by the dominant mode of popular, "conversational" poetry, such as Cintio Vitier and Eliseo Diego).

Of course, the other side of this divide, as personified by Neruda, was equally distrustful of Paz. The Chilean writer Jorge Edwards, who managed to maintain a friendship with both poets, has pointed out that Neruda used to like to conceive of himself in terms of a literary "family" that was more about instinct and excess than about intellectualism, espousing writers such as Rabelais, Victor Hugo, and Walt Whitman. "By contrast, Borges, Vicente Huidobro, Octavio Paz and some 'intellectual' poets from Brazil belonged to an opposing family, which Neruda always found suspect, a family, he felt, that was always susceptible to being dazzled by the artificial paradises show-cased by literary groups in the West."[11] Mario Vargas Llosa has also recently commented on this anti-intellectual "pose" that Neruda would adopt, in comparison to the ever scintillating Paz: "When someone floated an abstract, general topic, inviting a discussion about ideas—something that Paz shone at—Neruda's face fell."[12] Of course Neruda's anti-intellectualism was a pose—no one could write that range of poetry without being well-read—but this idea of two opposing families, the one more popular and nationalist, the other more intellectual and cosmopolitan reflected, in albeit crude terms, a division in the world of Latin American poetry, especially in the polarized moment of the early seventies.

Paz's close friend and the editor of the magazine *Diálogos,* Ramón Xirau knew where he stood in terms of this divide and he concurred with Paz's selection of poets. In an early issue of *Plural* (5, February 1972) he reviews several anthologies of Latin American poetry and holds up *The Penguin Book of Latin American Verse* for particular ridicule. Among the "significant and unpardonable" absences in this selection of poetry are the Mexican poets Bonifacio Nuño, Tomás Segovia, José Carlos Becerra, Gabriel Zaid, and Homero Aridjis; the Argentines Juarroz, Lozano, and Alejandra Pizarnik; the Cubans Vitier and Eliseo Diego; the poetry of Liscano and Sucre in Venezuela, and in Brazil, the concrete poetry of the de Campos brothers. (Ramón Xirau, "Poesía latinoamericana: tres visiones," *Plural* 5, p.14). These are all poets who we find in *Plural.* English-language poets published also coincide largely with Paz's particular interests. In the magazine we find the experimental musician John Cage, Elizabeth Bishop ("Visitas a St. Elizabeth," issue 19; also 49); John Ashbery (part of the homage to Joseph Cornell, issue 39, December 1974, also in issue 56, texts and commentary); "New Poetry from North America," selected by Mark Strand, issue 50, November 1975; a supplement on E.E. Cummings. Let us look at some areas that reflect these abiding interests of Paz and that are highlighted in the magazine.

In the late sixties, Paz was interested in exploring poetry as spatial form. We have seen his interest in haiku in earlier chapters and in 1968 he was to publish a group of poems called *Topoemas,* which experimented with shapes and forms. He developed this interest in exploring the visual form of poetry by publishing a series of avant garde texts in early issues of *Plural.* If we analyze the contribution of John Cage, entitled "Mesosticos," we find it in the issue of the journal the month before the publication of *Renga,* in a special section dedicated to "visual writing." Cage explains that his title means a central thread, in this case the name of his close collaborator, the dancer Merce Cunningham. The text is made up of syllables, words, and mixture of words determined by the *I Ching.* This mode of writing/representation is, as the translator Tomás Segovia points out, very much in keeping with the aesthetic principles of John Cage, against the author, the composer, the director, and against any form of control or determined programme.[13] In the same section, there is a playful contribution from Guillermo Cabrera Infante, which opens with a visual play on the words Dédalo and Minotauro, before moving on to a story about the Minotaur illustrated by Monty Python-esque cartoons provided by the author, in which the word-play within the printed text takes over from the "visual writing," with the Minotaur proving himself as adept at puns and palindromes as any of the characters in Cabrera's *Three Trapped Tigers*.

A more consistent exercise in visual writing is offered by the Mexican poet, Marco Antonio Montes de Oca, who talks of his own work as concrete poems, and stresses its ludic nature.[14] His own experimental work can be seen in the context of Paz's "Topoemas", a series of visual puns that were themselves dedicated to the Brazilian concrete poets, and also to the pioneering artist, Mathias Goeritz, the first concrete poet in Mexico (who would be the subject, of one of the first "artistic supplements" in April 1974).

In May 1972, *Plural* published a supplement on "Concrete Poetry," presented and selected by its two main Brazilian protagonists, Augusto and Haroldo de Campos. In their introduction they give an account of the development of the experimental Grupo Noigandres and their journal of the same name, a word that Pound had taken from the work of the Provencal poet Arnaut Daniel, as he wrote in Canto XX: "Noigandres, eh, noigandres, / Now what the DEFFIL can that mean."[15] Noigandres thus became synonymous with freedom of expression, as well as locating the poets within a tradition of poetic "inventors" such as Pound and Mallarmé. As well as giving a clear overview of the movement, the supplement also, usefully gives ways of reading individual poems by Ronaldo Azeredo, Augusto de Campos, Haroldo de Campos, and José Lino Grunewald. Haroldo de Campos would later sum up the intentions of the group: "The poem's structure is its true content. Only on the historical-cultural level will we be able to find a relationship between the concrete poem-object and a content external to it: a relationship, however, which, once again, will be a relationship of structures. Thus the 'physiognomy of our time' (the industrial revolution, the techniques of journalism and advertising, the theory of communication opened up by cybernetics, etc.) will be the likely structure of content related to the content structure of the concrete-poem."[16] The close collaboration with Paz in the sixties and early seventies would later be explored by

Haroldo de Campos in a book entitled *Transblanco*.[17] Paz also maintained a regular correspondence with Haroldo de Campos, and asked for his advice about which Brazilian and Portuguese writers to include in *Plural*. De Campos's reply was not overenthusiastic about current literature in Portuguese, but he did indicate the importance of Cabral ("he is the best we have"), as well as Clarice Lispector and the "best" literary critic, Antonio Cândido (Letter, Haroldo de Campos to Octavio Paz, São Paulo, 2 August 1971).

It is interesting that the de Campo brothers mention their interest in both the "Russian cubist-futurist" poets, especially Mayakovsky, for whom a "revolutionary form" was an inseparable element of poetic production (p.22), and also the work of E.E. Cummings. Both of these writers would be explored in separate supplements in the magazine, as we have indicated in chapter four. The Mayakovsky supplement consisting of two poems translated and introduced by Gerardo Deniz was published two months before the concrete poetry edition, in March 1972, while the E.E. Cummings dossier appeared in two parts, January 1975 and January 1976. The first part focused on his writing on poetry, while the second publish the poems themselves, in the translation of the poet Ulalume González de León. Mayakovsky's translator, Gerardo Deniz, does not share the de Campo brothers fascination with the poet. He remarks that the instigator of the project, as always, was Octavio Paz. "The reason for this translation is the usual one: one day Octavio Paz had the idea that it could be done, and since it was posed as something of a challenge, one had to accept it."[18] The challenge, however, became something of a burden, since, for Deniz, this poet should be in every anthology of the worst poetry of the twentieth century! In contrast to Deniz's humorous misanthropy, the supplement is produced in a handsome way, with photos from a family album, a photo of the poet in Mexico, and two drawings by Mayakovsky of the "Mexican landscape." The two supplements on E.E. Cummings, by contrast, are very clear in their support of this major figure in North American poetry, reviewing his poetics and translating his work. González de León quotes appreciatively William Carlos Williams' analysis of Cummings as a love poet, and concurs with Allen Tate's comments that Cummings was the only poet in the interwar years to have preserved his humanity and his poetry: "In my generation, some preserved their humanity and some their poetry, but no other poet than him, I think, preserved both." (*Plural* 42, p.50). In this way, *Plural* looked to offer a guide to its readers into the complexities of certain aspects of contemporary poetry. Of course, for Paz, the abiding interest is surrealism, and he uses the cultural supplements to provide Latin American readers with a context for reading the group of writers from earlier in the century associated with surrealism.

The main section of the magazine concerned with the dissemination of literary texts outside Latin America was the literary supplement. The brief analysis of the supplements made in chapter four revealed a predominance of contemporary poets—Mayakovsky, Brazilian concrete poetry, Holderin, E.E. Cummings, Pound and Chinese poetry, Mallarmé; and a reappraisal of the surrealist tradition and the interwar group of French intellectuals and associated with, or engaging, at a critical distance, with surrealism: Bataille, René Char, Benjamin Péret, René Daumal, Blaise Cendrars, Francis Ponge, and Alfred Jarry. Paz's most complete reappraisal of surrealism in the magazine is contained in a book review in *Plural* 35, an analysis of Stefan Baciu's *Antología de la poesía surrealista latinoamericana*. He begins the review with a surrealist enumeration of what surrealism means/has meant: "Surrealism has been the fiery apple in the tree of syntax...surrealism has been the cardboard crown of the headless critic and the viper that slides between the thighs of the critic's wife...Surrealism has been the seven league boots with which the prisoners of dialectical reasoning make their escape and Tom Thumb's axe which cuts through the knots of the poisonous thickets that cover the walls of the petrified revolutions of the twentieth century."[19] Paz later goes on to map his own work within this tradition.

With respect to poetry outside the Spanish-speaking world, the magazine was more successful in attracting poets of Paz's generation, with some exceptions. Paz always looked to publish special issues on young writers. There was a special section on young North American and French poets published in the fiftieth anniversary edition of the magazine. For the North American section, Paz would entrust the selection to the poet and translator Mark Strand, who had already worked on several translations of Paz's poems within the broader context of translating Mexican poetry. Paz acknowledges Strand's work by including and translating Strand's own poems in the anthology and presumably also—although the piece is unsigned—writing a short introduction to the poet. Strand's own selection of representative young poets—Charles Wright, Louise Gluck, Jon Anderson, Charles Simic, and James Tate—sought to mark out a field not dominated by the dominant vogue, in Strand's words, that young U.S. poets have to be both experimental and socially rebellious, or that they can be put into easy categories such as "beatnik" or "academic," or "confessional." His choice of poets favors "direct" and "naked" poems, "sincerity as form."[20] The selection of young French poets—Bernard Noel, Pierre Dhainaut, Jean Daive, Serge Sautreau, André Velter—is made by the poet Pierre Dhainaut, who had known Paz from the sixties. He calls his poets, echoing the phrase of Octavio Paz, *solitarios/solidarios*. Dhainaut, perhaps in deference to Paz, points out the ways in which the poets might or might not have been influenced by surrealism. But his strongest attack, which also chimes with the dominant discourse in *Plural*, is on the purported scientific criticism of, say, the *Tel Quel* group: "I fear that theory, like power, is totalitarian. Let us trust rather our contradiction: we will see clearly. These five poets might be located between surrealism and scientism."[21] These younger poets were well chosen and now appear in current French anthologies as the most important voices of the last third of the twentieth century.[22] Paz would also make sure that *Plural* would include an appreciation of his long-standing friend, the poet and critic Yves Bonnefoy.[23]

The influence of surrealism can be noted in the North American poets that *Plural* favors, in particular John Ashbery and the New York School. For Paz, Ashbery's work is "a personal and very American vision of Dada and surrealism." The influence of surrealism, for Paz, is also clear in abstract expressionism, pop art, and in the work of Joseph Cornell, whose work sees "the everyday object transfigured by the slow erosion of fantasy and humor."[24] *Plural* would publish a poem by Ashbery as a homage to Joseph Cornell in issue 39 (December 1974), and a further long poem in issue 56, May 1976. Paz would also publish a lead essay on Elizabeth Bishop in issue 49 of the magazine and translate two of her poems.[25]

The above describes the main parameters of the poetic world of Octavio Paz that we find in the magazine: his own work, his interests in certain literary developments, and his extraordinary range of contacts with fellow poets across the world. At this point we should broaden out the discussion to include a survey of poets writing in Spanish that the magazine publishes.

Spanish America and Spain

If the Brazilians were closest to Paz's interests in terms of literary experimentalism in the early seventies, his group of contacts would also largely dictate the choices of Spanish American and Spanish poets in the magazine. He wrote in a letter to Orfila in 1965 that he is interested in seeing Spanish American poetry as a whole, in exploring the links that bind different poets: "In every field, from economics to politics, Latin Americans are looking to unite or at least to integrate. Now, if there is something that really shows the unity of our America, that something is poetry: a world of great richness and variety but also, remarkably coherent."[26] When he had a chance to make this vision a reality he was in part successful. He would, in particular, maintain contact with different Argentine writers, whom he first met in the pages of *Sur* or on his frequent visits to Paris. One of what Alejandro Rossi would call the "subterranean links" with *Sur* was the poet Alberto Girri, who published with some frequency. Girri recognizes that *Plural* is a magazine that shares his values. Writing at a time when the military regime in Argentina was crumbling, when there was an increasing clamor for the return of Perón, when guerrilla groups were beginning to operate very openly, and when the whole intellectual field was becoming more and more politicized, Girri found some optimism in *Plural*'s project: "*Plural* has made the very best impression on me; I might add, it's almost unreal, since on top of the general excellence of the literary material, it has to its credit something that today seems more and more unusual: it is looking to be open to everything interesting written in these parts, without any extra-literary discrimination at work" (Letter, Alberto Girri to Tomás Segovia, Buenos Aires, 31 January 1972). Another *solitario/solidario* was the poet Roberto Juarroz who was published in the first issue of the magazine, and infrequently thereafter, as both poet and critic. Juarroz, for example, would edit the supplement introducing the Argentine poet Antonio Porchia. In his presentation of Porchia that reads like a prose poem, alternating observations about "depth" in poetry with italicized biographical memories of the poet, Juarroz describes an artistic practice very much akin to his own: "Depth is the opposite of politics. It is not strange that the word politics does not appear in the entire work of Porchia. Politics manipulates men and women, instrumentalizes them, mediates them, imposes priorities on them, subordinates them to power and ambition, submits them to causes and ideologies, depersonalizes them, turns them into a herd. Depth is the combination of men and women in their total being and has a vision of every single thing in relationship to all other things, without plans and strategies. One man, every man, not men in the plural."[27] This introduction was written, of course at a time in Argentina when the watchword was "everything is politics," as political turmoil increased in the mid-seventies.

Paz had known Alejandra Pizarnik from the early sixties, writing the introduction to her book of poetry *Arbol de Diana* in 1962. Pizarnik's own published essays on poetry also showed how she engaged with Paz's work. When she committed suicide in September 1972, the magazine published an interview with and a poem by Pizarnik as a "homage to a great friend and contributor to *Plural*." The interview with the Argentine Martha Moia explores some of the recurrent symbols in Pizarnik's poetry: the "garden," the "wood," while in an interview, Pizarnik explains her own conception of poetry: "I feel that signs and words make allusions. This complex way of feeling language leads me to think that language cannot express reality: that we can only talk about obvious matters. That is why I try to make terribly exact poems despite my innate surrealism and to work with inner shadows. That is what has characterized my poems."[28] Saúl Yurkievich would be another Argentine poet and critic who would become close to the magazine—and the magazine would on several occasions publish his joyful linguistic experimentation—as it would the Venezulean poets Juan Liscano and Guillermo Sucre. With all three writers, the fact that they worked as critics and poets, and also in the case of the Venezuelans, as magazine editors, made them attractive to the editorial team in *Plural*. It meant that many of the *Plural* contributors would already have been published by Liscano and Sucre. Liscano had founded the journal *Zona Franca* in 1964 and this magazine steered a course that concentrated on modern literature in Latin America and in particular, in its survey of the latest trends in U.S. literature and culture. He was also vehemently opposed to the proponents of armed struggle in Venezuela.[29] Guillermo Sucre edited the magazine *Imagen* in the late sixties before taking up a teaching post in the United States. When *Plural* appeared in 1971, Sucre was published in the second issue. He was announced as having a "privileged position" among "new Latin American poets."[30] The anti-academic Chilean poet Gonzalo Rojas, resident in Venezuela following the military coup, also contributes to the magazine. His violent images published in May 1975 are illustrated by a hazy photo of an image from the Chilean coup, thus rooting the work in a specific context.[31] Of the writers from Spain, it is Pere Gimferrer whose poetry is published with greatest frequency, with him often supplying his own translations from Catalan into Spanish, and there are occasional contributions from Jorge Guillén and José Angel Valente.

This coverage of Spanish language poetry in Spanish America and in Spain speaks, therefore, to a group with interlocking interests rather than an expansive view covering many different aesthetic and ideological tendencies and poets. Nicanor Parra's ironic, playful poems published in issue 6 of the magazine would find more favor, for example, than the conversational or epic poems that dealt directly with social issues and a specific Latin American "content": once again we can talk in shorthand of what we might call a Paz/Neruda divide, and their conflicting ideas as to what would constitute a political and an aesthetic vanguard.

Mexican Poets

We have noted on several occasions that Paz found it difficult to attract Mexican writers, despite (or perhaps because of) his best efforts: "We don't have enough Mexicans, that's clear, but we can't do anything except keep on insisting...I think that we must root *Plural* in the soil of Mexico, even if this soil is singularly hostile (mud and cement)" (Letter, Octavio Paz to Tomás, Segovia, 27 January 1972). Out of all the areas covered by *Plural* it was perhaps most successful in publishing Mexican poets. The two main promoters of the early magazine, Paz and Segovia were both poets and they had established contacts in that field. We have already seen that Paz had collaborated with two young poets, Homero Aridjis and José Emilio Pacheco along with Alí Chamucero on the anthology *Poesía en movimiento*, which came to a slightly uneasy consensus as to which were the most important voices in contemporary Mexican poetry, and these poets would be published in *Plural*.

Of the inner group of writers associated with the magazine, Tomás Segovia published his poetry on several occasions. Paz has described Segovia in the following terms. He belongs to:

> A group of writers who were victims of a double error. In 1939, almost children, they came to Mexico and they have been with us ever since. Are they Mexican or Spanish? That problem is of little interest to me, it is enough to know that they write in Spanish: language is the only nationality of a writer. But our critics insist on calling them foreign. And omit their names and their work in Mexican works of criticism and anthologies. Spanish critics, who are more arrogant and more categorical, ignore their very existence. Here talents as clear as Tomás Segovia and Ramón Xirau live in a sort of limbo, doubly orphaned, doubly exiled.[32]

In *Plural*, Segovia publishes a range of work, from direct erotic love poetry to rather more cerebral reflections on the nature of time and on the process of literary creation.[33]

Gabriel Zaid is most prominent in *Plural* as an essayist, but he published poetry on several occasions. Once again Octavio Paz is a sure guide into his world. We remember the biting satires of political figures and political corruption running through his work. For Paz, "In satire the three cardinal points of the Zaid's poetry intersect: love, thought and religion. Our lack of sensitivity to spirituality and the numinous has reached such proportions that no one, or almost no one has remarked on the religious tension that runs through Zaid's best poems. His desperation, his satire and his bitterness are like his ecstasy and enthusiasms, not those of an atheist, but those of a believer…Time, presence, death: love. A religious and metaphysical poet, Zaid is also—and for that very reason—a poet of love."[34] A good example of Zaid's direct satirical verse is the group of poems he published in *Plural* 49, October 1975.[35]

Outside the main group within the magazine, the most frequent contributors are Marco Antonio Montes de Oca, Homero Aridjis, José Emilio Pacheco, Gerardo Deniz, and Jaime Sabines. In his introduction to the edited volume of contemporary poetry, *Poesía en movimiento* published in 1966, Octavio Paz offers a brief survey of the literary field divided into generations. In terms of poets emerging in the fifties, he single out two groups: an older one comprising Rubén Bonifaz Nuño, Jaime Sabines, Jaime García Terrés, and Tomás Segovia and a younger cluster of poets that, he says, he has chosen and grouped together following the rules of *I Ching*: Marco Antonio Montes de Oca, Gabriel Zaid, José Emilio Pacheco, and Homero Aridjis.[36] These are the names that most frequently occur in the magazine ranging from the visual experiments of Montes de Oca to the angry, alienated, painful voice of Jaime Sabines to the laconic, conversational verses of José Emilio Pacheco. Pacheco outlines his own, very deliberately modest space in the literary world in the poem "Birds in the Night (Vallejo y Cernuda se encuentran en Lima)." As hungry marine birds die on the streets of Lima, the poet imagines César Vallejo wandering through streets of misery, fornicating, delirious, writing the occasional poem. Vallejo is now venerated and imitated, whereas in life he was spat on and left to die of hunger: "Cernuda said that no country / supports its living poets / But that's the way it should be / Isn't it worse / to be the National Poet / that everyone greets in the street?"[37] Pacheco, a poet, novelist, short story writer, chronicler, essayist, translator, and editor with a cultural breadth that could almost rival that of Octavio Paz, would always look to avoid the temptation of being the National Poet. Homero Aridjis would also attempt to explain the poetic process in a short poem dedicated to Octavio Paz: "The poem whirls around the head of a man / in narrowing and widening circles / discovering this the man tries to possess it / but the poem disappears. / With what the man can grasp / he makes the poem. / What escapes him / belongs to men in the future."[38]

Being published in the same magazine did not suggest any necessary friendship or meeting of minds. In issue 19 of the magazine, José Emilio Pacheco wrote a review of recent work by Aridjis in which he pointed out an excessive use of gerunds and other lapses in "craftsmanship." This elicited a furious response from Aridjis, who wrote to Paz demanding a right to reply in rather graphic, scatological terms. (Aridjis to Paz, 23 July 1973). Paz manages to keep Aridji's response within the bounds of the decorous, but the incident is an amusing example of rivalries and tensions simmering just under the surface.

A number of younger poets also appeared in the special issue on "joven literatura mexicana." Some remembered this time as being an important stepping-stone in their career. For example, Carlos Montemayor wrote a fine "Elegía 1968," reimagining the events of Tlatelolco ending with the lines; "impossible to forget / impossible to remain dead."[39] Montemayor would later write an appreciation of the impact that *Plural* had made on his generation. He was working as the editor of the *Revista de la Universidad de México*, with very limited resources and no office space or secretaries. *Plural* had an administrative structure that had not been seen before in Mexico. But more importantly, "*Plural* offered direct access to the outside world, to the essays, poetry and fiction of world class authors. We felt that, with *Plural*, Octavio Paz had definitively put Mexico in touch with the entire world."[40]

Other young writers published in that same issue were less complimentary about the magazine, as the case of José Joaquín Blanco. In an appraisal of poetry written in the seventies, Blanco, one of the editors responsible for the cultural supplement, *La Cultura en México*, began his review with an extensive commentary on Paz's work. He gives the clearest statement to date that while a number of critics still proclaimed that they benefited from reading Paz's poetry, his political writings were becoming more difficult to both ignore and to subscribe to. "Héctor Aguilar Camín has observed that the verbal greatness, the generosity, intelligence and beauty of the great moments of Paz are not in his political essays. Paz the polemicist is not Paz the poet." (*La Cultura en México* 745, 25 May 1976, p.III.) Allowing the political Paz to influence his reading of the poetic Paz, Blanco tries to evolve a theory about a writer who is too esoteric for contemporary society, because current Mexican poetry "has all the rage, the desperation and the lack of culture of the society that it inhabits" (p.IV).

He says, somewhat reluctantly, that he still profits from reading Paz, but he finds surprising that Paz lists as his "'utopian companions', Marcos Antonio Montes de Oca, Homero Aridjis, Carlos Montemayor, Ulíses Carrión, Daniel Leyva, Roberto Vallarino, Ulalume González de León and the El Zaguán group" (p.IV). He declares that there is a side to Paz, that of an "authoritarian mandarin, who surrounds himself with a secular court, demands veneration and disdains every-one who does not pay homage to him" (p.IV). The image used of Paz, which could also apply to the magazine, is that of a writer petri-fied into a cathedral. There are two options: one can enter the sacred space and chant mysterious prayers, or else throw stones and break all the windows (p.IV). On this analysis, Blanco perhaps thought that he had not broken too may windows, but such remarks clearly irritated Paz and gave him ammunition when, a year later, as we shall see, he would enter into a famous polemic with another editorial member of *La Cultura*, Carlos Monsiváis. Indeed, Paz countered Blanco's article directly in devastating fashion imagining the critic as an incontinent puppy urinating on his shoes, leaving a somewhat bruised Blanco to defend himself as best he could.[41]

This book has used the Paz/Neruda opposition as a shorthand for describing different political and literary options in the cultural field. In an essay review of the Chilean Roberto Bolaño's novel set in Mexico in the mid-seventies—*The Savage Detectives*—Carmen Boullosa uses the split between Paz and poet Efraín Huerta as a way of making the same division. Writing of her time as a university student, she comments:

> Those same university corridors were also frequented by the poets of my generation who had aligned themselves with pre-existing enemy camps. One camp admired the demotic poet Efraín Huerta, famous for his "minipoems." Packed with humor and nerve. The other looked to an exquisite magazine, *Plural*, published by the cosmopolitan intel-lectual and future Nobel laureate, Octavio Paz...It was the street smart types versus the aesthetes. Not that either camp corresponded exactly to its label. Paz and Huerta were descended from the same Mexican literary tradition...As young men, at the end of the 1930s, they had co-edited the magazine *Taller* (Workshop). But over these years they had drifted apart. Literary and political differences had arisen between them. Paz had denounced Communism and broken with the Cuban Revolution. Efraín had not. Paz's people said the Efrainites were Stalinists. The Efrainites called the Octavians reaction-aries. Neither tag was entirely accurate. The hostilities and affinities were both more and less complex than the insults implied.[42]

Her comments help to contextualize the criticism of *Plural* that we have seen in the pages of *La Cultura en México*.

Fiction Writers

Latin America and Spain

In this area, Argentine and Spanish writers are the most regular contributors. Significantly, there seems to be very little effort to translate contemporary fiction from other languages: most contributions are in the Spanish language.

As we have seen, Paz's closest literary friendship in Argentina is with José Bianco and the founding of the magazine dovetails with the publication of Bianco's only novel, *La pérdida del reino* ("The Loss of the Kingdom") that had been many years in the writing, as the Paz-Bianco correspondence over the years reveals. *Plural* published an extract from the novel, "En el colegio" in issue 9 (June 1972). This passage deals with the latent homoerotic tendencies of the schoolboys in the college. Bianco's work falls into what Daniel Balderston has classified as the second stage of gay and lesbian writing in Latin America, which sees, "the aestheticizing of homosexuality, with the homosexual posited as heir of the humanist tradition (Wilde and Gide), and the emergence of a homosexual subject without overt consciousness of community."[43] *Plural* would review the novel, but by far the most extensive and lyrical review would come in a letter from Paz to Bianco. In it, Paz gives a subtle reading of the novel suggesting that another title for the novel might be "the ambiguities of transparency." In the novel Paz finds a "play of transparencies," in which images of reality appear and fade, in which we are "given the image of a reality that we secretly desire and, as soon as we are given it, it is taken away from us." Paz captures well the allusive nature of this text. He goes on to gloss the homosexual content of the novel: "If Rufo had lived in a society in which his passion had not been seen as an abnormality (Greece or Rome), his natural duplicity would have taken another form" (Letter, Paz to Bianco, Mexico City, 8 December 1972). A delighted Bianco wrote in reply: "Your letter is the *only* satisfaction that my novel has given me." (Letter, Bianco to Paz, Buenos Aires, 18 January 1973.)

Paz had asked Bianco and Enrique Pezzoni to do a special issue of the magazine on Argentine culture and there are a number of letters from late 1972 and throughout 1973 suggesting that they were indeed far into the planning stage. Indeed there is an undated handwritten note from Bianco to Paz and Sakai (probably late 1973), indicating quite a precise content outline, including a number of short stories and poems. Their brief from Paz had been to do an issue on young writers, but Bianco pointed out that since the earlier issue on young Mexican writers had not, for Bianco, been "all that successful," then, "one must include certain more important figures which have inspired younger writers" (Letter from Bianco to Paz and Sakai, n.d.). In the end, for whatever reason, this issue did not appear, although through Bianco *Plural* did publish a short story by Silvina Ocampo, "El destino"[44] set in the Ocampo world of refined cruelty, dealing with adolescence, violence, and death. It would also publish several texts by Bianco's close friend, the writer Juan José Hernández, who would also pick a fight with Emir Rodríguez Monegal about the place that Monegal had given him in his article on the boom in Latin American fiction, where, according to Hérnandez, Monegal had not stressed enough his Tucumán origins (opposed to the hegemony of Buenos Aires) and had also slurred him by implying that he was influenced by Manuel Puig (*Plural* 10).

The contacts were mainly with the established *Sur* group of writers, through Bianco, and also with Julio Cortázar who, as we have seen, became very irritated when his short story published in issue 2 appeared with pages in the wrong order. Cortázar would only publish two works of fiction in *Plural*, but the magazine supported his fictional output asking the Uruguayan critic Angel Rama to write a review of *Libro de Manuel* (*A Manual for Manuel*), that appeared in 1973.[45] Interestingly, *Plural* finds here a reviewer sympathetic to the "political turn" in Cortázar's writing, while a few years later, Paz's magazine *Vuelta* would choose to try to undermine Cortázar's politics.

Younger writers such as Luisa Valenzuela would also publish in the magazine as would Héctor Bianciotti from Paris. Indeed, as the country spiraled into violence following the death of Perón in (July) 1974, Argentine writers became increasingly nervous as to what they could publish in their own country. Both direct and self-censorship increased, as the right-wing assassination squads, the AAA, went about their work of threats, murder, and "disappearance." Elvira Orphée offers Sakai a fictional text on torture, part of a novel in progress, seen from the perspective of the torturers. She remarks that the work is not publishable in the current climate in Argentina and she is looking for a Mexican publishing house that does not distribute in Buenos Aires, for reasons of personal safety: "although even though I find living ever more difficult, I wouldn't like to be murdered. And the consequence of publishing in my country might well be that, because people have been killed for much less" (Elvira

Orphée to Sakai, Buenos Aires, n.d [letter received on 9 April 1975 in the *Plural* offices]).

In the event, the Orphée text was not published. But *Plural* did publish an extract from *El beso de la mujer araña* (*Kiss of the Spider Woman*) by the most important of the post-*Sur* Argentine generation, Manuel Puig. This novel soon became recognized as one of the most important texts of late-twentieth-century Latin American literature with its "postmodern" blending of elite and mass culture texts, in particular, cinema, its fearless exploration of the limitations of fixed ideological positions, and the central place it gives to issues of homosexuality (Daniel Balderston has called it, "the founding text of a post-Stonewall gay literature in Latin America"[46]). The extract is published in *Plural* in its penultimate issue, June 1976, when there was still only an inkling that the spider webs of state power that entraps the central characters in the novel would also soon enmesh the magazine itself. *Plural* had also published an extract from Puig's previous novel, *The Buenos Aires Affair*, in issue 10, July 1972. This followed the pattern that defined most of the fiction published in *Plural*: extracts of novels appeared some months, or even years before their final publication in book form. Rodríguez Monegal also wrote a favorable review of it in *Plural* (issue 22, July 1973). It was a novel that found no favor at all in the heightened political climate of Argentina in late 1973 and early 1974. In January 1974 , the novel was banned as being pornographic. Puig had left Argentina in 1974 for fear of political reprisals against his family and himself and wrote *El beso* mainly in Mexico. This was a novel that was also banned in Argentina throughout the military dictatorship of 1976–1983. Here we see that *Plural* could offer a space to writers that were *non grata* in their own countries.

In an amusing letter to Tomás Segovia, dated 7 April 1972, Puig seeks to make sure that *Plural* will publish the revised version of his first chapter. He had given a first version to Paz in Harvard and had sent the revised version directly to Segovia in Mexico. He is looking to blame someone for his inadequate first draft: perhaps the pressure from publisher or former literary agent might be to blame. According to Puig's biographer, Jill Levine, Puig never quite forgave Barral and Balcells for not giving him enough support when his first novel, *La traición de Rita Hayworth* (*Betrayed by Rita Hayworth*) was to be published.[47] They become the butt of Puig's humor: "So I'd ask you to burn that other version in the Glorieta del Colón, so that it never appears, it's terrible and shouldn't see the light of day, maybe some enemy dictated it into my ear, perhaps Generalísimo Barral himself, or

Marchioness Balcells?" (Letter, Manuel Puig to Tomás Segovia, Buenos Aires, 7 April 1972). It is significant that, even though he has already published several critically acclaimed novels, Puig is still uncertain in the letter as to whether Paz will like the work and publish it.

Two of Puig's closest friends from the late sixties, the two Cuban exile writers Cabrera Infante and Sarduy, contribute to *Plural* with some regularity. Here one sees a continuity of interests with the writers that Emir Rodríguez Monegal had first supported from the pages of *Mundo Nuevo*. The magazine does not publish any writers from inside Cuba, not even Alejo Carpentier. And the magazine takes a cautiously anti-Cuban line, as we have seen earlier. Sarduy's published works are a mixture of his poems and prose poems (from *Big Bang*) and extracts from his novel *Cobra* (1972) and *Maitreya* (eventually published in 1978). His English translator, Jill Levine, offers an engaging portrait of Sarduy in the early seventies: "Severo, both as a person and as a writer, was a delightful brew of Baroque Cuban wit and French sophistication, with a cultural breadth akin to that of his good friend Roland Barthes. Barthes embraced Severo's third novel, *Cobra*, as an exemplar of his latest theory, elaborated in *The Pleasure of the Text*. What Manuel loved most about Severo was the equal pleasure that he seemed to take in sex and his *jeux de mots* and joie de vivre, his blend of *mulata rumbera* and avant-garde poet."[48] Even though *Plural* would publish Sarduy and the other persistent punster Cabrera Infante, the magazine's ethos was more "avant-garde poetry" than "mulata rumbera." Paz's sacred search, through Buddhism, or any form of sacred search, is far removed from the transvestites and leather fetishists that seek their nirvana on the streets of Amsterdam in Sarduy's *Cobra*. Paz's own treatise on the pleasure of reading, *El mono grámatico*, published at roughly the same time as Barthes's text gives the experience of pleasure and liberation, a woman's name, *Esplendor*, one woman, all women. Even though one can trace lineages of gay and lesbian writers in the pages of the magazine, it was not their sexuality but rather their value as writers that were highlighted. The experimentalism of Sarduy and Puig was supported by Rodríguez Monegal since the time of *Mundo Nuevo*, and most recently in his articles on the boom, though not all shared his views, as we saw in chapter four.

The other Latin American writer most closely associated with *Plural* in the second part of its short history was Mario Vargas Llosa. It was Vargas Llosa in particular who could partially locate the magazine within the orbit of the boom. In this period, Vargas Llosa was working on his comic novel about the military bureaucratic mind,

Pantaleón y las visitadoras (*Captain Pantoja and the Special Service*) and an extract from this novel was published in issue 21 (June 1973). It would show the reader that Vargas Llosa was exploring other terrains than the high seriousness and structural complexity of his novels of the sixties. Here he chose to offer a critique of the blinkered military mind through the weapons of parody and humor. The extract is taken from the moment in the novel when the recently promoted Captain Pantoja is given the orders for his mission by the upper echelons of the military: he must set up a mobile brothel in order to prevent the red-blooded young men of the Peruvian army stationed in the *selva* from turning their heterosexual desires into more "deviant" forms. Given the relatively long gestation period of novels, Vargas Llosa would contribute more to the magazine as an essayist than as a writer of fiction. It was, as we shall see, at the premiere of a screen adaptation of this novel that Vargas Llosa's famous parting of the ways with García Márquez would take place in February 1976.

García Márquez is absent from the magazine, although no particular inference should be drawn from this. Through all the period—1968 to 1975—that García Márquez was writing *El otoño del patriarca* (*The Autumn of the Patriarch*), after the runaway success of *Cien años de soledad* in 1967, he was not publishing fiction or journalism in any journals. After the publication of *El otoño* he famously remarked that he would not publish a novel until after Pinochet fell. Given Pinochet's endurance in power for some seventeen years, this was a promise that García Márquez would break. It was following the Chilean coup and his rapprochement with Cuba that he would begin again to write political journalism, but this coincided with the last months of *Plural* and the beginning of *Vuelta*. It would be in *Vuelta* that a political engagement with García Márquez would begin, which became more acerbic with the passing of the years. The Colombian writer who found most favor in the magazine was Alvaro Mutis—a friend of both Paz and García Márquez—who had been a long term resident in Mexico and was very well regarded by the Mexican intellectual community, with contacts across the political spectrum. We should remember that while the twenty-first century knows Mutis mainly as a successful novelist, he did not become established as a novelist until the mid-eighties, with the publication of *La nieve del almirante* (*Tae Snow of the Admiral* 1986). The pieces that *Plural* would infrequently publish were mainly prose poems, ("Lied" issue 58; also issue 43). *Plural* also published a fictional work entitled "El ultimo rostro," which can be seen as a precursor text to García Márquez's later novel on Bolívar, *El general en su laberinto* (*The General in his Labyrinth*, 1989).[49]

The most significant collection of fictional writers from Spain can be found in the special issue on Spain that was published in issue 25 (15 October 1973). Here there are extracts from several major novels: Juan Goytisolo's *Juan sin tierra* (*Juan the Landless*), Luis Goytisolo's *Recuento* ("Recount"), Juan Benet's *Horas en apariencia vacías* ("Empty Hours"), and Luís Martín-Santos's posthumous, uncompleted work, *Tiempo de destrucción* ("Time of Destruction"). This issue is edited by Pere Gimferrer and Julián Ríos and these two writers, along with the distinguished critic, J.M. Castellet, offer a clear and lucid explanation of what they perceive as the emergence of "new" literature in Spain. Castellet makes it clear that, for him, the term new or contemporary Spanish literature does not refer to the existence of a dynamic, coherent, and complex "literary field," but rather to the existence of certain writers and certain books that have opened up new possibilities in an overall barren landscape. Two significant moments in the development of the novel are outlined by the critics: the importance of Luis Martín-Santos's *Tiempo de silencio* (*Time of Silence*) published in 1962, and the increasing influence of Latin American writers in the sixties. The literary supplement section contains an appraisal of Martín-Santos and a reading of his posthumous novel, along with the publication of several extracts from this manuscript. At the planning stage for the special edition on Spain, Pere Gimferrer had written to Paz saying that Martín-Santos should be included, because he is "the real initiator... of the current revival of Spanish literature in all its forms" (Gimferrer to Paz, Barcelona, 18 June 1973).

Julián Ríos, in his introduction to the special issue, talks of the importance of the Latin American novel to those, like him, who had been born after the Spanish Civil War. He states: "*Our* contemporary literature was Paz, Cortázar, Lezama Lima, Fuentes, Sarduy... they were as much *ours* as they would be to an Argentine or a Peruvian reader."[50] For Ríos, an example of the bridge between Spain and Latin America was the friendship of Juan Goytisolo with key Latin American writers. Ríos is quite correct in pointing to the friendships that Juan Goytisolo had built up with key Latin American writers and his espousal as an honorary member of the boom by Carlos Fuentes. In his dedication to his novel, *Reivindicación del conde don Julián* (*Count Julian*, 1970), Goytisolo gave special thanks to Carlos Fuentes, Julio Cortázar, and Guillermo Cabrera Infante. We have already seen how Goytisolo tried to meld recent fiction in Spain with trends in Latin America through the pages of the short-lived, somewhat ill-fated magazine, *Libre*. In his autobiography, *Realms of Strife, 1957–1982*, he has mapped in great detail the fracturing of the intellectual community following the Padilla affair. As a result of this fracturing, he became more closely aligned with *Plural*.

Pere Gimferrer had already outlined in his letter to Paz of 18 June 1973 that the supplement would not contain many young fiction writers. He states quite bluntly, that leaving aside his coeditor, Julián Ríos, and himself, "The true new Spanish literature today...will come from writers born some forty years ago: Benet, Juan and Luis Goytisolo, Valente. We have been roundly disappointed with the work of younger writers. The hopes that existed—in 1969 and 1970—have come to nothing." When Gimferrer suggests to Paz that the supplement in the Spanish issue should be Martín-Santos's *Tiempo de destrucción*, he is not assuming that Paz already has prior knowledge of the importance of Martín-Santos. Gimferrer would also fulfill the role of interpreter of modern Spanish literature with an article on Juan Benet and other writers in later issues of *Plural*.

Some of Paz's closest contacts in Spain were publishers, often editors, like Gimferrer, who were involved in publishing Paz's voluminous work as a poet, essayist, and art critic. A writer close to Gimferrer, who published a book-length volume of interviews with Paz in 1973, Julián Ríos, also contributes to the magazine, organizing the Spanish special issue, writing notes for the supplement on Raymond Roussel, and publishing a "visual poem" in issue 25, and a fictional extract in issue 48 (September 1975). The work is dedicated to Paz and Paz finds an appropriate poetic image to describe the text: "traces of the sun's marks on the page...a long sentence that spreads out on the moving page of the beach covered bit by bit by the swelling tide of black ink on whose crests memory lights up its small fires." (Paz to Julián Ríos, 12 June 1975).

Paz was conscious of the lack of knowledge about Spanish letters in the broader Mexican public and also very aware of problems of distribution and censorship. For example, he asks the editor Carlos Barral to offer for publication an extract from Barral's memoirs— published in *Plural* 54—that is not too linked to specific Spanish people and events (Paz to Carlos Barral, Mexico, 3 March 1975). Indeed the whole issue of the book trade between Spain and Mexico was something that Paz would remark on frequently when, as the Franco regime entered into its final throes, issues of censorship became more acute. As Paz commented to Barral, Spanish publishers were not good at making their books available in Mexico and Mexican protectionist import laws also hindered the free circulation of ideas from Spain. (Paz to Barral, 3 March 1975). *Plural* pointed out in issue 48 (September 1975), as a prelude to a review of Goytisolo by Severo Sarduy, that the work of the Goytisolo brothers were faced with censorship in Spain. "*Juan sin tierra* by Juan Goytisolo was published by Seix Barral in Barcelona, but due to the express decision of the censors, it could not be distributed or sold. After a series of negotiations, the publishing house managed to obtain an export license for the book" (p.54). Luis Goytisolo's novel *Recuento* was published in Mexico, but was banned in Spain. In the final months of the dictatorship, censorship was as strong as ever.

Franco eventually died on 20 November 1975, after a lengthy illness. Anticipating his death by perhaps a few days, *Plural* 51 (December 1975), imagined a future Spain without Franco. Juan Marichal talks of the different options open in the transition to "another Spain" in the context of what he terms a "mesocratic modernization" of the country. He sees the affluence of the new middle class sectors that had emerged since the sixties as favoring a centrist political system, supported by a more progressive church, with military power much diminished and not likely to pose a threat. He talks about issues of federalism and predicts a republican future (pp.69–71). Juan Goytisolo, in an article written on 1 November 1975, three weeks before the death of Franco, speaks of the need to recover a voice. In a paragraph that could have been taken from *El otoño del patriarca*, published some months before, he talks of the need to give "expression" back to the people: to stop being "a country turned into deaf mutes by long, perennial, silence" (p.71). In the following issue of *Plural*, with Franco finally dead, Goytisolo writes, "In memoriam F.F.B. (1892–1975)" on 25 November 1975, five days after Franco's demise. He concentrates on the effect that Franco had on his generation of men and women, who were children during the Spanish Civil War, and the following generation, both of whom had spent almost their entire lives under the dictatorship. He talks of a devastating effect, a real "moral genocide." The options were either to emigrate or to "fall in with a situation that demanded of us silence or deception . . . Along with censorship, the regime created something worse: a system of self censorship and spiritual atrophy that has condemned Spaniards to the sinuous art of writing and reading between the lines, to always be aware of the existence of a censor invested with the monstrous power to mutilate them."[51] It was now the time to face up to the difficult task of teaching each and every Spaniard to think and act for themselves. Goytisolo sees his whole life as having been shaped by Franco. For him, Franco's death has come at least fifteen years too late. At that earlier time he was still enthusiastically caught up in debates about Spain and its progress. Now he finds himself to be a Spaniard, without any desire to be so, a Spaniard who is a Spaniard because he cannot be anything else.

Mexican Writers

A significant link between Spanish writers and Mexican writers was Carlos Fuentes, whose restless traveling and wide-ranging contacts found him frequently in Barcelona, where Gabriel García Márquez, Mario Vargas Llosa, José Donoso had taken up residence in the late sixties, and where Cortázar would be a frequent visitor from his Paris home. Fuentes would never live in Spain, but he had constant links with his novelist friends, with his agent Carmen Balcells, and with the Spanish writers—in particular Juan Goytisolo—especially associated with the "divine gauche." He was also very close to the Spanish exile community in Mexico, especially Luis Buñuel. In the first part of the seventies, his own fictional writing would be an extraordinarily ambitious novel that would finally be published under the title *Terra Nostra* in 1975. Ranging across time and space, the novel's main location is in the austere palace of El Escorial, where King Felipe is attempting to preserve a purity of race and of belief, while all around him heterodox forms and beliefs undermine this monological vision. In particular, the emblematic figures of Spanish literary history, Don Juan, Don Quixote, and Celestina play an important role in suggesting other forms, other ways of seeing. Fuentes would publish in *Plural* several short extracts from this work in progress that he initially called *Tantálo* (issue 4), then *Renacimiento* (issues 27 and 44), before finally deciding on the final title. The extract published in issue 4 based on a massacre of the *comuneros* in sixteenth-century Spain can be read as an allegory of a similar massacre that had taken place in Mexico only years earlier.

Another Mexican novelist in the throes of writing a gargantuan novel, Fernando del Paso, begins to publish in *Plural* in 1973, following an invitation from Octavio Paz. He remarked to Paz in a letter of 20 November 1972 that his work was taking a new direction after his novel *José Trigo* that had been published in 1966. Paz's letter found him working in London for the BBC after a two-year spell in the Writing Program at the University of Iowa. He describes his new approach to literature in the following terms: "In the novel I'm working on right now, humor and surrealism seem to be taking over in an uncontrollable fashion. It will be an ambitious, Rabelesian book, and, of course, a linguistic experiment" (Letter, Fernando del Paso to

Octavio Paz, 20 November 1972). The first extract published of what would eventually become chapter 21 of the novel *Palinuro de México* (*Palinuro of Mexico* 1977) would be an imagined meeting between the North American writer Ambrose Bierce—who had, in reality, traveled down to Mexico at the time of the Revolution and then disappeared— and Pancho Villa. In del Paso's version, the story is told to Palinuro by his grandfather who, it appears, was a captain in Villa's army and who serves in the story as both principle narrator and as an intermediary between Bierce and Villa trying to extract information from Bierce, who Villa believes is a spy working for his enemy Orozco. As another story within a story, del Paso imagines Bierce, the "Old Gringo" unafraid of his own death and seeking to rewrite the way one of his fictional characters, Parker Adderson had been executed as a prisoner of war in the U.S. civil war. In this way the literary imagination will triumph over physical death[52] ("Una bala muy cerca del corazón," *Plural* 19, pp.29–31). In a later letter to Paz, del Paso talks of the suc- cess of the story. He had met Fuentes in London, he says, recovering after an operation, and Fuentes had told him that Cortázar had enjoyed the story and that Fuentes himself had a "story about Ambrose Bierce" unpublished, in a drawer: "Now, he told me, he will have to bury it" (Del Paso to Paz, London, 1 July 1973). In the event it would take Fuentes some twelve years to unearth and develop his own story about Ambrose Bierce, which he published as *Gringo Viejo* (*The Old Gringo*) in 1985. More than a year later del Paso would introduce his two main characters Palinuro and Estefanía, his sister/cousin/lover/friend in a playful interlude discussing the nature of writing, in particular, the search for appropriate adjectives in a world in which adjectives had disappeared ("Una historia," *Plural* 33, pp.34–38). This extract is illustrated by del Paso's own drawings that were to be exhibited at the ICA in London in October 1973.

The two Mexican writers most closely identified with *Plural* were Salvador Elizondo and Juan García Ponce. They would become mem- bers of the Editorial Committee of the magazine and, as we have seen, would comment in the magazine on a whole range of cultural events and political developments. It is perhaps wrong to bracket Elizondo within the subheading, "writers of fiction" because he has always pointed out that he is bored by "literature," that his interest is in exploring the nature of "writing." In an interview with Elena Poniatowska published in *Plural* 45, he talks of his novel *Farabeuf* as a text "which does not have any climax or outcome, or which lacks the unities expected of a novelistic narration."[53] Instead, the search is for a "pure," "uncontaminated" art (p.33). This search reached its furthest limits in the text, *El grafógrafo*, and in *Plural* 14, Elizondo offers, as a lead article, a "Taller de autocrítica," discussing his work and imagining the ideal of the constant dialogue between criticism and writing: "the ideal would be to bring together in a single creative personality the poet and the critic, the one that sees and the one that is seen."[54] Sometimes that relationship between seeing and being seen is caught in the reflection of a mirror, reflecting not the world, but the process of writing itself, as in the famous phrase from *El grafógrafo*: "I am writing. I write that I am writing. Mentally I see myself writing that I am writing."

Juan García Ponce can also be seen as a writer's writer, as one of the main reviewers in *Plural*, José de la Colina, points out in a substantial article on the writer published in *Plural* 32 (May 1974). He states that García Ponce does not receive the critical acclaim of, say, a Rulfo or a Fuentes, but that his considerable oeuvre (nine novels and three books of short stories at the time of writing) does have a "modest number of very faithful readers" and a "timeless quality" that will ensure his lasting significance. He gives a brief overview of García Ponce's recent novels before focusing on his latest work, the novella *Unión*, which he sees as "a novel without psychology, almost without any reference to history and society, a novel about pure love and pure time, with characters that are no more than spirit."[55] The article is also illustrated by paintings from García Ponce's own private collection, works by Roger von Gunten, Vicente Rojo, Juan Soriano, and Rodolfo Zanabria, designed to his affinity with the work of contemporary artists, especially the formal elegance of a Vicente Rojo, or the eroticism of a von Gunten. The article quotes extensively from the novel, but this is the only direct quotation from García Ponce as a writer of fiction: his main presence in *Plural* would be as a cultural critic, in particular an art critic, and a book reviewer. But in the case of both Elizondo and García Ponce, the magazine gives directions on "how to read" these writers who formed the group of *solitarios solidarios* around Paz. Paz himself would point out in an early issue of *Vuelta* in a review of a novel that García Ponce first published in 1972, that the word innocence often comes up in Elizondo's work: "However, in almost all his novels and short stories, innocence is always allied to passions that we call *maudit* or perverse: cruelty, anger, excess, the delirium of an exasperated imagination, in short, the entire spectrum of pleasures that we disapprove of and yet, at the same time, fascinate us."[56]

There were, of course, other places where creative writers could get published, even within the umbrella of *Excélsior*. The newspaper *Excélsior* published its own supplement, *Diorama de la Cultura* and also a *Revista de Revistas*. Perhaps because the other publication came out weekly, writers were quite happy to publish there, rather than confront the rather more lengthy process of publishing in *Plural*. José de la Colina, talks of *Diorama de la Cultura* and *Plural* as "sister publications," "communicating vessels…Octavio and others, like Ibargüengoitia, Pacheco and I also collaborated in the other vessel, *Diorama*."[57] This is undoubtedly true, though José Emilio Pacheco, for example, published most of his essays, including a series entitled *Inventarios*, in *Diorama* rather than in *Plural,* although *Plural* would publish a story, "Tenga que se entretenga" in the June 1972 issue, which would appear later that year in his volume of short stories, *El principio del placer* (*The Pleasure Principle*), published by Joaquín Mortiz. In the same way, Ibargüengoitia would be a regular contributor to *Diorama* rather than to *Plural*. Elena Poniatowska would publish across a range of different magazines and supplements, and *Plural* would feature her work intermittently, including a short story "Los caballos" in issue 43. Only Augusto Monterroso, according to José de la Colina, would see the *Plural* project as too overblown for his tastes with the famous *boutade* that the magazine showed that the spirit is heavier than matter and that the magazine needed a cultural supplement in order to be comprehensible.[58]

Younger writers would appear in the magazine, but as essayists rather than as writer of fiction for the most part. Ignacio Solares, who worked in the editorial offices of *Plural* for a period, edited along with Esther Seligson and Carlos Montemayor, an anthology of young Mexican writers (born after 1940). Of the three editors, Esther Seligson appears most in the pages of *Plural*: she had had early success winning the Villaurrutia prize for 1973 for her fiction and she was also a well-published critic, showing an early interest in what would become a lifetime's work on Cioran who becomes known to a Latin American audience through the pages of *Plural*. All three editors would go on to have distinguished careers in the Mexican literary field and they had a good eye, according to Solares, at spotting the young talent of their generation. "We published in that issue a group of young writers: Gustavo Sainz, Agustín Monsreal, Carlos Montemayor, Hugo Hiriart, Ulises Carrión, Alejandro Aura, Federico Campbell, Esther Seligson, José Joaquín Blanco, Luis González de Alba, Daniel Leyva, Juan Tovar, José Agustín, Joaquín Xirau Icaza, Jorge Arturo Ojeda y otros."[59] Solares tells an amusing story that captures well Octavio Paz's enthusiasm for the magazine and his interest in monitoring its quality, even at a distance of several thousand miles. On occasion, when he worked in *Plural,* he would ring up

Paz in Harvard and read out every word of the next issue of the magazine, including all the commas and full stops. When it came to the special issue of young writers, Paz could not restrain his curiosity: "He asked us if he could have a look at the originals, just a quick look. We arrived at his flat in Río Lerma at seven in the evening and left after midnight. By that time he had read all the material out loud, expressing great enthusiasm and great disappointment. Every text, every line acquired with his voice a surprising significance that I am sure not even the author might have suspected."[60]

It is unclear from this anecdote of which young writers Paz approved. In a work published at the same time as the first issues of *Plural* in 1971, Margo Glantz edited a volume on the writers of what was known as "la onda."[61] In her introduction she talks about different tendencies among young writers, between novelists such as Sainz and Agustín who concentrated on vernacular writing, youth culture and protest, and urban stories, and more "writerly" options, personified in the work of Salvador Elizondo. Sainz is a writer who has some space in *Plural* as a critic as much as a writer of fiction. His early extract from what would become the novel *La princesa del Palacio de Hierro* (*The Princess of the Iron Palace*; the provisional title of the novel was initially *Paseo en trapecio*) was published as the lead contribution in the special edition of Mexican writers, while his fellow *onda* writer José Agustín appears later in the magazine with an extract entitled "Círculo vicioso." Sainz's novel would also be reviewed by Danubio Torres Fierro under the appropriate tagline, "La Molly Bloom defeña"[62] (*Plural* 39, December 1974, pp.84–86). In this review, Torres Fierro talks about the intentions of the *onda* group–colloquial language, urban culture—while seeing the narrative, a long monologue by the "princess"—a young woman working in Mexico City's most famous department store—as both inventive but ultimately rather monotonous.

José Agustín's published extract dealing with young men in prison on drug charges is based in part on Agustín's own experiences of having spent seven months in Lecumberri prison. He would later publish a novel and a play entitled *Círculo vicioso* in 1974. There was clearly, however, little rapport between Agustín and *Plural*. In his later survey of Mexican culture, Agustín would write of the elitism of *Plural*: "*Plural* made no attempt at all to honor its name and soon became a mafia comprising Gabriel Zaid, Enrique Krauze, Alejandro Rossi, José de la Colina, Ulalume González de León, Julieta Campos, Salvador Elizondo, Juan García Ponce and a few others that managed to attach themselves to the group, very elitist and as hermetic as the mysteries of Eulisis."[63] Later in the same study, he repeats the attack, stating that the name *Plural* was mere "wishful thinking," because in effect the magazine was an "unassailable fortress" (p.74). By contrast, Agustín has a good word to say about another *Excélsior* publication, the *Revista de Revistas* edited by Vicente Leñero, with its discussion of political and social issues. Salvador Elizondo is similarly parodied in a later novel by Agustín, *Cerca del fuego*, 1986, in a figure of fun entitled Dr. Salvador Elisetas. While some of Agustín's barbs are well-directed, others miss the mark: the image of the magazine as a fortress denying access to most Mexican writers is clearly overstated, as the above analysis has revealed.

Paz would have looked for different images to describe the magazine: building bridges across cultures perhaps, or opening windows to ventilate the stagnant air of populist nationalism, or translating. The image that we return to is that of the magazine title *Plural* that Agustín calls "wishful thinking." We have seen in these three chapters dealing with the content of the magazine that there was a correspondence between political and cultural criticism and the works of literature that the magazine published. The coherence was offered first of all by the drive of Octavio Paz himself: arguably no other writer in Latin America had the range and facility to cover so may areas and to keep alive debates within Mexico and in the wider world. A group of *solitarios/solidarios* formed around him. Together, they pursued a coherent, *critical*, intellectual, and aesthetic path which, in the highly ideological moment of the early seventies in Mexico and Latin America, would mean that certain writers would be excluded or would exclude themselves: maintaining a broad church would have been impossible, although the magazine did make some effort to publish dissonant and dissenting voices within its pages. Its pluralism is best expressed in its ability to communicate the world to Mexico and, to some extent, Mexico to the world while remaining true to international "avant-gardist" traditions.. Borges once wrote about the Argentine magazine *Sur* that its editor Victoria Ocampo "had a curious conception of a literary magazine and only wanted to publish texts by famous collaborators... and if a reader finds an article of forty pages signed Homer and another fifty page article signed Victor Hugo, that's just tedious."[64] Borges was being somewhat malicious here implying that Ocampo was something of a cultural head-hunter. He could not have leveled the same criticism at *Plural*: there are famous international names aplenty, but they are all there for a purpose, rather than as trophies. Together they form the magazine's own reading of contemporary politics and critical movements. The dialogue opened up between Mexican culture and the wider world defined the moment of *Plural*. And it was a dialogue that could still be conducted without too much discord, unlike the more openly polemical situation in Mexico a decade later. It is this movement from a certain fluid consensus to a hardening of positions that will be the subject of our final chapter.

Chapter 6

From *Plural* to *Vuelta*, 1976–1978

The *Excélsior* Affair

As a magazine published as part of the *Excélsior* newspaper group, *Plural*'s fortunes were tied to developments within that group. On 8 July 1976, in a fraught general Assembly meeting of the *Excélsior* cooperative, the editor Julio Scherer, along with a group of journalists loyal to him, were forced out of the *Excélsior* offices and out of the running of the newspaper.

In the pages of *Siempre!*, on 28 July, Paz and the members of the advisory committee of *Plural* printed their reaction to the internal coup: "Only an independent newspaper, like *Excélsior*, composed and written by free men and women, could publish a magazine devoted to criticism like *Plural*. We are thus indignant at the way in which *Excélsior* and its directors have been treated . . . It is impossible not to interpret what has happened as a sign that Mexico is moving towards the authoritarian darkness that covers almost all of our America."[1] This statement signaled the resignation of the *Plural* group: issue 58 bearing the date July 1976 was the last issue under Paz's directorship. *Excélsior* and *Plural* continued publication under a different editorial team, but Scherer and Paz would look to establish their own, independent magazines. The first issue of Scherer's weekly magazine *Proceso* appeared on 6 November 1976, while the first issue of Paz's new magazine, *Vuelta*, was dated December 1976 and was on sale from the middle of the previous month. At the same time, a former sub-director at *Excélsior*, Manuel Becerra Acosta was looking to found a new newspaper that would eventually be published in 1977 as *Unomásuno*.

How had the *Excélsior* crisis developed? A number of different accounts have been published that all point to the complicity of the Echeverría government in the process.[2] Echeverría, meanwhile, would keep insisting on his innocence despite widespread condemnation at home and abroad.[3] Why should the government choose this moment to act against *Excélsior*? Reports at the time suggest that even though there had been an uneasy alliance throughout the *sexenio* between "the two powers," in Becerra Acosta's phrase, matters became worse as *Excélsior* became more outspoken in its criticism of the government. Some commentators point to an incident on 14 March 1975, when the president had been attacked in UNAM by students hurling missiles. Even though the newspaper denounced the students, it also gave space for the student demands and showed photos of the president's slight head wound.[4] Others highlight the newspaper's opposition to Mexico support in late 1975 of the UN resolution that equated Zionism with racism and of helping to force the resignation of the Secretary of Foreign Relations, Emilio Rabasa.[5] If, early in 1976 Poniatowska could write that *Excélsior* was "an opposition authorized or at least tolerated by the government,"[6] it soon became clear that this tolerance was wearing thin. We remember the dinner at Daniel Cosío Villegas's house analyzed in chapter three, in which it was very clear that Echeverría did not see the difference between intellectuals serving power and intellectuals maintaining their critical independence, despite Octavio Paz's subtle distinctions.

There are many ways that newspapers can be put under pressure that fall short of direct sanctions. Two have been used quite frequently: the control of advertising, the main source of a newspaper's revenue, and the control of the price of paper, in Mexico a government monopoly. In 1972, the Comité Coordinador Empresarial (The Business Coordinating Committee), which represented organizations in the private sector felt that *Excélsior* was moving too far to the left. According to a statement given to Scherer by the head of the Committee, Juan Sánchez Navarro, Echeverría had suggested to them that they should withdraw advertising from the newspaper: this was the solution that they had readily available to them. But when the private boycott began to take effect, Echeverría arrived with a solution to the impasse: the government would offer advertising for state enterprises and thus stem the dwindling profits of the *Excélsior* cooperative. Faced with the government blocking the boycott that it had itself suggested, the private sector began advertising in *Excélsior* once again after a few months. Echeverría could claim in this way to be the champion of free speech. As he argued years after the *Excélsior* coup: "When *Excélsior* attacked Mexican businessmen from a Christian democrat point of view, they withdrew advertising from the newspaper. Thanks to the intervention of Licenciado Horacio Flores de la Peña, the magazine was given advertising for the Ciudad Sahagún complex and other state organizations."[7] The other area open to censorship, the cost of paper, would become significant when Paz and Scherer looked to set up new magazines in the aftermath of the events of July 1976.

Let us look more closely at the events leading up to the 8 July 1976. *Excélsior*, which was run as a cooperative, had purchased lands in Paseos de Taxqueña in the south of the city. They had compensated the former *ejido* owners with property in the states of Hidalgo and Veracruz, in 1959, as well offering a lump sum payment of 25 million pesos in 1974. Sure of their property rights, therefore, Scherer and others looked to develop this land. There was talk, for example, of moving the main editorial offices out of the center into this area and building a new industrial complex. However, on 10 June 1976, the *diputado* Humberto Serrano connected to the government Agrarian Reform Ministry invaded the Paseos de Taxqueña at the head of several hundred peasants, and claimed that these people had been illegally deprived of their land and would continue to occupy the land until they received some settlement. When asked whether this occupation was a government maneuver, Echeverría would avoid the question and say that: "If the cooperative had not been divided, but had been strong and united as in the past, they would have been able to deal with the situation."[8] Of course, it seemed that the government dirty tricks department was doing all that it could to create or exploit any divisions. The mass media, especially Televisa, made much of the occupation, painting Serrano as a latter day Emiliano Zapata. The leader of the agrarian reform ministry, Augusto Gómez Villanueva, stated that he could not intervene. Within *Excélsior*, a faction led by the editor of the evening section of the newspaper, Regino Díaz Redondo, looked to exploit this disquiet, and there were stories that the directors of the newspaper, through their intransigence, were endangering the patrimony of the workers and their families. Becerra Acosta lays a great deal of blame on Díaz Redondo and was greeted— when his book, *Dos poderes*, that contains these accusation, came out in 1985—to an extraordinarily virulent attack by Díaz Redondo on the front page of *Excélsior* (28 January).[9]

A number of those who participated in the assembly of the *Excélsior* cooperativists on 8 July pointed out that many people who were not members of the cooperative attended. These people seemed peculiarly reminiscent of the *halcones* paramilitary groups that were responsible for the 1971 massacre. They were wearing straw hats and other insignia that seemed to mark them out as a separate group, and they drowned out any discussion by jeering and creating an intimidating physical presence. According to Miguel Angel Granados Chapa, the Scherer group decided to leave the building before they were thrown out: "I think we were right to do so, because if we hadn't, there would have been fatalities...In *Excélsior* there were secret agents and police, so we could not call the police because they were already inside, not to protect us or restore order, but to attack us."[10] With Scherer out of the building, Díaz Redondo was elected as the new editor of the newspaper and the next day the paper contained an attack on the previous editor accusing him of embezzling funds and acting with unbridled power. His removal was, therefore, an "historic day, a day for rejoicing." A few days later, Echeverría would issue the first of his many denials: that what had happened in the newspaper was an internal matter and that the government had not intervened in any way. No one believed him of course, a feeling only reaffirmed when the occupation of the Paseos de Taxqueña land ended soon afterward, and the new directors eventually sold off the land, yielding a great profit.

Within days the incident had become a major national and international scandal. It was the correspondent of the *Washington Post*, Marlise Simons and Alan Riding of the *New York Times* who first covered the news of the internal coup. Simons wrote on 7 July that *Excélsior* was suffering a government-led campaign to overthrow Scherer. On 9 July Riding spoke of a conservative take-over of the newspaper, with the aid of President Echeverría, thus silencing independent opinion in Mexico. He also mentioned Paz's resignation. On 11 July Simons repeated the view that the coup had been orchestrated by Echeverría and she points out that sources had told her that Díaz Redondo was conspiring with government officials to bring down Scherer and that he had a government war chest to buy votes in the cooperative. There were further articles on the topic on 13 and 14 July. On 14 July the *Post* argued that what was not clear was whether Echeverría had moved against the paper for political reasons or to help consolidate his own financial interests in a rival newspaper consortium. Echeverría was a shareholder in Organización Editorial Mexicana (The Mexican Publishing Organization) that was looking to gain monopoly power over a number of newspapers, including *El Sol* and *El Universal* in Mexico City.

Perhaps goaded by this international response, Echeverría declared on 14 July, as quoted by *La Cultura en México*, that only U.S. newspapers, doubtless upset at his nationalist policies, were looking to blacken his name. No Mexican publications or media outlets had mentioned the case. He was wrong, because on 28 July, a number of declarations appeared in Mexico. Along with Paz's declaration on behalf of *Plural* in *Siempre!*, over two hundred intellectuals covering the whole cultural field signed a declaration published in *La Cultura en México*—the cultural supplement of that newspaper—praising the work of *Excélsior* (including the Sunday supplement *Diorama de La Cultura* and also *Plural*) and calling into question the "climate of public freedom" that Cosío had referred to in a tentative fashion back in 1971. *Excélsior* is seen as, "the most fertile adventure of the past decade, a high point of an organization that could express the demands of a well informed, uninhibited and free public consciousness."[11]

The events of 8 July took place a few days after López Portillo had been ratified as the next president of Mexico: he was to take up his post on 1 December. Echeverría was looking for life after the presidency in terms of securing the upcoming Secretary General of the UN post. He had also been put forward for the Nobel Peace Prize and was constructing a Third World Study Center in San Jerónimo near his house that he was looking to direct (this was opened in September 1976 by Kurt Waldheim, the Secretary General of the UN). A national and international scandal did not fit well with his future plans at home or abroad. Becerra Acosta states that the president called in the deposed group and first of all told Scherer that he should not fly to Washington to plead his case as an editor-in-exile. The president could only have known about this upcoming visit by bugging his phone.[12] The president said that he would investigate the cooperative meeting to see if it was illegal, but this was seen as a way of delaying and deflecting unpalatable actions, as had happened previously on 10 June 1971, the Corpus Christi affair. It was only under the next president, López Portillo, that a return to *Excélsior* might have been a possibility for Scherer.[13]

It became a matter of pride for Scherer to relaunch his team of journalists in a new, weekly magazine, *Proceso*, before the end of the Echeverría *sexenio*. He states that the government tried to stop him through direct threats from two high ranking government officials, Mario Moya Palencia and Javier Alejo. It was also very difficult to find a printer willing to bring out the magazine: in the event, Guillermo Mendizábal offered his now ageing printing press. The paper supplier, PIPSA, refused to sell them any paper and it was left to Fernando Canales, the editor of *Novedades*, to secretly supply the new enterprise with paper. It came out in time to launch a swingeing attack on Echeverría in the last weeks of his regime.

Vuelta: The Early Years

Octavio Paz was similarly committed to keeping up the impetus of *Plural*. But without the resources of *Excélsior*, this would be a difficult enterprise. Brazilian critic Tânia Maria Piacentini has interviewed a number of those involved in the early gestation of *Vuelta*. Alejandro Rossi maps out the situation: "There were two sources of money, one was the Tamayo painting that was raffled and produced a small amount of capital, no, there were three things really: the painting, the generous donation of some members of *Vuelta,* not extraordinary amounts, but sums that made a real difference. Then we picked up bits and pieces here and there and we were lucky to find a printer, Mendizábal, who had a small publishing company, and he charged us very little. It wasn't great quality printing, it was right at the limit of what was tolerable, what was legible."[14] *Proceso* and *Vuelta* would thus use the same printing press when their first issues came out at roughly the same time with the support of Mendizábal. With Sakai having moved the previous year to a post in the United States at the University of Texas in Austin, a young graphic artist, Abel Quezada Rueda, volunteered to design the first issues. He has talked about the poor quality of the paper that could be afforded and of the low production standards in first issues of the magazine due to lack of finance. Celia García Terrés—who had worked with Paz in the foreign ministry and was also a family friend—was asked by Paz to run the administration of the project. She also spoke to Piacentini about handling all the finances in the first years, running the administration on a shoestring initially, living hand to mouth: "The typewriter we used belonged to Octavio and he would always ask us to give him back his typewriter, so I said to him, you choose, you can either write or publish. That was of course until we got another machine and solved that problem."[15] All the contributors talk of rallying around to produce the magazine: Rossi acted as an interim director while Paz was teaching in Harvard, whilst José de la Colina acted as managing editor until Rossi invited Enrique Krauze to join the group from the fourth issue, in February 1977. Krauze was to become a central figure in the magazine from that moment bringing entrepreneurial experience as well as his training as a historian and as a commentator on contemporary affairs.

The first issue of *Vuelta* appeared some four months after Paz's resignation from *Plural*. The cover—the colors of the Mexican flag with a fold in the middle, presumably representing the turning of a page—proclaimed "Estamos de Vuelta", ("We are Back") with Paz's name underneath. The title, we note, is the same as that used by Paz for an anthology of his own poetry published by Seix Barral in Barcelona some months earlier in 1976, which covered the period from his return to Mexico in 1971. The title poem written in 1971 seems very relevant to the situation Paz and the writers faced. In the claustrophobic city, with its bureaucratic stagnation—"in the mailboxes/letters rot"—there was a sense of fracture and loss, of a world out of order: "languages in pieces / the signs were broken." Did I win or lose, the poet asks? The answer comes when he stresses the need for constant engagement, for continuing the journey, for the poet needs to be engaged: "I don't want / an intellectual hermit / in San Angel or Coyoacán."[16]

There is thus once again—we remember the title of the journal *El Hijo Pródigo* that had earlier suggested a correspondence between Paz's poetry and the journals that he contributed to—a very explicit link made between Paz's own poetic project and his work as an editor. The second page of the magazine contained the signatures of the entire editorial committee, the former stalwarts of *Plural*: José de la Colina, Salvador Elizondo, Juan García Ponce, Octavio Paz, Alejandro Rossi, Kazuya Sakai, Tomás Segovia, and Gabriel Zaid. Paz makes the continuity explicit: "*Vuelta,* as its name implies, is not a beginning but a return. In October 1971, a journal appeared, *Plural*. It continued, against the odds, for almost five years; when it reached issue 58, it disappeared; now it reappears, under a different name. Is it the same? Yes and no. The editorial board, the contributors and the intentions are the same."[17]

Paz excoriates the magazine still bearing the name of *Plural* published by *Excelsior*: it is not even a caricature, but rather a falsification of the original. A brief consideration of issue 59 of *Plural* published in August 1976 by new management of *Excélsior* shows how different the content had become, even though the new editorial team retained the same name, the same cover design, and the same categories *Crítica/Arte/Literatura*. It was obviously a rushed edition, but the whole tone is diametrically opposed to everything that *Plural* had looked espouse: it is overtly populist, anti-imperialist and third worldist. Articles denounce U.S. foreign policy and talk of fascism in Latin America. The Cuban critic Angel Augier offers an account of the Cuban revolution in the poetry of Nicolás Guillén (who had never been mentioned in the previous 58 issues of the magazine). There is a radical manifesto from Chomsky and an analysis of John Reed, "soldier of the Mexican Revolution." The artistic supplement focuses on an exhibition by the artist Enrique Estrada in the Poliforum, and a range of photos of his work, described as "graphic documents which focus on the most violent phase of political and revolutionary life in Mexico."[18] Solemn, somber, realist paintings of Zapata and Villa stare out at the reader as a reminder of Mexico's revolutionary roots. While the new *Plural* would later garner more respectable, regular columnists, it would maintain the same explicit nationalist, revolutionary focus, and many of the writers who had never appeared in Paz's day would parade their "Latin American," revolutionary credentials. It is little wonder that Paz sees the magazine as an irritation, a deliberate assault on his values.

Paz also enters the political debate by speculating as to the government's responsibility in the *Excélsior* "coup": "It is not easy to measure this responsibility, but it seems to me unquestionable that the coup would not have taken place if its instigators had not relied on at least the tacit support of government Power" (p.4). He goes on to analyze the current political situation, saying that the *Excélsior* affair had been disastrous for the government and for the nation. Bad for the government because, after vaunting their respect for open criticism for six years, it had closed down one the very few organizations committed to critical opinion in the country. Bad for the country because it coincided with a crisis in political parties: "the left is paralyzed by a dogmatic tradition and by its Stalinist past. The right does not exist, at least as political thought. We repeat once again: our obtuse right wing does not have ideas, only interests" (p.4). In this way the government grows at the expense of society. "Left and right, the union leader and the banker, the journalist and the bishop, all live prostrate in front of the Presidential Chair. That is why the *Excélsior* affair is so important: who will now criticize Power and the powerful?" (p.4).

Paz goes on to discuss the magazine's readership. He points out that *Plural* had always been accused of being "elitist" and had been constantly attacked from both right and left. This, he felt, was the fate of any living and lively magazine. But he had been very agreeably surprised at the interest and loyalty of their readers: "Never in the history of Spanish American literature has a literary magazine had so many and such attentive readers" (p.4). Putting its faith in this alert and curious readership that had been attracted to the independent vision of *Plural*, *Vuelta* had decided to go it alone trusting in the help and friendship of its readers.

As the first feature in the "Letras, letrillas, letrones" section (pp.46–47), the magazine reviews the press coverage of the *Excélsior* coup. The article argues that whereas most of the national press refused to publish the *Plural* statement in favor of Scherer and his group written on 7 July 1976, the international press had taken a great interest in this issue of press censorship. It quotes extracts of articles published in support of *Excélsior* and *Plural* from publications in Venezuela, Colombia, Buenos Aires, the United Kingdom and the

United States. It gives particular prominence to a letter published in the *NYRB*, which condemned the coup, blamed Echeverría, and encouraged readers to write to Echeverría to express their protest. The letter is signed by Hugo Estenssoro, Woody Allen, Noam Chomsky, Elisabeth Hardwick, John Kenneth Galbraith, Carey McWilliams, Arthur Miller, Philip Roth, Arthur M. Schlessinger Jr., I.F. Stone, and Gore Vidal, many of whom had been published in *Plural*. Reference is also made to comments in *Cambio 16* in Madrid, *Le Monde* in Paris, and the German newspaper *Die Zeit*. The magazine then maps out its community of friends and collaborators by printing the name of all the individuals from Mexico and abroad who supported *Plural*'s declaration or else sent individual messages. The feature ends with an elegant statement by Cioran, who talks about the range of *Plural* in contrast to the narrow provincialism of France and other countries in western Europe. "*Plural* was a reproach to the lack of curiosity shown in the West, a challenge, an elegant slap" (p.47).

The articles published in this first issue follow the format established by *Plural* over the previous five years: a blend of essays, fiction, poetry, book reviews, and art criticism. Italo Calvino's "Diálogo con Moctezuma" is the lead piece. This is followed by a short story by Jorge Luis Borges and Adolfo Bioy Casares penned by their parodic alter ego Bustos Domecq. The story has the evocative title of "El enemigo número uno de la censura," and, in a style that hyperbolizes the affectations of minor literary figures, imagines a literary world without any form of censorship (or critical intervention), where literally everything submitted to a publication is published. Of course, in such a Funes world of unclassified, unmediated freedom, freedom is tantamount to chaos.[19] The grant runs out for this first "Open Anthology of National Literature" half way through entries for the letter "a." The editorial group of the magazine makes a strong showing with a poem by Tomás Segovia, "El solsticio," a series of deliberations on the act of writing by Salvador Elizondo and an appreciation of the poetry and fiction of the Cuban writer José Lezama Lima. Kazuya Sakai writes on the fifteenth century text, *Libro de la transmisión secreta de la Flor*, a series of deliberations on poetics and the art of stagecraft of Noh theater by the Japanese Zeami. Two regular political commentators, Rafael Segovia and Gastón García Cantú, write on different aspects of the Mexican political and legislative systems. Both essays imply a critique of the current government and have words of warning for the next *sexenio*. Segovia states: "To silence criticism through silence or half truths is the worst temptation for a political class in crisis" (p.29). Alejandro Rossi supplies another entry in his "Manual del distraído," a rather more nimble parody of posturing literary figures than the rather self-indulgent tones of Bustos Domecq.

The review section contains two reviews by Pacheco, including a consideration of the work of the Colombian cultural journal *Mito* (1956–1962), in which Pacheco shows his enthusiasm for the work of little magazines. There are also two entries in the "Libros/Letras, letrillas, letrones" sections by Enrique Krauze. There are several reviews of artists and exhibitions, including an appreciation of Sakai's latest work by Jorge Alberto Manrique. The first organizations running advertisements in the magazine were UNAM, El Colegio Nacional, and different publishing houses including Fondo de Cultura Económica, Siglo XX1, Joaquín Mortiz ,and Monte Avila, along with bookshops and galleries. Advertisements and sales were all that the magazine had to survive on, as it sought to establish what Paz, in an interview with Elena Poniatowska in October 1976, would call his desire to, "find a greater financial independence, and the greatest autonomy possible from institutions. In general culture in Mexico is subject to the vicissitudes of politics or the protectors of culture. The best thing for any magazine is gradually to create the conditions that can sustain it."[20] These conditions could only be achieved through consolidating a readership. Paz went on to reiterate to Poniatowska that the new magazine would, like *Plural*, publish original works of literature, analyze Mexican and world culture, and "reflect on" what is happening "in the world and in our country." Let us follow these strands for the first two years of the magazine, as it establishes itself as an independent publication. We will end the study with an analysis of issues 21–24 (August to November 1978).

Between 1976 and 1978, Paz's interest in Mexican politics and in particular his critique of the left continues unabated. The magazine supported Carlos Fuentes when he resigned his Ambassadorship in Paris in April 1977 in protest at the appointment of Díaz Ordaz as Ambassador to Spain. Indeed the appointment of Díaz Ordaz caused a furious response from many, including Mexican writers such as Poniatowska and Monsiváis. Within a fortnight, Díaz Ordaz had resigned his post due to "ill health." Gabriel Zaid, Fuentes's erstwhile critic, defended Fuentes's actions and ridiculed the aspirations of Díaz Ordaz to represent Mexico in the diplomatic service.[21] In an article published the previous month, Poniatowska also gave an account of the protests that occurred in Mexico City in April 1977 at the appointment of Díaz Ordaz.[22] In the middle of this uproar over Díaz Ordaz, the new president López Portillo announced a reform of the electoral system in order to combat electoral abstention and offer opposition parties some official channels, including 25 percent of the seats in

Congress. New registration laws also allowed the Communist Party
to take part in elections for the first time since 1946, and there was a
limited possibility for different left-wing parties to form alliances. It
would be these reforms that Paz would later comment on in his essay
"el ogro filantrópico."

Another incident was more discordant within the intellectual field.
On 7 July 1977, the police were called in to the University City to
break a strike by STEUNAM, the UNAM Workers' Union. Responses
to this action varied. From the pages of *La Cultura en México* (20 July
1977), José Joaquín Blanco, Luis Miguel Aguilar, and Carlos Monsiváis
resigned from the editorial board of the *Revista de la Universidad de
México*. Paz, by contrast, argues that the Rector's hand was forced by
the intransigence of the union. He then goes on to state that the
union's actions reflected a wider problem of the lack of political debate
and political parties in Mexico. This situation was the fault of the PRI,
but it was also due to the atrophy of debates on the right and the left.
He points out that the intellectuals he published in *Plural* and now in
Vuelta could offer a nuanced liberal position: "In fact the most pene-
trating social and political criticism has been formulated by liberals
like Cosío Villegas or by writers with an intellectual perspective far
removed from the left, like Gabriel Zaid and Rafael Segovia. The intellectual sterility of the left has been as great as its incapacity to organize
itself and come together. There is a lack of ideas and a lack of leaders."[23]
In a provocative last paragraph, he returns to the dispute in the university and declares that a number of those who signed petitions against
the police action really thought that the strike was ridiculous, but they
protested anyway, as a sort of knee-jerk reaction.

Perhaps Paz was referring directly to Carlos Monsiváis in this aside.
In the event, Monsiváis replied to Paz's barbs when Paz reprised the
ideas contained in this article in a long interview with Julio Scherer
published in *Proceso* 57 and 58 (5 and 12 December 1977). Paz had
been awarded the Premio Nacional de Literatura and Scherer chose
this moment to record an extensive conversation with Paz covering
the trajectory of his political career. The second part of the interview
(*Proceso* 58) is entitled, "I see an absence of plans. Ideas have evapo-
rated." In it Paz warns against the power of the state, that he calls a
"cold monster" (his most famous metaphor is still some months away
from its definitive formulation). Answering a question from Scherer
about criticism, he contrasts the "severe and polite" criticism of a
Gabriel Zaid with the "howls of so many jackals" that inhabit the
world of literature (p.8). He then goes on to talk about "young radi-
cals, not without talent" who had attacked "liberal intellectuals" in a
special issue of the cultural supplement of *Siempre!* Later he refers to

the left in general as "muttering and rude," a group that "thinks little and talks a lot. A left without imagination." He contrasts the flexibility of Euro socialism with the stagnation of thinking in Mexico.

Monsiváis answered this direct provocation and over the next several issues of *Proceso*, a lively debate ensued.[24] The exchange is a mixture of choice invective but also of interesting discrepancies. For Paz, Monsiváis, "is a man full of jokes rather than ideas." Even now that he is supposedly discussing openly, he still uses "a method akin to 'amalgamation': isolating a paragraph from the main text, conferring on it absolute status and then condemning the author" (*Proceso* 61, 29). For Monsiváis, Paz is a great writer and poet, but he is prey to his obsessions: he looks to show that his opponents are Stalinist and intolerant by distorting, inventing, or decontextualizing their arguments. He has a mania for generalizations and for rounded phrases, his arguments are authoritarian, generalist, and dogmatic. Within these ritualistic insults, there is a genuine difference of opinions. Paz does not back away from his overall disappointment with the left and his critique of the PRI. Monsiváis looks to criticize some aspects of the dogmatic left, but he also says that these are very small in contrast to the "caciques, the latifundio system…the electoral fraud, intimidation, depoliticization as a means of personal safety, the control of workers' unions, the persecution and frequent assassination of independent leaders."[25] For Monsiváis, Paz represents a mandarin intellectual who is now being replaced by the view of the writer as just another worker: "The time when poets and writers were seen as olympian or celestial lightning conductors has now passed and with the decline of these mandarin intellectuals and their monopoly over Critical Consciousness, a process of cultural democratization can take place."[26]

This exchange published in Scherer's *Proceso* was reprinted in one of the first issues of *Nexos*, a cultural journal that started publishing in early 1978, a few months after the appearance of the newspaper *Unomásuno*. *Nexos* would come to be a space that would be seen as an alternative forum to *Vuelta*. The debate also received a great deal of press coverage and for several commentators, it triggered a more outspoken engagement with Paz. The Spanish writer Fernando Savater would preface an interview with Paz in April 1979 by writing that, "the assassination and devouring of father Paz is now a rite of passage for young Mexican intellectuals…They watch over him, make demands of him, insult him: today, in Mexico, writing, thinking creating always means, in some form or another, taking on Octavio Paz."[27] One should be careful here, not to see Paz in some sort of victim role: he greatly enjoyed polemic, he was quite happy to engage in confrontation, even to provoke it. And the history of *Vuelta*, especially from the late seventies, would see increasing polemic across a series of political issues and with individual writers. But that is a chapter in another book.

An early intimation of a more polarized intellectual field can be seen in an exchange between Danubio Torres Fierro and Julio Cortázar. Throughout the *Plural* period Cortázar could publish in the magazine without his increasingly radical politics becoming an area of discussion or contention: old friendships, it seemed, could override political difference. There was space for "plural" difference. This was to change in *Vuelta*. Torres Fierro wrote a long review of Cortázar's volume of short stories, *Alguien que anda por ahí*, in issue 11 of *Vuelta*[28] (October 1977). He makes a distinction between Cortázar as a "narrator of fantasy" and as a "denunciatory narrator" arguing that when he writes about politics, his art suffers. Cortázar is splendid when he talks about "life," but fails when he talks about "reality." For the reviewer, life and reality are not the same thing: literature concerns itself with life, but it has little or no connection with reality (p.36). While Torres Fierro understands Cortázar's engagement with the horrors of the Argentine dictatorship, he is less forgiving about his adherence to Cuba and also in his inability openly to denounce the Soviet Union. In a series of rather provocative asides, he says that Cortázar practices a "kind-hearted, rose colored social-ism," and that his political opinions are "naïve and clumsy," either unsustainable or indefensible (p.37). In the book under review, Torres Fierro approves of the short story published in *Vuelta* 7, "Usted se tendió a su lado," but denigrates several other stories which he con-siders to be "denunciatory." This is a direct assault on Cortázar, an assault with a very clear political intent.

In the same issue of the magazine, Torres Fierro provides a ten-page interview with Guillermo Cabrera Infante, the central feature in the magazine. Although the interview mainly offers an engaging account of Cabrera Infante's literary development focusing mainly on *Tres tristes tigres*, there are still sufficient references to tyranny and censorship to remind readers of the magazine's consistent anti-Castro sentiments. When Cabrera talks of the lack of intellectual freedom and the absence of dissident voices within Cuba—comparing Cuba to Bulgaria in its tight control of all aspects of society (p.22)—he paints a portrait of an oppressive society that Torres Fierro, some pages later, would accuse Cortázar of supporting. Torres Fierro's review also fol-lows Emmanuel Ladurie's analysis of Boris Suvarin's famous biography of Stalin written in the thirties, one of the first and most detailed denunciations of Stalinist tyranny. There is thus a sequence that goes from Cuba, a tin-pot, "Bulgarian" tyranny, to a critique of Stalin, to a critique of Cortázar as a foolish fellow traveler of the Soviet Union, still enamored of Caribbean dictators. In a later issue of *Plural* (issue 14), Juan Goytisolo also attacked Cortázar for stating that the Soviet Union was going through a "phase or moment" which could be read as negative, but did not constitute a fatal flaw in the system. How, for Goytisolo, can the Gulag, the purges, the state bureaucracy, be seen as mere "accidents en route?"[29]

Cortázar responded explicitly to Torres Fierro's review, and implicitly to Goytisolo, in issue 15.[30] He declares that he never answers critics publicly but that he feels compelled to do so given the ideas being mooted about the nature of Latin American literature (Cortázar, in fact, is quite willing on occasion to respond to criticism: see his polemic with David Viñas in the Argentine magazine *El Escarabajo de Oro*, 46, June 1973, when Viñas accuses him of "sanctifying" Paris). He reaffirms his commitment to socialism, "because socialism as a *plan for reality* is the only decent road for history to take" (p.48). While condemning the violation of human rights in the USSR, he argues that these can be corrected, whilst the abuses of capitalism are inherent to the capitalist system. He then goes on to ridicule Torres Fierro's affirmation that life and reality are not the same thing and that literature has no truck with reality. He uses as a counter argument the fact that within two years of his writing his story, "Apocalípsis en Solentiname," the national guard of the Somoza dictatorship in Nicaragaua had invaded the Christian community in Solentiname organized by the poet-priest Ernesto Cardenal amongst a group of agricultural workers and fishermen. The community was destroyed and Cardenal had been forced into exile. The story had anticipated some of these outcomes, which Cortázar had based in part on his own experiences living in the community. Cortázar argues that the events in Solentiname are an irrefutable proof of the necessary and constant osmosis between writing and reality, between art and reality: "and if that is not *life*, please tell me what it is?" (p.49). He regards the latest critical trends that just talk of text as text, as shameful elitism, unmasked in such arguments that the presence of immediate reality has no place in creative works. For Cortázar, by contrast, literature is life and reality and art blended in a single "dizzying operation." After this response, *Vuelta* publishes a conversation between Cortázar and Saúl Yurkievich about poetry and fiction (*Vuelta* 17), but after that, Córtazar never published in the magazine. In an obituary for Cortázar published in *Vuelta* 88, March 1984, Paz talks about the "fervor and naiveté" with which Cortázar embraced politics from the late sixties, taking up positions that Paz thought "reprehensible." "I stopped seeing him, but never stopped liking him. I think that he, also, never stopped being my friend. Through the barriers of words and paper that separated us, we showed signs of friendship" (p.5). Certainly a significant "barrier of words and paper" was the Torres Fierro review. Interestingly, also, the polemic focused on a story set in Nicaragua. The views on Nicaragua and El Salvador expressed in the magazine from the late seventies would also spark important controversies.

There is a danger here of retrospective readings, to bring into play the reviews in *Vuelta* that would cause rifts with Carlos Fuentes and Elena Poniatowska in the 1980s. While one can see an increasingly polemical attitude in my defined period, up to the second anniversary of the magazine, the major rifts take place after this time. Perhaps what we are observing is an increasing drift away from the "plural" model, toward more clearly defined confrontation. There are fault lines here in the intellectual community that are waiting to open up. At this moment, both Poniatowska and Fuentes publish quite regularly in *Vuelta*. Fuentes publishes two short stories, "El día de las madres" ("Mother's Day") in issue 4 and "Estos fueron los palacios" ("These Were the Palaces") in issue 12,—family dramas set in different areas of Mexico City later published in his celebrated collection of four interlocking stories, *Agua quemada* (*Burnt Water*, 1981 the epigraph is taken from Paz's poem "Vuelta"). Soon after his resignation from the Ambassadorship in Paris, he begins to write what is announced in issue 13 as a monthly column entitled "Diario de ayer y hoy" ("Yesterday's and Today's Diary"), covering a range of topics from Buñuel to Pinochet. He does not keep quite to a monthly column, but this is the period of his closest cooperation with any magazine edited by Paz. He remembers his time as an Ambassador in Paris through his appreciation of the former Minister of Culture, Françoise Giroud who, less than a year after leaving politics—at the same time as Fuentes—wrote a book entitled *La Comédie du pouvoir*.[31] Fuentes had already lived through the "comedy of power" for several years, attacked for his adherence to Echeverría, attacked for joining the diplomatic service. He remembers his final night in Paris, a dinner with Giroud, Galbraith and others—"before returning to Mexico, to its vicious cannibalism, compared to which French politics is a delicate pavane" (30). In Giroud's book and in her personal integrity, Fuentes finds an answer to his critics: state officials are not strong figures representing an all powerful "tutelary Father": they are just more or less intelligent people trying to make a difference: In Giroud's words, "the king and his court are naked; the sooner we recognize this, the sooner there will be opportunities to change the relations of authority and the structures of power vis a vis the state" (p.30).

In another evocation of his years in Paris, Fuentes describes a party in his official residence, to celebrate his wedding anniversary with his wife Sylvia.[32] He outlines his guest list: Luis Buñuel, Julio Cortázar, Octavio Paz and Marie-José, Gabriel García Márquez, Milan Kundera and his wife Vera, and Régis Debray. It is interesting to compare this list with the "family friends" of *Vuelta*. Luis Buñuel is a shared friendship, a shared appreciation of a man that Fuentes called "the greatest artist of surrealism." Kundera also appears in the pages of *Vuelta*, in his analyses of modern writers (for example, on Kafka in *Vuelta* 6). We have already explored the fissures appearing between *Vuelta* and Julio Cortázar, while García Márquez remains a significant absence until Paz begins to state openly his opposition to García Márquez's political views. Another uneasy guest for *Vuelta* is Régis Debray. Even though Fuentes declares that one day he will write a column on "my very dear friend Régis Debray," it seems very unlikely that *Vuelta* would have published it. Debray, after all, was still seen as the major apologist of Guevarist style guerrilla tactics, an ex-student of Althusser who had exchanged revolutionary theory in Paris for revolutionary practice in Bolivia. Already in the same issue of the magazine that publishes the appreciation of Buñuel, there is an article by Mario Vargas Llosa on terrorism ("El homicida indelicado," 42–45), in which, inter alia, he criticizes Debráy's misguided proclamation of the "foco" theory that led to the deaths of so many *guerrilleros* at the hands of the armies in Bolivia, Peru, Venezuela, Guatemala, Colombia, and Argentina (p.42). Indeed, Vargas Llosa was already researching a novel, *La guerra del fin del mundo* (*The War of the End of the World*, 1981), set in late-nineteenth-century Brazil, which has a misguided revolutionary figure, Galileo Gall, who might be seen as a Régis Debray of sorts. Vargas's Llosa's attacks were not confined to fiction: he later conducts a polemic with Debray, and with other writers such as Mario Benedetti, and Günter Grass that would often take place in the pages of *Vuelta*. Even though Fuentes's family of friends extends to Octavio Paz and Marie-José, it is clear that Fuentes might soon find coexistence in the pages of *Vuelta* somewhat problematic as personal and political divisions began to widen.

At this moment, however, Fuentes is moving between Mexico and Princeton, becoming immersed in Mexican debates about the possible reforms of the PRI. He pens a humorous political conversation between a utopian political thinker and a pragmatist. In this, he rehearses all the pros and the cons of the PRI, but without tipping the balance in any specific direction.[33] Significantly, this article appears in the same issue as Paz's essay "El ogro filantrópico" and an article by Manuel Camacho on possible ways of reforming the PRI. In an later interview with Torres Fierro—*Vuelta* 43, June 1980—Fuentes would argue that democracy in Mexico would only come about through the democratization of both the PRI and other parties, such as the Mexican Communist Party (p.43). He affirms that he has never belonged to the PRI and has often been a critic of the PRI, but that the regime had guaranteed that Mexico had remained an "island of tranquility" in a continent beset by dictatorships. Other articles written by Fuentes in these first two years of *Vuelta* also explore the craft of fiction and, in the second anniversary edition of the magazine, he publishes a long lecture on the development of the novel and on the importance of literature in society, proclaiming the robustness of the form. In this second year of the magazine's existence, Fuentes publishes fiction, political commentary, and essays on culture in the magazine. This is the time of his closest adherence.

Elena Poniatowska also appears intermittently in the magazine, with major articles on the legacy of 68 and also an appreciation of Jesusa, the subject of her novel *Hasta no verte Jesús mío* (*Until We Meet Again*, 1969). She also publishes a long extract from her novel in preparation, *Querido Diego, te abraza Quiela* (*Dear Diego*) (*Vuelta* 15, 5–15), focusing on an imaginary correspondence by Angelina Beloff, directed at her former lover, Diego Rivera. We are still a number of years from a rift with Paz over her interest in Tina Modotti, who Paz saw as a talentless Stalinist (His article, "Tina Stalinísima" appeared in *Vuelta* 82, when Poniatowska had just begun her research on her novel, *Tinísima* that was to appear some nine years later.) Indeed, when Paz looked to broaden the scope of the editorial committee by admitting two women writers for the first time—the Uruguayan Ulalume González de León and the Cuban Julieta Campos, who join the committee from issue 18—he also asks Poniatowska onto the board. Poniatowska declined, she says, because she did not want to be seen to be taking sides in what was becoming a more polarized intellectual world, where her close friend, Carlos Monsiváis, Paz's sparring partner, edited the pages of *La Cultura en México*.

The group identified with *Plural* remained the stable base of *Vuelta*, with Gabriel Zaid as the most frequent contributor covering a range of political and economic topics. Perhaps Zaid's most memorable polemic was his article on Luis Echeverría published in the second issue of the magazine. Jorge Ibargüengoitia joins the editorial board at the same time as González de León and Campos and for the first years of the magazine his quirky, ironic humorous column covers a range of topics, in the first person, from the latest novel by Fuentes to his own impressions of the *Excélsior* coup. He would also publish an extract from his novel, *Las muertas* (*The Dead Girls*), in issue 5 (April 1977).

In terms of contributors outside Latin America, a significant presence in these early issues is Isaiah Berlin. Berlin provides *Vuelta* and its contributors—Vargas Llosa would become very influenced by Berlin from the late seventies, Krauze would be a consistent admirer—with certain ways of expressing a liberal credo, like the term "negative" liberty that allows individuals to do what they want, as long as this did not impinge on other people's freedom, as opposed to "positive" liberty—the basis of socialism and communism—which seeks to use politics to liberate people from either inner or outer barriers or repressions. Democratic government, offers a better guarantee of negative freedom than other regimes. Berlin argues that values underlying democracy—equality, freedom, and justice—usually contradict each other leading to possible conflict and loss. It was because of these contradictory values inherent in society that Berlin would reject any notion of an ideal society or ideal human behavior, an insight that would chime with *Vuelta's* critique of utopias, in particular the utopia of socialism. Berlin would also offer a reading of historical thinkers that would point out the roots and the dangers of cultural nationalism in, say, the German Romantic movement with its insistence on a distinctive German *Kultur*. Berlin was less interested in commenting on contemporary politics, and when he did so, he lacked the subtlety of his philosophical/historical essays. Enrique Krauze would later interview Berlin in All Soul's College in Oxford in November 1981 and published this interview in *Vuelta* 66 (May 1982).

The Polish political philosopher, Leszek Kolakowski, forced into exile in 1968 and now teaching in Oxford, would be an example of the heterodox thinker, in opposition to Stalinism, that the contributors to *Vuelta* would always admire. His first publication in the magazine—in March 1977—would be a coauthored account of the Polish resistance movement, an account of the strikes and of the repression in the country. It is a plea for international solidarity and an exploration of how many groups in society were willing to fight against an authoritarian regime: workers movements, intellectuals, the Church, amongst others. *Vuelta* would follow the development of this resistance movement throughout the late seventies and through the eighties, and Kolakowski would be a source of knowledge about Poland in particular, as well as philosopher seeking to unravel classic Marxist theory.

The economist John Kenneth Galbraith would also publish a book review and five articles in the magazine in the first ten issues under the title, "Reflections of a solitary economist." Galbraith is introduced in the magazine as an economist recently willing to engage with monetarist policies, "a very different response to the simple formulations of ignorant people who seek to refute or support monetarism in terms of politics."[34] Galbraith is seen as a model of an independent economic thinker, a respected figure on the left wing of the Democrat Party. After a cluster of five articles on different aspects of the economy, including a very forthright defense of women's rights in the workforce, Galbraith appeared once more in the magazine, warning later of the dangers of neoliberalism, in an article entitled "Predictions for the Eighties" (*Vuelta* 41, April 1980).

While the magazine would always seek dialogue with international intellectual figures, the core group of contributors would be Mexican with some Spanish and Spanish American writers and critics, in particular Juan Goytisolo, Guillermo Cabrera Infante, Severo Sarduy, Mario Vargas Llosa and critics such as the Peruvian José Miguel Oviedo. The magazine, as we have seen, would become increasingly outspoken in its critique of what it saw as the dogmatic left in Mexico and in the wider world. The touchstone for such dogmatism would, for *Vuelta*, be attitudes toward Cuba and, by extension, to the Soviet Union. Guillermo Cabrera Infante would lead the charge against the Cuban regime with a series of increasingly outspoken articles through the late seventies on the repression of homosexuality, on the persecution of intellectuals, and on imprisoned writers. From a different perspective, Gabriel García Márquez published a series of articles in the political journal *Alternativa* in Colombia, from 1975, some of which were reprinted in *Excélsior*, which sang the praises of the Cuban regime, at home and at war in Angola. From 1976, according to his biographer Gerald Martin, he began to develop a very close friendship with Fidel Castro. There was no place for this outspoken journalism and for such friendships in the pages of *Vuelta*. In a significant parting of the ways, at the premiere in Mexico of *Pantaleón*, a movie based on Vargas Llosa's recently published comic novel, the two friends parted company in a public manner. Whatever the reasons for this parting of the ways, it is clear from the articles they were publishing at the time that the two writers, the closest of friends for many years, were moving apart in terms of their analysis of politics and the social function of literature. *Vuelta* would be the home for Vargas Llosa's developing commitment to liberalism; García Márquez was either ignored or else rebutted.

Perhaps one can see the political-intellectual "moment" of *Plural* drawing to a close in 1978, with two issues in particular, 21 and 23, August and October. Issue 23 discusses the legacy of 1968. The cover reads "1968/1978. Mexico, Estados Unidos, Francia: Ensayos y Testimonios." ("Mexico, the United States, France: Essays and Testimonies"). These are the dates that frame our study. The countries in the title also refer to the dialogue that always took place in *Plural*, and now in *Vuelta*, between Mexico (Latin America), the United States, and Europe. Here the main focus is on the tenth anniversary of Tlatelolco, with three analytical essays and the testimonial accounts of José Revueltas. Zaid offers a caustic appraisal of the aftermath of 1968 pointing out that Echeverría had thrown money at the universities in order to neutralize dissent. He shows that between 1968 and 1978, the budget for higher education had increased over 1,000 percent, with the grant to UNAM increasing by 1,688 percent, while per capita spending on food had decreased some 6 percent in this period. It causes much less aggravation, Zaid argues, for the government to repress peasants in the countryside than to repress university students in the city: "improving the lives of a minority who can speak in favor of the majority works out much cheaper than improving the lives of a majority" (p.7). Eduardo Lizalde talks about the anniversary of both the repression at Tlatelolco and also of the railway workers in 1958/1959. He argues that analyses of these events have been at the level more of moral outrage than of political analysis and he points out, quoting José Revueltas, that the student leaders had very little power: they were led by events, rather than leading events. He concludes that both events showed the lack of any "ideological or political impulse capable of influencing a true political or social movement within a democratic framework" (p.11). Julián Meza argues, in contrast, that some gains *have* been made as a result of 1968—the enlightened despotism of Echeverría and the electoral reforms of López Portillo—but that the festive or ludic elements of student protest were stifled by brutality and political solemnity. The section on Mexico ends with extracts from the writing of José Revueltas, the critical conscience of the Movement. Placing Mexico 68 in a wider context, there are also essays by Edgar Morin on May 68 in France and its legacy and by David Riesman on movements in the United States.

In its coverage of Tlatelolco, the *Vuelta* analysis chimed to some extent with the opinions of Carlos Monsiváis and Elena Poniatowska, who were seen as the most consistent and vocal defenders of the student movement of 1968. It is interesting that in an article published in *Proceso* on 9 October 1978, Carlos Monsiváis chooses a line from Paz's Tlatelolco poem as the title for his piece: "Si una nación entera se avergüenza" ("If an entire nation is shamed"). Despite their robust polemic of the previous year, Monsiváis is willing to acknowledge the moral authority of Paz's position in 1968 and his continuing interest in exploring the legacy of Tlatelolco. Further articles by Monsiváis in *La Cultura en México* (11 October 1978) and by Poniatowska in *Proceso* (2 October 1978) cover the demonstration that took place to commemorate the tenth anniversary. Whilst decrying the abuses of power, both argue that the student movement and its survival in different forms is part of the process of democratization in Mexico. Poniatowska argues that the student leaders are now prominent in opposition politics and Monsiváis concurs with this point. While Paz might disagree with the relative weight and importance given to these opposition parties—Monsiváis stressed the importance of the student movement in effecting political change—the overall sense of the coverage of Tlatelolco, ten years on, is of a relative hope for democratic change, a truce between the different factions in the field.

Two issues earlier, Paz had published what is arguably his best-known essay, "El ogro filantrópico," in the "Letras, letrillas, letrones" section of the magazine.[35] Even though the phrase, the philanthropic ogre, has gone into common currency as an evocative description of the blandishments and coercion of state power, Paz's article is a specific contribution to the debate over the political reform being introduced in Mexico in 1978 and also a commentary on the tenth anniversary of Tlatelolco. In order to understand political processes, it is necessary, Paz argues, to understand the particular nature of the Mexican state that is not dictatorial or totalitarian, but rather rests on a balance between different interest groups.[36] These different groups can be summed up as: "The government bureaucracy, which is more or less stable ...; the heterogeneous conglomerate of friends, favorites, family members, private and protected, an inheritance from seventeenth and eighteenth century courtly society; the political bureaucracy of the PRI, made up of professional politicians, an association that is not so much ideological as based on factional and individual interests" (p.41). The courtesans are the friends and allies of the President, who always sees the state as his personal patrimony. This sets up a tension between a modernizing, "technocratic" bureaucracy made up of professionals, and a set of courtesans who are mainly replaced every six years with every new six-year presidential term. The conflicts between these groups makes running the state both difficult and "sinuous." The other integral part of state power is the political bureaucracy of the PRI. The PRI, Paz argues, now wishes to reform, but it knows that its reform is inseparable from the reform of the country: "The question that history has posed Mexico since 1968 is not just whether the State could govern without the PRI, but whether we Mexicans would allow ourselves to be governed without a PRI" (p.41).

The PRI, for Paz, was born out of necessity: to guarantee the continuity of the postrevolutionary regime. In its essence was a compromise between an authentic, democratic, party system and a caudillo dictatorship. This regime had lasted for many years without anyone questioning its legitimacy. "The events of 1968, which culminated in the killing of several hundred students, severely fractured this legitimacy, that had already been eroded by half a century of uninterrupted domination" (p.42). Since 1968, successive governments have sought a new legitimacy. The recent attempt by the government at recognizing the existence of other parties, at introducing pluralism is, for Paz, a step toward democracy. Yet this step will be faltering given the lack of established political parties: The PAN is weak, the Mexican Communist Party is small and is only influential in the universities, although left-wing intellectuals have had no influence on the development of the party itself. The Partido Democrático Mexicano, for Paz, is also in crisis. For him the one glimmer of hope is the Partido Mexicano de los Trabajadores—with which he had flirted earlier in the decade—although, to date, it does not have a clear, democratic programme. This is the problem faced by the political reform process. Thinking through a process of democratic reform that would incorporate all aspects of Mexican society will require extraordinary imagination. But that, after all, is the task of intellectuals, of magazines like *Plural* and *Vuelta*. In the end, therefore, Paz is giving the PRI the benefit of the doubt, as long as it commits itself to more "pluralist" reforms. Paz ends his essay with a project that binds creative writing to intellectual responsibility, to critical intelligence. It serves as a useful resume of the moment of *Plural* and a statement of intent for the further development of *Vuelta*: "I do not need to point out that the rebirth of the imagination, in art and in politics, has always been prepared and preceded by analysis and criticism. I think that our generation and the one following it have been given this task. But before undertaking the criticism of our societies, their history and their present circumstances, we Spanish American writers must begin with a criticism of ourselves. The first thing we must do is to cure ourselves of simplistic and simplifying ideologies" (p.44).

Notes

Introduction

All nonpublished correspondence quoted in this book was authorized by Octavio Paz during his lifetime, as the introduction explains. I have, however, adhered closely to the copyright laws of "fair usage" and have thus directly quoted only sparingly from these letters. All the translations used in this book are my own.

Note on translation of book titles. When a work of fiction or poetry has been translated into English, the English title is given in italics. When no published translation exists, the title is given in quotation marks.

1. Guillermo Sheridan, "Octavio Paz: editor," *Letras Libres* 96 (December 2006): 67.
2. Christopher Domínguez Michael, "Un árbol hemerográfico de la literatura mexicana," *Letras Libres* 7 (July 1999): v.
3. Raymond Williams, "The Bloomsbury Fraction," in *Problems in Materialism and Culture*. (London: Verso, 1980): 148–150.
4. See John King, *El Di Tella y el desarrollo cultural argentino en la década del sesenta* (Buenos Aires: La Marca Editora, 2007).
5. For a commentary on this "happening" and other avant garde events in Argentina, see, Octavio Paz, "Letter to Eduardo Costa," in *Listen, Look, Now! Argentine Art of the 1960s: Writings of the Avant Garde*, ed. Inés Katzenstein (New York: Museum of Modern Art, 2004), 233–236.
6. Octavio Paz, "Antevíspera: *Taller* (1938–1941)," *Vuelta* 76 (March 1983): 12.
7. Among the many titles that cover this area, see: Roderic Camp, *Intellectuals and the State in Twentieth Century Mexico* (Austin: University of Texas Press, 1985); Alan Knight, "The Peculiarities of Mexican History; Mexico Compared to Latin America," *Journal of Latin American Studies* 24 (1992): 99–144; Nicola Miller, *In the Shadow of the State: Intellectuals and the Quest for National Identity in Twentieth-Century Spanish America* (London: Verso, 1999); Deborah Cohn, "The Mexican Intelligentsia, 1950–1968: Cosmopolitanism, National Identity

and the State," *Mexican Studies/Estudios Mexicanos* 21, I (Winter 2005): 141–182; Kristine Vanden Berghe, "La cultura en México (1959–1972) en dos suplementos: *México en la Cultura* de *Novedades* y *La Cultura en México* de *Siempre!*" (MA thesis, UNAM, Mexico City, 1989); Jorge Volpi, *La imaginación y el poder. Una historia intelectual de 1968* (Mexico City: Era, 1998); Claire Brewster, *Responding to Crisis in Contemporary Mexico. The Political Writings of Paz, Fuentes, Monsiváis and Poniatowska* (Tucson: The University of Arizona Press, 2005).

  8. Alfonso Reyes and Victoria Ocampo, *Cartas echadas: Correspondencia 1927–1959,* (Mexico City: UAM, 1983), 32.

  9. See Enrique Krauze, "La comedia mexicana de Carlos Fuentes," *Vuelta* 139 (June 1988): 15–27, reprinted in Krauze, *Mexicanos eminentes* (Mexico City: Tusquets, 1999).

 10. See in particular, Guillermo Sheridan, *Los Contemporáneos ayer* (Mexico City: Fondo de Cultura Económica, 1985); *México 1932: la polémica nacionalista* (Mexico City: Fondo de Cultura Económica, 1999); *Poeta con paisaje: ensayos sobre la vida de Octavio Paz* (Mexico City: Era, 2004).

 11. See *Le discours culturel dans les revues latinoaméricaines de l'entre-deux guerres, 1919–1939, América, Cahiers du CRICCAL* 4–5 (Sorbonne: Paris, 1989). Two further volumes on the topic of literary magazines covering the periods 1940–1970 and 1970–1990 were published in *América, Cahiers du CRICCAL* no. 9–10, 1992 and no. 15–16, 1996.

 12. The most relevant studies to this book are María Eugenia Mudrovcic, *Mundo Nuevo: Cultura y guerra fría en la década del sesenta* (Rosario: Beatriz Viterbo, 1997); and Saúl Sosnowski, ed. *La cultura de un siglo: América Latina en sus revistas* (Buenos Aires: Alianza, 1999).

1 Mapping the Field: Paz, Politics, and Little Magazines, 1931–1968

 1. Octavio Paz, "Nocturno de San Ildefonso," *Plural* 38 (September 1974): 24–27.

 2. Enrique Krauze, "Octavio Paz: Facing the Century. A Reading of *Tiempo nublado,*" *Salmagundi* 70–71 (1986): 130.

 3. Enrique Krauze, "Octavio Paz. Y el mantel olía a pólvora...," in *Mexicanos eminentes* (Mexico City: Tusquets, 1999): 154.

 4. The best single guide to the world of Vasconcelos is Claude Fell, *José Vasconcelos: los años del águila (1920–1925)* (Mexico City: UNAM, 1989).

 5. Lorenzo Meyer, "Mexico in the 1920s," in *Mexico Since Independence,* ed. Leslie Bethell (Cambridge: Cambridge University Press, 1991), 207–210.

 6. Meyer, 210.

 7. Guillermo Sheridan, *Poeta con paisaje: ensayos sobre la vida de Octavio Paz* (Mexico City: Ediciones Era, 2004), 126.

8. Octavio Paz, "Itinerario," in *Ideas y costumbres I. La letra y el cetro. Obras Completas* 9 (Mexico City: Fondo de Cultura Económica, 1995): 20.

9. For Paz's views on Gide and an analysis of this episode, see Octavio Paz, "La verdad frente al compromiso," introduction to Alberto Ruy Sánchez, *Tristeza de la verdad: André Gide regresa de Rusia* (Mexico City: Joaquín Mortiz, 1991).

10. See in particular Sebastiaan Faber, *Exile and Cultural Hegemony: Spanish Intellectuals in Mexico, 1939–1975* (Nashville: Vanderbilt University Press, 2002).

11. Diana Ylizarriturri, "Entrevista con Octavio Paz, editor de revistas," *Letras Libres* 7 (July 1999): 54.

12. Paz, "Itinerario," 29.

13. Octavio Paz, "Profesión de fe," in *El peregrino en su patria, Obras Completas* 8 (Mexico City: Fondo de Cultura Económica, 1994): 569.

14. *El Hijo Pródigo* 1 (April 1943): 8 I have consulted the facsimile edition of the magazine published in the Revistas Literarias Mexicanas Modernas series, published by the Fondo de Cultura Económica in Mexico in 1983.

15. See Sheridan, "Octavio Paz: editor," 73.

16. Octavio Paz, "Poesía de soledad y poesía de comunión," *El Hijo Pródigo* 5 (15 August 1943): 278.

17. Octavio Paz, "Un catálogo descabellado" and "Cronología del surrealismo," *Plural* 17 (February 1973): 36–42.

18. Octavio Paz, *¿Aguila o sol?* (Mexico City: Fondo de Cultura Económica, 1951): 117.

19. Kristal argues that one must see Paz's writings in their totality at every stage in his career. Here he teases out the affinities between Paz's own poetry and his reading of the paintings of Rufino Tamayo. See Efraín Kristal, "La palabra y la mirada de Octavio Paz: eros y transfiguración," *Boletín de la Fundación Federico García Lorca* 9 (June 1991): 125.

20. Paz wrote of his friendships in Paris in this period in an introduction to a book of poems by Blanca Varela published in 1959. See "*Destiempos* de Blanca Varela," in Octavio Paz, *Obras Completas* 4 (Mexico City: Fondo de Cultura Económica, 1994): 349–353.

21. Quoted in Mariella Balbi, *Szyszlo: Travesía* (Lima: Universidad Peruana de Ciencias Aplicadas, 2001), 55.

22. See Octavio Paz, "Itinerario," 41–42.

23. Interview with Sergio Marras, in Octavio Paz, *Obras Completas* 9, 144.

24. For an excessive and passionate account of the Paz-Garro-Bioy triangle from a daughter's point of view, see Helena Paz Garro, *Memorias* (Mexico City: Océano, 2004).

25. Octavio Paz, "De Octavio Paz," *Sur* 346 (January–June 1980): 92.

26. This would be a constant theme in a number of the discussions I had with Paz over the years. Knowing my work on *Sur*, he would always point out the similarities and, more importantly, the differences between *Sur* and his later magazines, *Plural* and *Vuelta*. This comparison will be developed in later chapters. For an analysis of *Sur*, see J. King, *Sur: An Analysis of the Argentine Literary Journal and its Role in the Development of a Culture, 1931–1970* (Cambridge University Press: Cambridge, 1986).

27. Sheridan, *Poeta*, 407.

28. Octavio Paz, "Los campos de concentración soviéticos," in *Obras Completas* 9: 167.

29. Ibid., 170.

30. Elena Poniatowska, *Octavio Paz: Las palabras del árbol* (Barcelona: Plaza Janés, 1998), 58.

31. Interview in *Excélsior*, January 1954, quoted in Poniatowska, 56.

32. Quotations from José Luis Martínez, "Esquema de la cultura mexicana actual," *Revista Mexicana de Literatura* 8 (November–December 1956): 39–45 and 55–56.

33. José Emilio Pacheco, "El Puente de Nonalco y el avión de balderas," *La Jornada,* 8 October 1995.

34. Ibid.

35. T. Segovia, "Periodistas y escritores," *Revista de la Universidad de México* 12, 10 (June 1959): 28.

36. *La Cultura en México* 1 (1961).

37. Gabriel Zaid, "Tres momentos de la cultura en México," *Plural* 43 (April 1975): 14. Reprinted in G. Zaid, *Como leer en bicicleta: problemas de la cultura y el poder en México* (Mexico City: Joaquín Mortiz, 1975), 189.

38. Cohn, "The Mexican Intelligentsia," 158–159. For a detailed analysis of the two supplements, see Kristine Vanden Berghe, "La cultura en México (1959–1972) en dos suplementos: *México en la Cultura*, de *Novedades* y *La Cultura en México*, de *Siempre!*" (MA thesis, UNAM, Mexico City, 1989). Dr. Vanden Berghe kindly provided me with a copy of this thesis.

39. Annick Lempérière, *Intellectuels, États et Société au Mexique. Les Clercs de la Nation* (Paris: L'Harmattan, 1992).

40. Typescript copy of the conversation, "Los espacios de la literatura: *Revista de La Universidad,*" between Jaime García Terrés and Alvaro Matute, Wednesday 29 June 1983, Museo Carrillo Gil, Mexico City, 1983, 4–5. Jaime García Terrés kindly gave me a copy of this typescript.

41. Interview with the author, Mexico City, 28 August 1985.

42. "Los espacios de la literatura," 9. For a detailed account of the activities of the Casa del Lago, see Ana Luisa Vega, *Casa del Lago: Un anhelo colectivo* (Mexico City: UNAM, 1988).

43. For an analysis of the Joaquín Mortiz publishing house, see Danny J. Anderson, "Creating Cultural Prestige: Editorial Joaquín Mortiz," *Latin American Research Review* 31, 2 (1996): 3–37.

44. Juan García Ponce, *Pasado presente* (Mexico City: Fondo de Cultura Económica, 1993).

45. For an account of the activities of the Centro Mexicano de Escritores, see Martha Domínguez, *Los becarios del Centro Mexicano de Escritores* (Mexico: Aldus, 1999).

46. Huberto Batis, *Lo que 'Cuadernos de Viento' nos dejó* (Mexico City: Diógenes, 1984), 27.

47. Michael K. Schuster, *Elenísima: Ingenio y figura de Elena Poniatowska* (Mexico City: Diana, 2003).

48. Carlos Monsiváis, *La Cultura en México* 202 (1965): 4. Quoted in Kristine Vanden Berghe, "Los mafiosos del boom. Literatura y mercado en los años setenta," in *Literatura y dinero en Hispanoamérica*, eds. N. Lie and Y. Montalvo Aponte (Brussels: Vlaams kennis-en Cultuurforum, 2000), 54–55.

49. *Revista Mexicana de Literatura* 6 (July–August 1956): 68.

50. R.X., "Epígrafe," *Diálogos: Revista Bimestral de Letras y Artes* 1 (November–December 1964): 2.

51. "Entrevista con Salvador Elizondo a cargo de Héctor de Mauleón," *Confabulario* 21 (11 September 2004), reprinted in the facsimile edition of *S.Nob*, (Mexico City: Editorial Aldus).

52. For a thorough study of the development of counterculture in Mexico, see, Eric Zolov, *Refried Elvis: The Rise of Mexican Counterculture* (Berkeley: University of California Press, 1999).

53. Gerald Martin, "The Boom of Spanish American Fiction and the 1960s Revolutions," in *The Blackwell Companion to Latin American Culture and Literature*, ed. Sara Castro Klaren (New York: Blackwell, 2007, forthcoming).

54. Mario Vargas Llosa, *García Márquez: historia de un deicidio* (Barcelona: Seix Barral, 1971).

55. Marshall Berman, *All That is Solid Melts into Air: The Experience of Modernity* (London: Verso, 1983), 33.

56. Mario Vargas Llosa, *Making Waves* (London: Faber and Faber, 1996), 73.

57. Jean Franco, *The Decline and Fall of the Lettered City: Latin America in the Cold War* (Cambridge, Mass.: Harvard University Press, 2002). For an analysis of U.S. cultural policies toward the arts in the sixties, see, J. King, *El Di Tella*.

58. Quoted in Valerie Fraser, *Building the New World: Studies in the Modern Architecture of Latin America, 1930–1960* (London: Verso, 2000), 244.

59. Angel Rama, "El boom en perspectiva," in *Más allá del boom. Literatura y mercado* (Mexico: Siglo XXI, 1981), 98.

60. Gabriel García Márquez, *Vivir para contarla* (Barcelona: Mondadori, 2002), 137–138.
61. José Donoso, *Historia personal del boom* (Barcelona: Anagrama, 1972), 113.
62. "Dialogue. Carlos Fuentes, "Situación del escritor en América Latina," *Mundo Nuevo* 1 (July 1966): 5–21.
63. Both these letters are printed in *L'Herne: Fuentes*, eds. Claude Fell and Jorge Volpi (Paris: Éditions de L'Herne, 2006), 54–57.
64. For extracts from this correspondence see María Eugenia Mudrovcic, *Mundo Nuevo: Cultura y guerra fría en la década del 60* (Rosario: Beatriz Viterbo, 1997), 11–13.
65. "Carta abierta de los intelectuales cubanos a Pablo Neruda," *Marcha* 1315 (5 August 1966).
66. Letter, Carlos Fuentes to Pablo Neruda, Paris, 2 November 1966, quoted in *L'Herne: Fuentes*, 72–73.
67. *L'Herne*, 73.
68. In an interesting analysis of Paz's work in this decade, Anthony Stanton sees that: "three fundamental encounters shape this period: a careful reading of Mallarmé, a deep interest in the theories of structuralism, and a passionate study of the history and thought of Indian religion and civilization, especially those of Buddhism." See Anthony Stanton, "Poetics of the Apocalypse, Spatial Form and Indetermination: the Prose of Octavio Paz in the 1960s," *Siglo XX/20th Century Critique and Cultural Discourse* 10, 1–2 (1992): 127.
69. Octavio Paz and Arnaldo Orfila, *Cartas cruzadas* (Mexico City: Siglo XXI, 2005), 145. I am very grateful to Adolfo Castañon for sending me this book and other material relating to *Plural*.
70. *Cartas cruzadas*, 150.
71. *Cartas cruzadas*, 155–156.
72. See Kristal, "La palabra y la mirada" for an analysis of Paz's reading of Lévi-Strauss and Duchamp in the late sixties.
73. *Cartas cruzadas*, 162.
74. *Cartas cruzadas*, 180.

2   The Genesis and Birth of *Plural*

1. On responses of intellectuals printed in *La Cultura en México*, see Jorge Volpi, *La imaginación y el poder. Una historia intelectual de 1968* (Mexico City: Era, 1998).
2. "Octavio Paz ante el detector de mentiras," *La Cultura en México* 297 (18 October 1967): 1.
3. For an analysis of Monsiváis's writings on the student movement, see Brewster, 40–47.
4. Quoted in Julio Scherer García and Carlos Monsiváis, *Parte de Guerra. Tlatelolco 1968* (Mexico City: Aguilar, 1999), 167.

5. Quoted in Volpi, 486.
6. For a discussion of these texts, see Volpi, 353–356 and 374–376.
7. Quoted in Scherer and Monsiváis, 246.
8. "Le parti gouvernmental est un obstacle au développement du pays, nous declare M.Octavio Paz," interview with Jean Wetz, *Le Monde*, 14 November 1968, 2.
9. *Cartas cruzadas*, 183.
10. *Cartas cruzadas*, 189.
11. *Cartas cruzadas*, 225.
12. For a critique of the "mythic" elements of *Posdata*, see Javier Rodríguez Ledesma, *El pensamiento político de Octavio Paz: las trampas de la ideología* (Mexico City: Plaza y Valdés, 1996), 303–316; Roger Bartra, *La jaula de la melancolía: identidad y metamorfosis del mexicano* (Mexico City: Grijalbo, 1987).
13. Octavio Paz, *Posdata*, first edition, Mexico 1970. I am using the text of *Posdata* in Octavio Paz, *El peregrino en su patria. Historia y política de México. Obras completas* 8 (Mexico City: Fondo de Cultura Económica, 1994), 269–324. Further references will appear in parentheses in the text.
14. See David Brading, *Octavio Paz y la poética de la historia mexicana* (Mexico City: Fondo de Cultura Económica, 2002), 77–87.
15. *Cartas cruzadas*, 243.
16. "En vísperas de sus 80 años, Octavio Paz hace relación y recuento de su pensamiento," interview with Julio Scherer, *Proceso* 885 (18 October 1993): 8.
17. Carlos Monsiváis, "Octavio Paz y la izquierda," *Letras Libres* 4 (April 1999): 32–33.
18. Octavio Paz, "Historia y prehistoria de *Vuelta*," interview with Samuel de Villar and Rafael Segovia in 1981, quoted in Marie-José Paz, Adolfo Castañon, and Danubio Torres Fierro, eds., *A treinta años de Plural (1971–1976)* (Mexico City: Fondo de Cultura Económica, 2001), 18–19.
19. *Cartas cruzadas*, 262.
20. See in particular Fuentes's appreciation of Goytisolo in *La nueva novela hispanoamericana* (Mexico City: Joaquín Mortiz, 1969).
21. Juan Goytisolo, *Realms of Strife: The Memoirs of Juan Goytisolo 1957–1982* (London: Quartet Books, 1990), 132.
22. All quotations from Goytisolo, 134.
23. Plinio Apuleyo Mendoza, "Introducción," *Libre. Revista de Crítica Literaria (1971–1972)*, facsimile edition (Madrid: El Equilibrista/ Ediciones Turner/Sociedad Estatal Quinto Centenario, 1990), x.
24. Goytisolo, *Realms of Strife*, 132.
25. For the text of these statements, see *Libre 1*, facsimile edition, 95–145.
26. Roberto Fernández Retamar would return on several occasions to the topic of Caliban revising some of his earlier opinions, but never

quite apologizing to Fuentes. For a collection of his articles, see, *Todo Calibán, Milenio* 3 (November 1995).

27. Octavio Paz, "La autohumillación de los incrédulos," *La Cultura en México* 484 (19 May 1971): iv.

28. Carlos Fuentes, "La verdadera solidaridad con Cuba," *La Cultura en México* 484 (19 May 1971): v.

29. Goytisolo, 164.

30. *Libre*, xi.

31. Jorge Castañeda, *Perpetuating Power: How Mexican Presidents were Chosen*, (New York: The New Press, 2000), 22–23.

32. Daniel Cosío Villegas, *Memorias* (Mexico City: Joaquín Mortiz, 1976), 269.

33. Ibid., 271.

34. For the real reformist achievements of María Esther Zuno as well as her nationalist displays, see Sara Sefchovich, *La suerte de la consorte* (Mexico City: Océano, 2000), 345–362.

35. Héctor Aguilar Camín and Enrique Krauze, "La saña y el terror," Sergio Sarmiento, "Traían efigies del Che," both articles dated 14 June 1971, in *La Cultura en México* 490 (30 June 1971): I and II.

36. José Agustin, *Tragicomedia mexicana*, vol. 2 (Mexico City: Planeta, 1992), 26.

37. Interview with Jaime García Terrés, Mexico City, 22 August 1985.

38. Interview with Octavio Paz, Mexico City, 4 March 1995.

39. Interview with Octavio Paz, Mexico City, 9 September 1993.

40. *La Cultura en México* 500 (8 September 1971): II.

41. *A treinta años*, 3.

42. All the correspondence quoted is taken from the personal files of Octavio Paz and from the *Plural* archive, which, at the time I consulted it, in 1993, was in the possession of the magazine *Vuelta*. Paz personally gave me a number of photocopied letters from his archive and also had his staff at *Vuelta* photocopy material for me from the *Plural* archive.

43. *La Cultura en México* 479 (14 April 1971): II.

44. Interview with Alejandro Rossi, Mexico City, August 1985.

45. His book on Lévi-Strauss, *Claude Lévi-Strauss o el nuevo festín de Esopo*, was published by Joaquín Mortiz in Mexico in 1967.

46. Poniatowska, *Octavio Paz*, 81.

47. Interview with Elena Poniatowska, Mexico, 25 August 1985.

48. See Margo Glantz, *Onda y escritura en México: jóvenes de 20 a 33* (Mexico City: Siglo XXI, 1971).

49. Zolov, *Refried Elvis*, 217–218.

50. Interview, Adolfo Castañon with Efraín Kristal, Paris, December 2006.

51. Susan Sontag, "En memoria de Paul Goodman," *Plural* 17 (February 1973): 11.

3 Politics in *Plural*, 1971–1976

1. See Sergio Zermeño, "Intellectuals and the State in the 'Lost Decade,'" in *Mexico: Dilemmas of Transition*, ed. Neil Harvey (London: Institute of Latin American Studies, 1993), 279–298.

2. Carlos Fuentes, *Tiempo mexicano* (Mexico City: Joaquín Mortiz, 1971).

3. *Excélsior* 22 June 1972.

4. Carlos Fuentes, "Opciones críticas en el verano de nuestro descontento," *Plural* 11 (August 1972): 3–9. Further references will appear in parentheses in the text.

5. Maarten van Delden, *Carlos Fuentes, Mexico and Modernity* (Nashville: Vanderbilt University Press), 125.

6. In a recent homage to Zaid, on the occasion of his seventieth birthday, critic Xavier Rodríguez Ledesma argues that Zaid took the letter initially to *La Cultura en México*, which refused to publish it, on the advice of Pagés Llergo. From that moment, according to Rodríguez Ledesma, Zaid would not contribute to *La Cultura* and would instead publish in *Plural*. See, "Por la Academia en bicicleta," *Metapolítica* 38 (December 2004–January 2005): 69. Special edition entitled "Gabriel Zaid: el poeta en la ciudad."

7. Gabriel Zaid, "Carta a Carlos Fuentes," *Plural* 12 (September 1972): 53. Further references will appear in parentheses in the text.

8. José Emilio Pachecho, "México 1972. Los escritores y la política,"*Plural* 13 (October 1972): 25. Further references to this special issues appear in parentheses in the text.

9. Van Delden, *Carlos Fuentes*, 128.

10. Jaime Sánchez Sussarey, *El debate politico e intelectual en México* (Mexico City: Grijalbo, 1993), 33–34.

11. "La crítica de los papagayos," *Plural* 11 (August 1972): 41–42.

12. Octavio Paz, "La pregunta de Carlos Fuentes," *Plural* 14 (November 1972): 8.

13. Enrique Krauze, *Daniel Cosío Villegas: una biografía intelectual* (Mexico City: Joaquín Mortiz, 1980), 262.

14. Daniel Cosío Villegas, "Política: acción estudiada y estudio accionado," *Plural* 7 (April 1972): 4.

15. Rafael Segovia and Daniel Cosío Villegas, "¿Controversia?" *Plural* 18 (March 1973): 13–14.

16. Daniel Cosío Villegas, *Memorias* (Mexico City: Joaquín Mortiz, 1976), 294.

17. Daniel Cosío Villegas, "Pasan atropelladamente periódicos, gobierno e intelectuales," *Plural* 32 (April 1974): 62.

18. Cosío, *Memorias*, 295.

19. Julio Scherer, *Los presidentes* (Mexico City: Grijalbo, 1986), 80.

20. Ibid., 83.

21. Daniel Cosío Villegas, *El estilo personal de gobernar* (Mexico City: Joaquín Mortiz, 1974), 125.
22. Octavio Paz, "Daniel Cosío Villegas: las ilusiones y las convicciones," *Plural* 55 (April 1976): 80.
23. See Gabriel Zaid, "Este era un gato," in *Cómo leer en bicicleta: problemas de la cultura y el poder en México* (Mexico City: Joaquín Mortiz, 2nd edition, 1979), which contains a number of these *Plural* essays.
24. Mauricio Tenorio Trillo, "Zaidianas," *Istor* 19 (Winter 2004): 84. This edition of *Istor* has three essays on Zaid by Adolfo Castañon, Rafael Rojas, and Tenorio to celebrate his seventieth birthday.
25. Gabriel Zaid, "Anacrónico y hasta impertinente," *Plural* 40 (January 1975): 73.
26. Quoted in Tenorio, "Zaidianas," 83.
27. Gabriel Zaid, "Frágil: cuidado al acarrear," *Plural* 35 (August 1974): 80.
28. Gabriel Zaid, "Esa mayo...!," *Plural* 53 (February 1976): 76. See also Octavio Paz, "El desayuno del candidato," ibid., 74–75.
29. Gabriel Zaid, "Tres momentos de la cultura en México," *Plural* 43 (April 1975): 16.
30. Gabriel Zaid, "Para entender la política mexicana," *Plural* 48 (September 1975): 50.
31. "Denuncias sin respuesta," *Plural* 48 (September 1975): 71.
32. Octavio Paz, "Carta a Adolfo Gilly," *Plural* 5 (February 1972): 16.
33. John Womack, Frederick C.Turner, and Octavio Paz, "México: presente y futuro," *Plural* 6 (March 1972): 3–8.
34. "Una bocanada de oxígeno," *Plural* 30 (March 1974): 77.
35. Octavio Paz, "Entre Viriato y Fántomas," *Plural* 21 (June 1973): 40.
36. "Los misterios del pedregal II," *Plural* 15 (December 1972): 39.
37. "Los misterios del pedregal III," *Plural* 16 (January 1973): 37.
38. Octavio Paz, "Monólogo en forma de diálogo," *Plural* 43 (April 1975): 79–80.
39. Octavio Paz, "El desierto político," *Plural* 22 (July 1973): 38.
40. Carlos Salinas, "Tríptico de la dependencia: frustración, concesión y limitación en la visión," *Plural* 38 (November 1974): 26–30.
41. Octavio Paz, "Hacia una política de población en México," *Plural* 12 (September 1972): 29; "Entre Herodes y la píldora," *Plural* 31 (April 1974): 79–80; "Ixtlilxóchitl y el control de la natalidad," *Plural* 46 (July 1975): 79–80.
42. Elena Poniatowska, "Octavio Paz y *Plural*," *A treinta años de Plural*, 132.
43. Mario Ojeda, "La política internacional," *Plural* 22 (July 1973): 15.
44. I.F. Stone, "La traición de la psiquiatría," *Plural* 6 (March 1972): 38.
45. Octavio Paz, "Polvo de aquellos lodos," *Plural* 30 (March 1974): 18. Further references are in parentheses in the text.

46. Octavio Paz, "Gulag: entre Isaías y Job," *Plural* 51 (December 1975): 74–77.

47. Mario Vargas Llosa, "Un franco tirador tranquilo," *Plural* 39 (December 1974): 74. Further quotations are given in parentheses in the text.

48. Octavio Paz, "Los centuriones de Santiago," *Plural* 25 (October 1973): 49. Further quotations are given in parentheses in the text.

49. Alejandro Rossi, "Manual del Distraído," *Plural* 25 (October 1973): 52.

50. "La lección chilena," *Plural* 27 (December 1973): 64–65. See also, "Chile: los 'antis' y sus cómplices inesperados," *Plural* 31 (April 1974): 80–81.

51. "Onetti, 'Marcha' y los militares," *Plural* 30 (March 1974): 77.

52. "Uruguay: cultura y represión," *Plural* 57 (June 1976): 70–72.

53. "La censura o el nuevo Buenos Aires Affair," *Plural* 31 (April 1974): 81–82.

54. Octavio Paz, "El espejo indiscreto," *Plural* 58 (July 1976): 74.

55. Gabriel Zaid, "Lo que pedía nacer," *A treinta años de Plural*, 51. I did not find that note in the correspondence. There is, however, a letter from Paz to Galbraith apologizing for the amount that he could pay for an article.

56. Octavio Paz, "Historia y prehistoria de *Vuelta*," in Octavio Paz, *Pasión Crítica* (Barcelona: Seix Barral, 1985): 264.

57. *Plural* 50 (November 1975): 91.

58. Nadezda Mandelstam, "Mi testamento," *Plural* 10 (July 1972): 16.

59. Joseph Brodsky, "Más allá del consuelo," *Plural* 39 (December 1974): 20.

60. See Kostas Papaioannou's articles on "Superdesarrollo y revolución," published in issues 54 and 55 of *Plural* (March 1976): 6–11 and (April 1976): 26–31.

61. See, for example, Leszek Kolakowski, "Ambivalencia del dinero," *Plural* 17 (February 1973): 3–7 and "Georges Sorel: un marxismo jansenista," *Plural* 44 (May 1975): 6–18.

62. See, for example, Pierre Klossowski's article on "Sade y Fourier," *Plural* 11 (August 1972): 29–34.

4 Cultural Criticism in *Plural*: Literature and Art

1. Jason Wilson, "Alejandra Pizarnik, Surrealism and Reading," in *Arbol de Alejandra: Pizarnik Reassessed*, ed. Fiona J Mackintosh with Karl Posso (London: Tamesis, 2007, forthcoming).

2. Interview with the author, 4 March 1995.

3. Ernesto Sábato, "El escritor y sus fantasmas, entrevista con Danubio Torres Fierro," *Plural* 41 (February 1975): 23–32; Silvina Ocampo,

"Correspondencia entre Silvina Ocampo y Danubio Torres Fierro," *Plural* 50 (November 1975): 57–60; "Victoria Ocampo, entrevista de Danubio Torres Fierro," *Plural* 51 (December 1975): 18–25; "José Bianco, entrevista de Danubio Torres Fierro," Plural 52 (January 1976): 23–27; Adolfo Bioy Casares, "Las utopias pesimistas, entrevista de Danubio Torres Fierro," *Plural* 55 (April 1976): 47–53; Alberto Girri, "Alberto Girri: repaso a una obsesión, entrevista de Danubio Torres Fierro," *Plural* 58 (July 1976): 48–51.

4. "Borges juzga a Borges," *Plural* 35 (August 1974): 17–22.

5. José Bianco, "En torno a Marcel Proust," *Plural* 2 (November 1971): 36; José Bianco, "El ángel de las tinieblas (Paúl Léataud y Proust)," part 1, *Plural* 31 (April 1974): 18–22; and part II, *Plural* 32 (May 1974): 34–41.

6. Julio Cortázar, "Neruda entre nosotros," *Plural* 30 (March 1974): 39.

7. For the remaining quotations, ibid., 40–41.

8. Octavio Paz, "Polvos de aquellos lodos," 18.

9. Efraín Kristal, *The Temptation of the Word: The Novels of Mario Vargas Llosa* (Nashville: Vanderbilt University Press, 1998), 80–81.

10. Mario Vargas Llosa, "Albert Camus y la moral de los límites," *Plural* 51 (December 1975): 14. Further quotations are given in parentheses in the text.

11. Kristal, *The Temptation*, 81.

12. Mario Vargas Llosa, "Una pasión no correspondida," *Plural* 37 (October 1974): 35.

13. Ibid., 37.

14. Mario Vargas Llosa, "Historia de una sedición permanente," Entrevista de Danubio Torres Fierro, *Plural* 47 (August 1975): 25 and 27.

15. Mario Vargas Llosa, "La excepción a la regla," *Plural* 57 (June 1976): 56.

16. Ibid., 56.

17. Severo Sarduy, "Gran Mandala," *Plural* 3 (December 1971): 14; "Big bang," *Plural* 14 (November 1972): 6–7.

18. Severo Sarduy, "Sobre *Juan sin tierra* de Juan Goytisolo," *Plural* 48 (September 1975): 54.

19. Vargas Llosa, "Historia," 28.

20. Emir Rodríguez Monegal, "Notas sobre (hacia) el Boom," 1, *Plural* 4 (January 1972): 29; 2: "Los maestros de la nueva novela, *Plural* 6 (March 1972): 35; 3: "Nueva y vieja novela," *Plural* 7 (April 1972): 13; 4: "Los nuevos novelistas," *Plural* 8 (May 1972): 11. The book is entitled *El boom de la novela latinoamericana* (Caracas: Tiempo Nuevo, 1972).

21. See Gerald Martin, "The Boom of Spanish American Fiction and the 1960s Revolutions," in *The Blackwell Companion to Latin*

American Culture and Literature (New York: Blackwell, 2007, forthcoming).

22. See Kristine Vanden Berghe, "Hacia una cartografía del boom. Una polémica en *Zona Franca*," in *Le discours culturel dans les revues latinoamericaines de 1970 a 1990*, ed. Claude Fell, *América, Cahiers du CRICCAL*, 15–16 (1996): 21–30.

23. Anthony Stanton, "Poetics of Apocalypse," *SigloXX/20th Century* (1992): 127.

24. Interview with the author, Mexico City, August 1985.

25. Claude Lévi-Strauss, "Etnología y literatura. Discurso del ingreso en la Academia Francesa"; Roger Caillois, "Las paradojas de la etnología. Discurso de recepción de Claude Lévi-Strauss en la Academia Francesa, *Plural* 37 (October 1974): 6–12 and 13–21.

26. Roman Jakobson, "Los oximoros dialécticos de Fernando Pessoa (1)," *Plural* 7 (April 1972): 5; "Los oximoros dialécticos de Fernando Pessoa (2)," *Plural* 8 (May 1972): 36.

27. Roman Jakobson, "P.S. (sobre lingüística y poesía)," *Plural* 27 (December 1973): 6–9.

28. Roman Jakobson, "Ojeada al desarrollo de la semiótica (primera parte)," *Plural* 48 (September 1975): 6–11; "Ojeada al desarrollo de la semiótica (final)," *Plural* 49 (October 1975): 13–18.

29. Roland Barthes, *Plural* 26 (November 1973): 18–21; Gillo Dorfles, "Los mass-media y la enfermedad del lenguaje," *Plural* 27 (December 1973): 33–34; Umberto Eco, "Acerca de la posibilidad de generar mensajes estéticos en una lengua edénica," *Plural* 29 (February 1974): 17–34.

30. Harry Levin, "La tierra baldía: de ur a echt," *Plural* 13 (October 1972): 3–6; "Una enormidad literaria," *Plural* 16 (January 1973): 34–36.

31. Norman O. Brown, "Dafne o la metamorfosis," *Plural* 8 (May 1972): 5–8.

32. Juan Goytisolo, "In memoriam F.F.B. (1892–1975)," *Plural* 52 (January 1976): 12–14.

33. Octavio Paz, "El parlón y la parleta," *Plural* 18 (March 1973): 37–38.

34. Octavio Paz, "La tradición del haiku," *La Cultura en México* 479 (April 1971): II.

35. Ibid., II.

36. Interview with Octavio Paz,, Mexico City, August 1985.

37. Octavio Paz, Kazuya Sakai, "Cambio y continuidad," *Plural* 42 (March 1975): 82.

38. Interview with José de la Colina, Mexico City, 7 February 1993.

39. See Octavio Paz, "Lecho y mesa," *Plural* 2 (November 1971): 17–20 and "La mesa y el lecho," in *El ogro filantrópico* (Mexico City: Joaquín Mortiz, 1979), 212–234.

40. For both quotations, see Octavio Paz, "¿Por qué Fourier?" *Plural* 11 (August 1972): 10.

41. Paz, "Lecho y mesa," 20.

42. Salvador Elizondo, "Introducción: Georges Bataille, *Madame Edwarda*," *Plural* 26 (November 1973): 31.

43. Octavio Paz, "El ocaso de la vanguardia I parte," *Plural* 26 (November 1973): 4–8; "El ocaso de la vanguardia, II parte," *Plural* 27 (December 1973): 18–23; "El ocaso de la vanguardia, III parte," *Plural* 28 (January 1974): 20–24.

44. Jason Wilson, *Octavio Paz* (Boston: Twayne, 1986), 132.

45. José Miguel Oviedo, "Octavio Paz y el drama de la modernidad," *Plural* 39 (December 1974): 82–83.

46. Paz, *Plural* 26 (November 1973): 6.

47. Quoted in Sheridan, *Poeta con paisaje*, 97.

48. Kazuya Sakai, "Gato Barbieri: hacia un auténtico jazz latinoamericano," *Plural* 37 (October 1974), 80–81.

49. Claude Lévi-Strauss, "'Bolero' de Maurice Ravel," *Plural* 9 (June 1972): 9; "Escritos de Eric Satie," *Plural* 56 (April 1976): 32–42.

50. Interview with José de la Colina, Mexico City, 7 February 1993.

51. For an analysis of the circumstances surrounding the screening of *Los olvidados* in Cannes, see the beautifully illustrated study *Los olvidados* (Mexico City: Televisa 2004). I am very grateful to Ignacio Durán for donating this book to me and for facilitating my work on Mexican cinema over many years.

52. Octavio Paz, "Razón y elogio de María Félix," in *María Félix* (Mexico City: Secretaría de Gobernación, Cineteca Nacional, 1992).

53. Juan Villoro, "Alejandro Rossi," at www.sololiteratura.com/vill/villactalejandro,htm, accessed on 3 September 2005.

54. Rossi in *A treinta años*, 42.

55. Interview with Alejandro Rossi, Mexico City, August 1985.

56. Adolfo Castañon, "El ensayo en México a fin de siglo: Brevísima relación de los que ensayaron y sobrevivieron," *Cuadernos Hispanoamericanos* 544–550 (March–April 1996): 70.

57. Interview with Rossi, Mexico City, August 1985.

58. Octavio Paz, *Obras Completas 7. Los privilegios de la vista II. Arte de México* (Mexico City: Fondo de Cultura Económica, 1995), 13.

59. Octavio Paz, *El signo y el garabato* (Mexico City: Joaquín Mortiz, 1973).

60. Octavio Paz, "Tamayo: transfiguraciones," *Plural* 7 (April 1972): 17.

61. JGP, "El caso del museo Tamayo," *Plural* 56 (May 1976): 75.

62. Juan García Ponce, "La obra de José Luis Cuevas," *Plural* 54 (March 1976): 43–46.

63. Kazuya Sakai, "Ocho ejercicios para un homenaje a Ogata Korin," *Plural* 50 (November 1975): 52. Article reprinted in Kazuya Sakai, *Itinerarios* (Buenos Aires: Centro Cultural Recoleta, 2005), 106.

64. See John King, *El Di Tella*.

65. For an appreciation of the work of Romero Brest, see the articles in the section, "Jorge Romero Brest: rewriting Modernism," in *Listen, Look, Now,* 76–153.
66. U.S. scholar Claire Fox is writing a history of the Pan American Union Arts Programme. I am grateful to her for sharing with me her ideas and her bibliography on this organization and on the broader context of inter-American cultural relations in this period.
67. Conversation with Sumiko Sakai, February 2007.
68. Donald Goodall, "Exposición *Plural*," *Plural* 50 (November 1975): 93.
69. "Exposición *Plural*: Doce artistas latinoamericanos," *Plural* 50 (November 1975): 95.
70. Damián Bayón, "Reflexiones sobre un simposio de arte," *Plural* 52 (January 1976): 78.
71. See Serge Guilbaut, *How New York Stole the Idea of Modern Art: Abstract Expressionism, Freedom, and the Cold War* (Chicago, University of Chicago Press, 1983), 11.
72. Mario Vargas Llosa, "La pintura de Fernando de Szyszlo," *Plural* 55 (April 1976): 43. My comments on Traba in this paragraph have been influenced by the ideas of Claire Fox.
73. For Cuevas's account of the Austin seminar, see José Luis Cuevas. *Gato macho.* (Mexico City: Fondo de Cultura Económica, 1994), 21; and José Luis Cuevas, *Confrontaciones.* (Mexico City: UAM, 1984), 28. For the attack on Bayón, see José Luis Cuevas, "La era de los tontos," *El Sol de México* 13 July 1975, 3–5.
74. Tomás Segovia, "Nunca más," in *A treinta años,* 46.

5 Literary "Creation"

1. Octavio Paz *Traducción: literatura y literalidad.* (Barcelona: Tusquets, 1971). Further references will appear in parentheses in the text. For a collection of Paz's translations of poetry, see Octavio Paz, *Versiones y diversiones* (Madrid: Círculo de Lectores, 2002).
2. See in particular, Efraín Kristal, "Jorge Luis Borges y Octavio Paz: Poéticas de la traducción y traducción poética," *Studi Ispanici* (2002): 261–270; and Maya Scharer-Nussberger, *Octavio Paz. Trayectoria y visiones* (Mexico City: Fondo de Cultura Económica, 1989).
3. Tomás Segovia, "Un lenguaje intraducible," *Plural* 8 (May 1972): 32–35 .
4. Salvador Elizondo, "Traducciones: la poesía transformada," *Plural* 44. (May 1975): 75–76.
5. Octavio Paz, "Centro móvil," *Plural* 6 (March 1972): 29.
6. Ibid., 30.
7. Wilson, *Octavio Paz,* 128.
8. Octavio Paz, "Manuel Alvarez Bravo," *Plural* 11 (August 1972): 37.

9. Octavio Paz, "Nocturno de San Ildefonso," *Plural* 36 (September 1974): 26.
10. Octavio Paz, "Aunque es de noche," *Plural* 30 (March 1974): 7.
11. Jorge Edwards, *Adios poeta...* (Barcelona: Tusquets, 1990): 164.
12. Quoted in Mario Vargas Llosa, *Touchtones* (London: Faber and Faber, 2007).
13. John Cage, "Mesosticos," *Plural* 5 (February 1972): 3–4.
14. Marco A. Montes de Oca, "Lugares donde el espacio cicatriza," *Plural* 5 (February 1972): 9–11.
15. Augusto and Haroldo de Campos, "Poesía concreta: configuración/ textos," *Plural* 8 (May 1972): 21.
16. Haroldo de Campos, in Augusto de Campos, Haroldo de Campos, and Décio Pignatari, *Teoria de poesia concreta: textos críticos e manifestos, 1950–1960* (São Paulo: Duas Cidades, 1975), 151. I am using the translation by David Treece in Mike González and David Treece, *The Gathering of Voices: The Twentieth Century Poetry of Latin America* (London: Verso, 1992), 244–245.
17. Octavio Paz and Haroldo de Campos, *Transblanco (em torno a Blanco de Octavio Paz)* (Rio de Janeiro: Editora Guanabara, 1986).
18. Quoted in *Plural* 6 (March 1972): 21.
19. *Plural* 35 (August 1974): 74.
20. Mark Strand, "Nueva poesía norteamericana," *Plural* 50 (November 1975): 29.
21. Pierre Dhainaut, *Plural* 50 (November 1975): 41.
22. See Jean-Baptiste Para, ed., *Anthologie de la poésie française du XXe Siècle*. Vol. II (Paris: Gallimard, 2000).
23. See Claude Esteban, "El eco de una morada (la obra poética de Yves Bonnefoy)"; Yves Bonnefoy, "Dans le leurre du seuil," *Plural* 53 (February 1976): 10–16.
24. Octavio Paz, Roberto González Echeverría, and Emir Rodríguez Monegal, "Cuatro o cinco puntos cardinales," *Plural* 18 (March 1973): 18.
25. Octavio Paz, "Elizabeth Bishop o el poder de la reticencia"; Elizabeth Bishop, "El fin de marzo, Duxbury," *Plural* 49 (October 1975): 6–9.
26. Paz to Orfila, 20 October 1965, *Cartas cruzadas*, 32.
27. Roberto Juarroz, "Antonio Porchia o la profundidad recuperada," *Plural* 47 (August 1975): 34.
28. Alejandra Pizarnik, "Algunas claves," *Plural* 18 (March 1973): 8.
29. Julio Miranda, "Lucha armada, lucha escrita: *Zona Franca* e *Imagen* en la Venezuela de los '60,'" in Sosnowski, *La cultura de un siglo*, 409–419.
30. Guillermo Sucre, "Frases y poemas," *Plural* 2 (November 1971): 7.
31. Gonzalo Rojas, "Poemas," *Plural* 44 (May 1975): 19–20.
32. Quoted in Guillermo Sheridan, "Tomás Segovia: Premio Octavio Paz de Poesía y Ensayo 2000," *La Gaceta de Fondo de Cultura Económica* 355 (July 2000): 22.

33. See, for example, Tomás Segovia, "El mirlo en la ciudad," *Plural* 27 (December 1973): 11; and "Secuencia del tiempo," *Plural* 42 (March 1975): 23–24.

34. Octavio Paz, "Respuestas a *Cuestionario*—y algo más: Gabriel Zaid," in *Obras Completas 3. Fundación y disidencia. Dominio Hispánico* (Mexico City: Fondo de Cultura Económica, 1993), 317 and 320.

35. Gabriel Zaid, "Poemas," *Plural* 49 (October 1975): 12.

36. Octavio Paz, "Prólogo," in Octavio Paz, Homero Aridjis, Alí Chumacero, and Jose Emilio Pacheco, eds., *Poesía en movimiento: México 1915–1966* (Mexico City: Fondo de Cultura Económica, 1966), 26–27.

37. José Emilio Pacheco, "Canciones tristes y otras conversaciones," *Plural* 19 (April 1973): 11.

38. Homero Aridjis, "Poemas," *Plural* 42 (March 1975): 30–31.

39. Carlos Montemayor, "Elegía 1968," *Plural* 20 (May 1973): 8.

40. Carlos Montemayor, "Cuando apareció *Plural*," in *A treinta años*, 126.

41. See José Joaquín Blanco, "Respuesta a Octavio Paz," in *Crónica literaria: un siglo de escritores mexicanos* (Mexico City: Cal y Arena, 1996)

42. Carmen Boullosa, "Bolaño in Mexico," *The Nation* 23 April 2007.

43. Daniel Balderston and José Maristany, "The Lesbian and Gay Novel in Latin America," in *The Cambridge Companion to the Latin American Novel*, ed. Efraín Kristal (Cambridge: Cambridge University Press, 2005), 204.

44. *Plural* 14 (November 1972): 15–16.

45. Angel Rama, "El libro de las divergencias," *Plural* 22 (July 1973): 36–37.

46. Balderston and Maristany, "The Lesbian and Gay Novel," 208.

47. Suzanne Jill Levine, *Manuel Puig and the Spider Woman: His Life and Fictions* (London: Faber and Faber, 2000), 177–184.

48. Ibid., 171.

49. Alvaro Mutis, "El último rostro," *Plural* 31 (April 1974): 23–26.

50. Julián Ríos, "Las huellas de Robinson," *Plural* 48 (September 1975): 24–31.

51. In *Plural* 52 (January 1976): 13.

52. Fernando del Paso, "Una bala muy cerca del corazón," *Plural* 19 (April 1973): 29–31.

53. Elena Poniatowska, "Entrevista a Salvador Elizondo," *Plural* 45 (June 1975): 28–35.

54. Salvador Elizondo, "Taller de autocrítica," *Plural* 14 (November 1972): 5.

55. José de la Colina, "Juan García Ponce: la narración ensimismada," *Plural* 32 (May 1974): 61.

56. Octavio Paz, "*Encuentros* de Juan García Ponce," *Vuelta* 31 (June 1979): 34–35.

57. *A treinta años*, 35.
58. Ibid., 35.
59. Ibid., 68.
60. Ibid., 67.
61. Margo Glantz, *Onda y escritura en México: jóvenes de 20 a 33* (Mexico City: Siglo XXI, 1971).
62. *Plural* 39 (December 1974): 84–86.
63. José Agustín, *Tragicomedia mexicana 2: La vida en México de 1970 a 1988* (Mexico City: Planeta, 1992), 20.
64. Jean de Milleret, *Entretiens avec Jorge Luis Borges* (Paris: Pierre Belfond, 1967), 60.

6 From *Plural* to *Vuelta*, 1976–1978

1. Quoted in Julio Scherer, *Los presidentes* (Mexico City: Grijalbo, 1986), 221.
2. See in particular, the accounts of several of the major protagonists: Julio Scherer, *Los presidentes* (Mexico City: Grijalbo, 1986); Vicente Leñero, *Los periodistas* (Mexico City: Joaquín Mortiz, 1978); Manuel Becerra Acosta, *Dos poderes* (Mexico City: Grijalbo, 1984).
3. See, for example, Luis Suárez, *Echeverría en el sexenio de López Portillo*, (Mexico City: Grijalbo, Mexico, 1983), 275–280.
4. Kenneth Johnson mentions this moment, while Claire Brewster has analyzed *Excélsior's* coverage of the incident. See Kenneth Johnson, *Mexican Democracy: A Critical View* (New York: Praeger, 1978), 60–61 and Claire Brewster, *Responding to Crisis*, 89.
5. See Marlise Simons's articles in the *Washington Post*, 7 and 11 July 1976.
6. Quoted in Brewster, 89.
7. Suárez, *Echeverría*, 279–280.
8. Suárez, *Echeverría*, 279.
9. See Scherer, *Los presidentes*, 243.
10. Quoted in *Dos poderes*, 153.
11. Ibid., 227–228.
12. Scherer would also include García Cantú's recollection of this meeting in *Los presidentes*, 237–240. García Cantú's article, published in *Siempre!* 20 December 1978 is entitled "Posdata para Vicente Leñero. Con Echeverría, en el Salón Colima de Los Pinos."
13. This would happen in May 1977. Scherer had apparently told Alan Riding that he was looking to return to the newspaper with the backing of the new president. Riding's article was read on the teletext in the *Excélsior* offices and the newspaper ran a spoiler on 14 May 1977 that effectively put an end to this plan.
14. Tânia Maria Piacentini, "*Vuelta*; uma revista de autor" (Phd thesis, Universidade Estadual de Campinas, Brazil, 1996), 125. I am very

grateful to Dr. Piacentini for sending me her valuable and engaging study.

15. Ibid., 116.

16. Paz published this poem in several places before it became part of the 1976 collection. I have chosen to quote the text from the book of photographs edited in Buenos Aires by Sara Facio and Alicia D'Amico. Paz sent them this poem as a "self portrait." See "Vuelta" in Sara Facio and Alicia D'Amico, *Retratos y autoretratos* (Buenos Aires: Ediciones de Crisis, 1973), 140–142. This book was published by the journal and publishing house Crisis. By 1976, Crisis had been closed down by the military coup in Argentina and its executive director, Federico Vogelius, and its editors Eduardo Galeano and Juan Gelman were in exile. When Fuentes speaks in this chapter about Mexico as an "island of tranquility," he is perhaps thinking of his fellow writers such as Galeano or Tomás Eloy Martínez, forced into exile after consistent death threats.

17. *Vuelta* 1 (December 1967): 4. Further quotations are in parentheses in the text.

18. *Plural* 59 (August 1976): 45.

19. One might add as an aside that while Adolfo Bioy Casares anticipated the invention of holography in his novel *The Invention of Morel* (1940), in this story he also seems to be anticipating the unchecked freedoms of the internet.

20. Quoted in Poniatowska, *Octavio Paz*, 173.

21. Gabriel Zaid. "Legítimo repudio," *Vuelta* 8 (July 1977): 50–51.

22. Elena Poniatowska, "El movimiento estudiantil de 1968," *Vuelta* 7 (June 1977): 15–27.

23. *Vuelta* 10 (September 1977): 46.

24. For the developing dispute, see Carlos Monsiváis, "Respuesta a Octavio Paz," *Proceso* 59 (19 December 1977): 39–41; Octavio Paz, "Aclaraciones y reiteraciones," *Proceso* 61 (2 January 1978): 29–31; Monsiváis, "Rectificaciones y relecturas: y sin embargo lo dijo," *Proceso* 62 (9 January 1978): 31–33; Paz, "Repaso y despedida," *Proceso* 63 (16 January 1978): 31–33; Monsiváis, "Recapitulación y conclusiones a cargo del lector," *Proceso* 64 (23 January 1978), 31–32.

25. *Proceso* 62, 31.

26. *Proceso* 64, 32.

27. Octavio Paz, *Pasión crítica* (Barcelona: Seix Barral, 1985), 180.

28. Danubio Torres Fierro in *Vuelta* 11 (October 1977). Further references are given in parentheses in the text.

29. Juan Goytisolo, *Vuelta* 14 (January 1978), 18.

30. Julio Cortázar in *Vuelta* 15 (February 1978). Further references are quoted in parentheses in the text.

31. In *Vuelta* 15, 28–30.

32. Carlos Fuentes, "El límpido deseo de Luis Bunuel," *Vuelta* 14 (January 1978): 30–32.

33. Carlos Fuentes, "Tomás y Nicolás hablan de política," *Vuelta* 21 (August 1978): 29–32.

34. In *Vuelta* 5 (April 1977): 5.

35. Octavio Paz, "El ogro filantrópico," *Vuelta* 21 (August 1978): 38–44. Further references are quoted in parentheses in the text.

36. We remember of course the famous falling out among friends some twelve years later, in 1990, when Mario Vargas Llosa announced at a symposium organized by Paz and in a session chaired by Paz that Mexico was the "perfect dictatorship." This was a temporary rift, though opinion divided as to whether Vargas Llosa's phrase was ungrateful or well-aimed, or both.

Select Bibliography

For a complete list of all books and articles cited, see the endnotes.

Primary Sources
Literary Magazines and Supplements

Plural 1971–1976. Issues 1–58.
Vuelta 1976–1978. Issues 1–24.

Contemporáneos, 1928–1931. Facsimile edition. Mexico City: Fondo de Cultura Económica, 1981.
El Hijo Pródigo, 1943–1946. Facsimile edition. Mexico City: Fondo de Cultura Económica, 1983.
La Cultura en México.
Libre, 1971–1972. Facsimile edition. Madrid: Turner Libros/Ediciones del Equlibrista, 1990.
Revista de Literatura Mexicana.
S.Nob. Facsimile edition. Mexico City: CONACULTA, 2004.
Taller, 1938–1941. Facsimile edition. Mexico City: Fondo de Cultura Económica, 1983.

Principal Works by Plural Contributors Cited in the Book

Cosío Villegas, Daniel. *El estilo personal de gobernar.* Mexico City: Joaquín Mortiz, 1974.
———. *Memorias.* Mexico City: Joaquín Mortiz, 1976.
Cuevas, José Luis. *Gato macho.* Mexico City: Fondo de Cultura Económica, 1994.
Fuentes, Carlos. *La nueva novela hispanomericana.* Mexico City: Joaquín Mortiz, 1969.
———. *Tiempo mexicano.* Mexico City: Joaquín Mortiz, 1971.
García Ponce, Juan. *Pasado presente.* Mexico City: Fondo de Cultura Económica, 1993.
Paz, Octavio. *Claude Lévi-Strauss o el nuevo festín de Esopo.* Mexico City: Joaquín Mortiz, 1967.

Paz, Octavio. *Posdata*. Mexico City: Siglo XXI, 1970.

———. *El ogro filantrópico: historia y política 1971–1978*. Mexico City: Joaquín Mortiz, 1979.

———. *Obras completas (edición del autor)*. Barcelona: Círculo de Lectores; Mexico City: Fondo de Cultura Económica:

Vol. 3. *Fundación y disidencia. Dominio hispánico*. 1993.

Vol. 4. *Generaciones y semblanzas. Dominio mexicano*. 1994.

Vol. 7. *Los privilegios de la vista II. Arte de México*. 1995.

Vol. 8. *El peregrino en su patria. Historia y política de México*. 1994.

Vol. 9. *Ideas y costumbres I. La letra y el cetro*. 1995.

———. *Primeras letras*. Mexico City: Vuelta, 1988.

———. *Traducción: literatura y literalidad*. Barcelona: Tusquets, 1971.

———. *Versiones y diversiones*. Madrid: Círculo de Lectores, 2002.

———. *Vuelta*. Barcelona: Seix Barral, 1976.

Poniatowska, Elena. *La noche de Tlatelolco*. Mexico City: Era, 1971.

———. *Las palabras del árbol*. Mexico City: Plaza y Janés, 1998.

Zaid, Gabriel. *Como leer en bicicleta: problemas de la cultura y el poder en México*. Mexico City: Joaquín Mortiz, 2nd edition, 1979.

———. *El progreso improductivo*. Mexico City: Siglo XXI, 1979.

Interviews

I spoke to many people about *Plural*. The following list just refers to taped interviews.

Adolfo Castañon. Mexico City, August 1985; interview with Efraín Kristal, Paris, December 2006.

José de la Colina. Mexico City, 6 September 1993.

Jaime García Terrés. Mexico City, 22 August 1985.

Enrique Krauze. Mexico City, 30 August 1985.

Jaime Labastida. Mexico City, 6 September 1993.

Carlos Monsiváis. Stratford-on-Avon, 1 October 2005.

Octavio Paz. Mexico City, 28 August 1985; Mexico City, 9 September 1993; Mexico City, 4 March 1995; Oxford University, 11 June 1996.

Elena Poniatowska. Mexico City, August 1985.

Alejandro Rossi. Mexico City, August 1985.

Danubio Torres Fierro. Mexico City, 7 September 1993.

Gabriel Zaid. Mexico City, August 1985.

Secondary Sources

A treinta años de Plural (1971–1976). Eds. Marie-José Paz, Adolfo Castañon, and Danubio Torres Fierro. Mexico City: Fondo de Cultura Económica, 2001.

Agustín, José. *Tragicomedia mexicana*. 3 vols., Mexico City: Planeta, 1990, 1992, 1998.

Bartra, Roger. *La jaula de la melancolía: Identidad y metamorfosis del mexicano*. Mexico City: Grijalbo, 1987.

Batis, Humberto. *Lo que "Cuadernos de viento" nos dejó*. Mexico City: Diógenes, 1984.

Becerra Acosta, Manuel. *Dos poderes*. Mexico City: Grijalbo, 1984.

Blanco, José Joaquín. *Crónica literaria: un siglo de escritores mexicanos*. Mexico City: Cal y Arena, 1996.

Brading, David. *Octavio Paz y la poética de la historia mexicana*. Mexico City: Fondo de Cultura Económica, 2002.

Brewster, Claire. *Responding to Crisis in Contemporary Mexico: The Political Writings of Paz, Fuentes, Monsiváis and Poniatowska*. Tucson: University of Arizona Press, 2005.

Camp, Roderic. *Intellectuals and the State in Twentieth Century Mexico*. Austin: University of Texas Press, 1985.

Castañeda, Jorge. *Utopia Unarmed: the Latin American Left after the Cold War*. New York: Vintage, 1994.

———. *Perpetuating Power: How Mexican Presidents were Chosen*. New York: The New Press, 2000.

Cohn, Deborah. "The Mexican Intelligentsia, 1950–1968: Cosmopolitanism, National Identity and the State." *Mexican Studies/Estudios Mexicanos* 21, 1 (2005): 141–182.

Egan, Linda. *Carlos Monsiváis, Culture and Chronicle in Contemporary Mexico*. Tucson: University of Arizona Press, 2001.

Faber, Sebastiaan. *Exile and Cultural Hegemony: Spanish Intellectuals in Mexico, 1939-1975*. Nashville: Vanderbilt University Press, 2002.

Fell, Claude. *José Vasconcelos: los años del águila (1920–1925)*. Mexico City: UNAM, 1989.

Fell, Claude and Jorge Volpi. Ed. *L'Herne: Fuentes*, Paris: Editions de L'Herne, 2006.

Glantz, Margo. *Onda y escritura en México jóvenes de 20 a 33*. Mexico City: Grijalbo, 1971.

González Torres, Armando. *Las guerras culturales de Octavio Paz*. Mexico City: Editorial Colibrí, 2002.

Goytisolo, Juan. *Realms of Strife: The Memoirs of Juan Goytisolo 1957–1982*. London: Quartet Books, 1990.

Joseph, Gilbert, Anne Rubenstein, and Eric Zolov. Eds. *Fragments of a Golden Age: The Politics of Culture in Mexico since 1940*. Durham and London: Duke University Press, 2001.

Katzenstein, Inés. Ed. *Listen, Here, Now! Argentine Art of the 1960s: writings of the Avant-Garde*. New York: Museum of Modern Art, 2004.

King, John. *Sur: A Study of the Argentine Literary Journal and its Role in the Development of a Culture, 1931–1970*. Cambridge: Cambridge University Press, 1986.

———. *El Di Tella y la cultura argentina en la década del sesenta*. Buenos Aires: La Marca Editora, 2007.

Krauze, Enrique. *Daniel Cosío Villegas: una biografía intelectual.* Mexico City: Joaquín Mortiz, 1980.

Krauze, Enrique. "Octavio Paz: Facing the Century. A Reading of *Tiempo nublado.*" *Salmagundi* 70–71 (1986): 129–163.

———. "The Guerrilla Dandy." *New Republic,* 27 June 1988, 28–38.

Kristal, Efraín. "La palabra y la mirada de Octavio Paz: eros y transfiguración." *Boletín de la Fundación Federico García Lorca* IV (1991): 119–135.

———. *The Temptation of the Word: The Novels of Mario Vargas Llosa.* Nashville: Vanderbilt University Press, 1998.

———. "Jorge Luis Borges y Octavio Paz: poéticas de la traducción y traducción poética." *Studi Ispanici* (2002): 261–270.

Lempérière, Annick. *Intellectuels, États et Société au Mexique: Les clercs de la nation (1910–1968).* Paris: L'Harmattan, 1992.

Leñero, Vicente. *Los periodistas.* Mexico City: Joaquín Mortiz, 1978.

Miller, Nicola. *In the Shadow of the State: Intellectuals and the Quest for National Identity in Twentieth-Century Spanish America.* London: Verso, 1999.

Monsiváis, Carlos. *Amor perdido.* Mexico City: Era, 1977.

———. *Días de guardar.* Mexico City: Era, 1970.

———. "No con un sollozo, sino entre disparos." *Revista Iberoamericana* 55 (1989): 715–735.

Mudrovcic, María Eugenia. *Mundo Nuevo: Cultura y guerra fría en la década del sesenta.* Rosario: Beatriz Viterbo, 1997.

Paz Garro, Helena. *Memorias.* Mexico City: Océano, 2003.

Piacentini, Tânia Maria. "*Vuelta:* uma revista de autor" (PhD thesis, State University of Campinas, Brazil, 1996).

Reyes, Alfonso and Victoria Ocampo. *Cartas echadas: Correspondencia 1927–1959.* Mexico City, UAM, 1983.

Rodríguez Ledesma, Xavier. *El pensamiento político de Octavio Paz: las trampas de la ideología.* Mexico City: Plaza y Valdés, 1996.

Ruy Sánchez, Alberto. *Una introducción a Octavio Paz.* Mexico City: Joaquín Mortiz, 1990.

Sánchez Susarrey, Jaime, *El debate político e intelectual en México: 1968–1992.* Mexico City: Grijalbo, 1993.

Santí, Enrico Mario. *El acto de las palabras. Estudios y diálogos con Octavio Paz.* Mexico City: Fondo de Cultura Económica, 1997.

Scharer-Nussberger, Maya. *Octavio Paz: trayectorias y visiones.* Mexico City: Fondo de Cultura Económica, 1987.

Scherer, Julio. *Los presidentes.* Mexico City: Grijalbo, 1986.

Sefchovich, Sara. *México: país de ideas, país de novelas.* Mexico City: Grijalbo, 1987.

———. *La suerte de la consorte.* Mexico: Océano 1999.

Sheridan, Guillermo. *Los contemporáneos ayer.* Mexico City: Fondo de Cultura Económica, 1985.

———. *México 1932: la polémica nacionalista.* Mexico City: Fondo de Cultura Económica, 1999.

————. *Poeta con paisaje: ensayos sobre la vida de Octavio Paz.* Mexico City: Era, 2004.

Sosnowski, Saúl. Ed. *La cultura de un siglo: América Latina en sus revistas.* Buenos Aires: Alianza, 1999.

Steele, Cynthia. *Politics, Gender and the Mexican Novel, 1968–1988.* Austin: University of Texas Press, 1992.

Suárez, Luis. *Echeverría en el sexenio de López Portillo.* Mexico City: Grijalbo, 1983.

Van Delden, Maarten. *Carlos Fuentes, Mexico and Modernity.* Nashville: Vanderbilt University Press, 1998.

Vanden Berghe, Kristine. "La Cultura en México (1959–1972) en dos suplementos: *México en la Cultura* de *Novedades* y *La Cultura en México* de *Siempre!*" (MA thesis, UNAM, Mexico City, 1989).

Vizcaíno, Fernando. *Biografía política de Octavio Paz o la razón ardiente.* Malaga: Algazara, 1993.

Volpi, Jorge. *La imaginación y el poder: una historia intelectual de 1968.* Mexico City: Era, 1998.

————. "The End of the Conspiracy: Intellectuals and Power in 20th-Century Mexico." *Discourse* 23, 2 (2001): 144–154.

Wilson, Jason. *Octavio Paz.* Boston: Twayne, 1986.

Zolov, Eric, *Refried Elvis: The Rise of Mexican Counterculture.* Berkeley: University of California Press, 1999.

Index

Sanguinetti, Edoardo, 126, 149
  with Octavio Paz, Jacque
    Roubaud and Charles
    Tomlinson: *Renga*, 125,
    149, 152
Sarduy, Severo, 54, 62, 96, 118,
    119, 120, 127, 135, 139, 151,
    166, 168, 170, 197
  "Big Bang", 118, 151
  Big Bang, 166
  Cobra (1972), 118, 166
  Maitreya (1978), 166
Sarmiento, Sergio, 52, 59
Sartre, Jean Paul, 116, 122, 124,
    130
Satie, Eric, 134
Sautreau, Serge, 156
Savater, Fernando, 190
Scherer, Julio, 1, 10, 50, 52, 57, 60,
    61, 64, 65, 84, 85, 179, 180,
    181, 182, 183, 186, 189, 190
Schlessinger Jr., Arthur, 187
Second International Writers'
    Congress for the Defence of
    Culture, Valencia, Spain
    (1937), 16
Segovia, Rafael, 8, 25, 44, 61, 62,
    63, 64, 65, 66, 68, 69, 70, 73,
    76, 81, 83, 88, 91, 94, 102,
    103, 111, 112, 118, 126, 133,
    138, 148, 152, 157, 159, 165,
    187, 189
Segovia, Tomás, 1, 7, 8, 24, 25, 26,
    31, 43, 44, 48, 54, 61, 62, 63,
    64, 65, 66, 68, 69, 70, 73, 75,
    76, 80, 81, 83, 88, 94, 102,
    103, 111, 112, 118, 121, 123,
    126, 127, 129, 133, 135, 138,
    146, 147, 148, 152, 153, 157,
    159, 160, 165, 166, 185, 187
  "El solsticio", 187
Seix Barral, publishing house, 36,
    123, 170, 184
Seligson, Esther, 174
semiotics, 122

Semprún, Jorge, 57
Serge, Victor, 22, 135, 156
Serrano, Humberto, 181
Sheridan, Guillermo, 1, 5, 6, 15, 17,
    19, 22, 132
Shikubu, Murasaki, 126
Siempre!, 25, 50, 60, 88, 179, 183,
    189
Siglo XXI, publishing house, 28,
    30, 33, 39, 44, 45
Silva Herzog, Jesús, 19
Simic, Charles, 155
Simons, Marlise, 182
Siqueiros, David Alfaro, 15, 17, 26
Solares, Ignacio, 110, 128, 135,
    174
Solzhenitsyn, Aleksandr, 94, 95,
    104, 105, 109, 110
  The Gulag Archipelago, 95, 105
Somoza, Anastasio, 192
Sontag, Susan, 7, 71, 123
Sor Juana Inés de la Cruz, 8
Sora, Kawai, 125
Sorbonne University, 5, 6
Soriano, Juan, 29, 173
South America, 14, 53
Spain, 16, 17, 31, 39, 68, 111, 139,
    156, 158, 163, 168, 169, 170,
    171, 188
Spanish Civil War, 9, 16, 18, 168
Spoletto, Italy, 47
Stalin, Josef, 17, 105, 150, 191,
    192
Stanton, Anthony, 121
Steiner, George, 62
STEUNAM Sindicato de
    Trabajadores y Empleados de la
    UNAM, 90, 189
Stone, I.F., 66, 94, 103, 105, 109,
    110, 187
Strand, Mark, 152, 155
Stravinsky, Igor, 28
structuralism, 47, 66, 121–2
Sucre, Guillermo, 71, 121, 135,
    151, 152, 158

Vallarino, Roberto, 162
Vallejo, César, 89, 151, 160
Vallejo, Demetrio, 89
van Delden, Maarten, 78
Vanden Berghe, Christine, 26–27
Varela, Blanca, 21, 62, 151
Vargas Llosa, Mario, 7, 34, 35, 36,
    37, 53, 54, 56, 57, 96, 97, 109,
    110, 115, 116, 117, 118, 124,
    127, 135, 145, 151, 166, 167,
    171, 194, 196, 197
    La ciudad y los perros (1962), 36
    La guerra del fin del mundo
        (1981), 194
    Pantaleón (film), 115, 167,
        197
    Pantaleón y las visitadoras (1973),
        115, 167
Vasconcelos, José, 14, 15
Velazco Alvarado, Juan, 78
Velázquez Sánchez, Fidel, 59
Velter, André, 156
Venezuela, 120, 121, 152, 158,
    186, 194
Veracruz, Mexico, 181
Vermont, 20
Vidal, Gore, 187
Villa, Pancho, 50, 172, 185
Villaurrutia, Xavier, 15, 16, 18, 19,
    29, 150, 174
Villoro, Luis, 30, 80, 127, 135
Viñas, David, 192
Vitier, Cintio, 31, 151, 152
Von Gunten, Roger, 141
Vuelta (1976–1998), 1, 3, 4, 5, 6, 7,
    9, 11, 76, 119, 128, 164, 167,
    173, 179, 181, 183, 184, 185,
    186, 187, 189, 190, 191, 192,
    193, 194, 195, 196, 197, 198,
    199, 200

Waldheim, Kurt, 183
Washington Post, 47, 182
Weil, Simone, 31
Weston, Edward, 150

Westphalen, Emilio, 31
Whitman, Walt, 151
Wilde, Oscar, 163
William, William Carlos, 154
Williams, Raymond, 2
Wilson, Jason, 110, 131, 149
Womack, John, 78, 89, 149
Wordsworth, William, 131
    The Prelude, 131
Wright Mills, Charles, 26
Wright, Charles, 155

Xirau Icaza, Joaquín, 174
Xirau, Ramón, 28, 31, 32, 67, 110,
    135, 152, 159, 174
XIX Olympic Games, Mexico 1968,
    48, 49, 51

Yale University, 120, 121
Yáñez, Agustín, 26
Yevtushenko, Yevgeny, 32
Yucatán, Mexico, 16
Yunkers, Adja, 68, 138
Yurkievich, Saúl, 115, 121, 135,
    143, 151, 158, 192

Zabludovsky, Jacobo, 59
Zaid, Gabriel, 4, 8, 24, 26, 27, 60,
    72, 79, 80, 81, 86, 87, 90, 92,
    103, 104, 106, 110, 117, 127,
    135, 152, 159, 160, 175, 185,
    188, 189, 195, 198
    Cómo leer en bicicleta, 117
Zanabria, Rodolfo, 173
Zapata, Emiliano, 181,
    185
Zapata, Fausto, 84
Zea, Leopoldo, 19
Zhdanov, Andrei, 41, 82
Zisman, Alex, 119
Zócalo, Mexico, 13
Zolov, Eric, 67
Zona Franca, 120, 158
zona rosa, 25, 35
Zuno, María Esther, 59